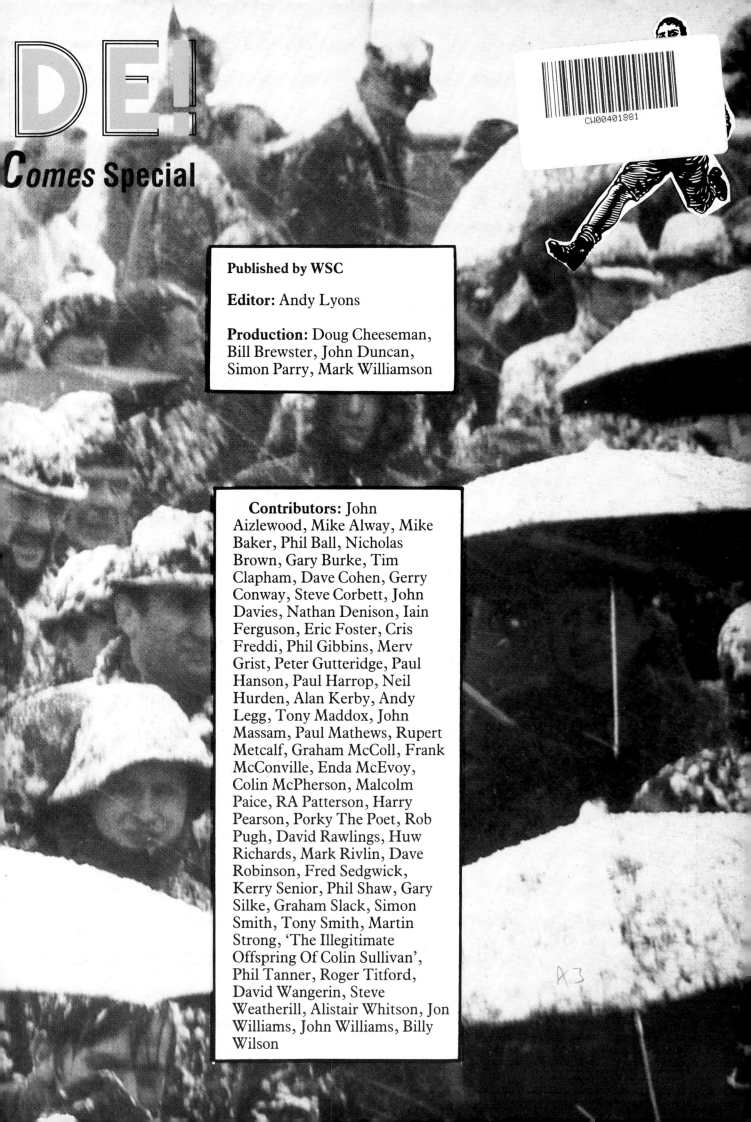

DE!
Comes Special

Published by WSC

Editor: Andy Lyons

Production: Doug Cheeseman, Bill Brewster, John Duncan, Simon Parry, Mark Williamson

Contributors: John Aizlewood, Mike Alway, Mike Baker, Phil Ball, Nicholas Brown, Gary Burke, Tim Clapham, Dave Cohen, Gerry Conway, Steve Corbett, John Davies, Nathan Denison, Iain Ferguson, Eric Foster, Cris Freddi, Phil Gibbins, Merv Grist, Peter Gutteridge, Paul Hanson, Paul Harrop, Neil Hurden, Alan Kerby, Andy Legg, Tony Maddox, John Massam, Paul Mathews, Rupert Metcalf, Graham McColl, Frank McConville, Enda McEvoy, Colin McPherson, Malcolm Paice, RA Patterson, Harry Pearson, Porky The Poet, Rob Pugh, David Rawlings, Huw Richards, Mark Rivlin, Dave Robinson, Fred Sedgwick, Kerry Senior, Phil Shaw, Gary Silke, Graham Slack, Simon Smith, Tony Smith, Martin Strong, 'The Illegitimate Offspring Of Colin Sullivan', Phil Tanner, Roger Titford, David Wangerin, Steve Weatherill, Alistair Whitson, Jon Williams, John Williams, Billy Wilson

OFFSIDE!

The *When Saturday Comes* Special

ALL NEW MATERIAL

All Football Books Have Them, So Here Is Our ...

"*Here We Go, Here We Go, Here We Go*" is a popular chant among Britain's football faithful, but when exactly did things start to "*Go*"? That's a question soccer fans ask themselves most Saturdays and now, thanks to modern carbon-dating techniques, scientists think they may have the answer. Tests recently carried out on a beefburger discovered at the Victoria Ground, Hartlepool, indicate it is at least 235 million years old. Staggering proof that the game of soccer originated in the primordial slime which covered the Earth prior to the first Ice Age. Naturally, in those days, the game was very different from league football as we now know it. It was played between teams of microscopic, mud-dwelling amoeba, with a ball no bigger than a grain of sand, in a stadium the size of the smallest thing you can think of, halved.

Obviously, it was to be several million years before the laws of the game were conclusively established by a conclave of eminent Victorian freemasons with improbable first names such as Jedekiah and Aloysius, so the rules tended to vary according to the players' position on the evolutionary scale.

Geological evidence suggests that the coming of the first Ice Age had a profound effect on prehistoric micro-football and almost certainly led to the creation of the first Pools Panel. Probably made up of half a dozen sort-of-jellyfish-type-things, the newly formed committee may have been forced to meet every Saturday for 148,000 consecutive seasons. It was around this time that the Littlewoods Company was set up by John Moores, a young amphibean with a sense of destiny and a liking for civic patronage.

The first evidence of mankind's interest in football is to be found in Paleolithic cave paintings near the villages of Lobo, Solti and Botsford in the Glanville region of Southern Italy (equally famous for its extraordinary local dialect, which is peppered with peculiar adjectives and makes little sense to outsiders). For a short while in recent times, the periodical *Football Today* captured the essence of these primitive etchings in its series of (genuinely remarkable) centre-page illustrations, the like of which had never previously been seen in a professional magazine.

Although in many respects the game depicted contrasts sharply with modern soccer, one aspect of it is familiar: the Stone Age manager's decision to play a pair of bison in the centre of defence.

Ancient Greece was the scene of soccer's first golden age. The cradle of civilisation boasted a globally-reknowned team, the stars including highly creative playmaker Sophocles, seminal left-winger Plato, and goalkeeper Archimedes, whose knowledge of angles made him almost impossible to beat.

Rome At Last

The Romans adapted the Greek prototype to create their own version of the game in which the result was often decided in advance. Many players were imported from across the Empire, the most successful coming form the Germanic tribes of Northern Europe. Occasionally, muscular captives from the British Isles would be brought over to play. News of their achievements (often exaggerated) were relayed back home by messengers known as 'Unsatisfactory TV Anchormen' to a populace which was otherwise ill-informed about events in the rest of the continent.

The Roman Empire also witnessed the first instance of player power when, in 45 BC, Spartacus led a revolt against the maximum wage. The rebellion was a success, but its results were to be shortlived. Weakened by complacency, decadence and a betting scandal, Rome's once-impregnable defences began to crumble and eventually fell apart under ceaseless pressure from Barbarian Wanderers, an undisciplined but competitive collection of grizzled veterans, whose string of victories were marked by numerous instances of boisterous behaviour in nightclubs throughout the continent.

Morale had been badly affected some time previously when large crowds began turning out to see rival Real David City's talented but wayward striker, Jesus Christ. He was the Martin Peters of his day, forever holy-ghosting through on the blind side to get on the end of crosses. His success was shortlived, however, as he sparked off considerable disquiet in the dressing room through his unconventional views on the value of money, insistence on washing his team-mates' feet after each match and his turning of the other shin to brutal opponents.

Soccer flourished in the Ancient World yet it was to be all but obliterated in the centuries that followed. Nomadic, horse-bound people such as the Avars, the Khazars and (most fearsome of all) the Three-Day-Eventers, detested this most civilised of games, preferring instead to charge about hitting sheeps' heads with mallets. This bizarre practice was followed in later centuries by other preposterous equestrian sports, all of which, then as now, appear to have involved members of the ruling dynasty falling off their mounts with tiresome regularity.

In the Stygian gloom of the Dark Ages, the flickering flame of football was kept alive by communities of monks. The greatest of all was the Trappist XI from Lindisfarne in Northumbria, who, curiously, always fared better in knockout competitions than in league play. On their tiny island, the friars erected a magnificent stadium which every Sabbath day would echo to the sound of 40,000 fans chanting an

The Game

early Christian hymn, "*Saaaaack Theee Boardddd....*"

Sadly, many talented players of this period perished during intermittent raids by fearsome Vikings, who showed scant regard for the intricacies of the noble game. They preferred to indulge in seemingly random acts of pointless violence, often aimed at one another. Many such attacks had been planned, to the tiniest detail, months in advance, though you wouldn't know it. Scholars claim this as proof of the Norsemen's 'discovery' of the American continent, because a strikingly similar ritual, known as 'Gridiron' (usually accompanied by another folk custom, 'Steroid Test') is now phenomenally popular in that sadly misguided land.

During the 14th century, football was embroiled in the Wars Of The Roses, with the two opposing factions, Lancaster and York each seeking to impose their influence on England's sporting habits. The Lancastrians enjoyed a long period of footballing hegemony at national level, their era being characterised by the prominence of men with names like Stan and Arthur, and also by a widespread affliction known as 'Unbelievably Crap Goalkeeping' which no-one seems to have been aware of at the time.

Their rivals on the other side of the Pennines foreswore football in favour of a game involving a willow bat and small leather ball. They briefly excelled at this pastime, but then underwent a long period without any success at all. Curiously, this bleak spell was greeted with great rejoicing throughout the rest of the country.

Oblivious to the dynastic wars raging all about them, the monasteries remained havens of footballing enlightenment until the reign of Henry VIII. He destroyed many of these footballing academies, believing that soccer undermined the warlike spirit of the English. The game was banned and replaced by a game of the monarch's invention, known as 'Ye Rugge Bugge', in which thirty men spent eighty minutes alternately punching one another and sticking their heads up each other's bottoms. The 'game' concluded with the players jumping in the bath together and singing praise songs to their genitals, to their drinking prowess, and to the educational establishments where they first learned how to punch one another and stick their heads up each other's bottoms.

Ball Artists

The Dark Ages could not last forever. The 15th Century saw a bright new dawn for painting, philosophy, poetry, architecture and football. A central figure in this fresh awakening was Michelangelo, whose artistic eye for colour helped him create some of the most fabulous football kits the world has ever seen (striped, halved, hooped and quartered shirts, with no squiggles on the sleeves or chests, and *not a manufacturers' name in sight*). Equally influential was Leonardo Da Vinci, whose designs for flying machines and submarines were centuries ahead of their time, although the plans that most puzzled his contemporaries were those for what looked like a plain brick wall. Only today can we recognise them for what they are — a prototype for the design of the Ayresome Park urinals. The Renaissance also saw the publication of the first classic work of soccer literature, Dante Aligheri's prophetic *Divine Comedy*, which foretold Malcolm Allison's ill-advised return to Manchester City in 1977.

The 18th Century witnessed one of the most bizarre experiments in football's

colourful history. The insistence of the Metaphysical philosophers that the material world did not exist had a profound effect on Maximillian Robespierre, the President of UEFA, with the result that for two seasons football (or foot as it became known) was played without a ball, the referee basing his decisions on the relative merits of tactical hypotheses advanced by opposing players. Soccer's 'Age Of Reason' came to an end in 1793 when a youthful Arthur Schopenhauer, one of the top coaches of his day, conclusively proved the existence of matter to Robespierre by kicking him in the groin during a game between Heidelberg and Racing Paris. Hence forwards, logic was to have little or no place in the minds of the game's administrators.

British soccer took little notice of the philosophical discourses indulged in by its counterparts on the continent. It was largely pre-occupied with a crisis of its own, sparked off in 1837 when Victoria came to the throne. The reign of the 'Widow of Windsor Park' saw the expansion of the Empire, increased economic prosperity and the repeal of the draconian Hot Bovril Laws, yet it had a near disastrous effect on the nation's football.

The stiff moral climate of the day had an impact on every aspect of the game. Shooting and passing were impeded by the long-johns, trousers, petticoats, bussels and whalebone corsets which had become compulsory items of kit; the players' top hats made heading highly inaccurate; and a new offside law, under which to remain on-side an attacker had to have six defenders, four chaperones, two cousins and a maiden aunt between him and goal, made scoring impossible.

Despite these problems the period saw many positive developments: the invention of the bobble hat, the replacement of the title 'trainer' with the more scientific-sounding 'physio', and the foundation of the Football Association and the Football League. These two fine organisations were to lead soccer into the Edwardian Era and, who knows, maybe one day even beyond it.

Whe

History teacher **Rob Pugh** *explains how Brighton and Hove Albion have threatened the tranquillity of his happy existence in the Fens.*

Whe

The role of Brighton and Hove Albion in the education of the young might seem irrelevant, but hold on. For the last seven years all the classes I have taught history to have become very familiar with the fortunes of the Seagulls.

I am convinced many pupils have come to school after a Brighton defeat just to give me the benefit of their wit. The relegation season of 1986-7 was indeed the 'happiest days of their lives' for many of 3PH who, with the opportunism of Lineker, never missed the chance to remind me of what a useless team I supported.

Thankfully I have always ignored the advice received from my college adviser who, after observing a lesson on Slavery, warned me of the dangers of engaging in a conversation with one boy about the fortunes of Tottenham. The historical parallel between certain slave owners and the Tottenham Board of Directors in their respective treatment of slaves and supporters surely goes without saying. Ironically the boy in question (one Barry Smith, 14 at the time) went on to play for Brighton reserves, despite his barely concealed contempt for my team at the time I taught him. Unfortunately he never made the progress in history that he made in football.

After the euphoria of seeing my team at Wembley, I set off for my first teaching job in the football wilderness of Cambridgeshire. The vast majority of kids in the quiet market town of Ransey seemed to have spurned the excitement of following Peterborough or Cambridge United in favour of supporting Liverpool, Man Utd, or Arsenal. Few had even heard of Brighton. Livingston in Africa never set about a missionary task with such zeal as I did. Success however was limited. Despite frequent stories about the goals of Peter Ward, the tenacity of Brian Horton, the elegance of Mark Lawrenson, and the aerobatics of Graham Moseley, a Brighton and Hove Albion Appreciation Society never developed.

Clown Time Is Over

I did gain some credibility in that first difficult year of teaching, when the club got rid of a clown and appointed a manager (ie Chris Cattlin took over from Jimmy Melia). I also had sweet revenge over the

perpetrators of many a cruel joke, when, for the second season running, we knocked Liverpool out of the Cup. But such moments were rare in a season of mediocrity.

In an effort to introduce some locals to their own team I organised a few trips to Peterborough. For those brought up on TV with the Anfields, Old Traffords and Wembleys of this world, London Road must have been something of a culture shock. The standard of football was also generally shocking, with John Wile's team relying more on brawn than brain. Still, a few moments linger in the mind; the afternoon the outrageously talented John Byrne of York (later QPR) scored a goal of great individual skill; the night when the ground attracted a full house (needless to say Peterborough weren't playing) to see England Under 21's draw with Yugoslavia.

Here my boast about the talents of Terry Connor, playing as an over age player, were fulfilled as an ex Seagull (may he be kicked all over the park by Larry May next season for joining Pompey) scored England's goal and played a blinder.

Probably my worst moment in the Fens came in February 1986. Cup fever gripped that area as Peterborough, languishing in Division Four swept aside those giants of

e Seagulls Dare

the football world, Bishop Stortford and Bath, to reach the third round for the first time since the Great Fire of London. Unbelievably, Carlisle and Leeds were also seen off. Wembley was only three games away. As the draw for the Fifth Round approached my formroom was packed, as the new band of Posh supporters waited to hear who would be their next victims.

Silence descended as the draw began. *"Please God, no"*, I prayed *"Give us a trip to Anfield or Goodison. Anything but…"*. Then it happened. *"Number 8… Peterborough… will play…..number 2 ….Brighton and Hove Albion."* Cheers echoed around the room as I sat back and moaned quietly. After away wins at Newcastle and Hull surely this was a travesty of justice. I could never mention my team again in Cambridgeshire if Peterborough knocked us out of the Cup.

In the week before the game I couldn't walk past a pupil at school without being told what was going to happen on Saturday. Score predictions ranged from a conservative 1-0 to some supremely confident 3 or 4-0.

Sleep just wouldn't come on the Friday night as I fretted anxiously about the morrow. Saturday morning seemed to foreshadow disaster. Snow and ice covered the ground but the game was on. How could

artists like Dean Saunders and Dennis Mortimer cope with these conditions?

I must have been the only Brighton supporter on the packed East Terrace. Worse, three or four kids from school were stood close behind me, and my three adult friends were all solidly anti-Seagull. Conditions were farcical as players could hardly stand let alone run. Still, we reached half time with no score. Then disaster struck as Brighton went 1-0 down. Thankfully, the equaliser came soon after, but with ten minutes left the world caved in. Peterborough's only skilful player, Errington Kelly, scored.

Jacobs' Cracker

I was already thinking of my excuse to be off school for a month when indescribable joy returned. The much maligned Steve Jacobs had bundled in another equaliser. I jumped and screamed with delight, forgetting for the only time in my life, the golden rule of football supporting; keep quiet and say nothing when supporting the away team surrounded by home supporters.

The replay was safely negotiated 1-0 and Southampton loomed in the Quarter Finals. The handicap of having Mick Ferguson as our No 9 couldn't be overcome and we lost 2-0. But even my deep gloom was lifted somewhat by the knowledge that no-one at school supported Southampton.

From one footballing outpost to another. I now teach at Broadstairs, where support for the county's teams, Gillingham and Maidstone, is virtually non existent. Travel to Brighton games is easier generally, but the reaction of the kids the same. Frequent complaints that they cannot concentrate on what Garibaldi's role in Italian unification or why World War 1 began because of the 1988-89 Brighton squad staring down at them from the classroom wall, are ignored.

The delights of teaching the fifth year on a Friday afternoon are made just that bit more bearable as a glimpse of my team reminds me once again that it is nearly Saturday, and surely Nelson will be at his most exhilirating, surely Wilkins will score his first goal at the Goldstone in a League game, surely Lloyd will play Chapman at left back…

"Now then you lot, lets examine the causes of the Cuban missile crisis…"

R Pugh

FOCUS ON

... the 1890s

Professional Ambition: To complete a match without sustaining a wound or fracture of any kind.

Best Countries Visited: The Orange Free State, Mesopotamia (Old Unacceptables Tour, 1876)

Car: Pardon?

Music: Dame Nelly Melba

Favourite Reading: Jules Verne; The Bible

Biggest Disappointment: The surrender of Khartoum

Greatest Influence On Career: My Housemaster at Eton

Miscellaneous Likes: Billiards at the Piccadilly Sporting Club, boating, pig-sticking

Miscellaneous Dislikes: Anarchists, pamphleteers and G R T Farquharson, the Royal Engineers' rather boorish left back

Favourite Pre-Match Meal: Quails Eggs, Saddle Of Venison

If Not A Footballer What Do You Think You'd Be: An explorer, lexicographer, botanist, sculptor and military historian

Person Most Like To Meet: My Father, believed to be gun running in Zanzibar

Favourite Phrase: *"Gadzooks!"*

...the 1930s

Professional Ambition: To win the FA Cup with Gateshead

Biggest Disappointment: Finishing second in the annual mile race at our textile mill

Greatest Influence On Career: My old Battery Sergeant, who sadly left us at Anzio

Miscellaneous Likes: Smoking, Drinking, Queueing

Best Countries Visited: Wales and Lake District

Car: Brough Superior motorcycle and sidecar

Music: Hartley Moore And His Mandolin Syncopators

Favourite Reading: *Radio Times; Radio Fun*

Miscellaneous Dislikes: Travelling to work on the no 35 tram (the ribbing we receive from fellow passengers would have to be heard to be believed!)

Pre Match Meal: Some nourishing offcuts

If Not A Footballer....: I'd return to being a chief gutterer operating thrakestops on a steam engine

Person Most Like To Meet: The new German Chancellor, Mr Hitler (a man of admirable purpose!) and Arthur Askey ("*Hello Playmates!*").

Favourite Phrase: *"There won't be another war"*

Living For The City

The City have finally made it! What do you mean, which City? Gloucester City, of course, aka God's gift to football. After a nervous end of season finale, they finally clinched the championship of the Beazer Homes League Midland Division, and have returned to the forefront of English football — they're back on the Pools coupon, three times a season.

The Beazer Homes League trips delightfully off the tongue. When I was a lad, it was the good old Southern League. No sponsors titles in those far off days when my mate Phil would say *"Are you going to the City this afternoon?" "Who are they playing?"* I'd reply. *"Sittingbourne". "You bet, it'll be a cracker!"* The innocence of youth.

Gloucester has always been a rugby city. The Kingsholm Rugby Union ground still attracts crowds in their thousands. By adding together the crowd, players, officials, those watching for free through the fence and those who only came to the clubhouse for a game of skittles, City watchers would number in the middle hundreds. Evening matches, without the competition of the local amateur leagues, might draw in a few more.

For years, City were one of the few Clubs in the League without floodlights. This meant that evening matches, played on Thursday, the traditional payday, kicked off at 6 30 in September and then didn't kickoff at all from then until April. Eventually a blanket was paraded at home games into which the faithful would lob their coppers (if you were accurate, in off the linesman). Rumour had it so little was collected, that the club used the cash to buy a new blanket.

Chris Townsend and fan club

The old home of the Gods was Horton Road Stadium, though 'Stadium' was a slight misnomer, as three sides of the ground consisted of grass banks set too far away from the pitch to actually recognise the players. The remaining side consisted of a small stand, clubhouse and a covered terrace, the latter housing the vocal Tea End . Led by one Don Mann, known to the masses as 'Manhole' we sang the City onward to victory (sometimes). The classics included such as

Brian Godfrey (left) enjoying a cuddle

"We all agree
Jones is better than Yashin
Stevens is better than Eusebio
And Hinckley are in for a thrashin" .

Wit was rather a scarce commodity, though one memorable moment of spontaneity was produced. City had a winger called Bob McCool, a Charlie Cooke-type who opposing full backs would love to clobber into Row G. The Tea End chant for their favourite was the traditional *"He's here, he's there, He's every f***** where, Bob McCool…"* which brought a warning from the FA about the bad language being used! During the game following this dictatorial decree, McCool set off on another mazy dribble which ended with the Tea End singing *"He's here, he's there, we're not allowed to swear, Bob McCool…"*

City possessed several other entertainers in their side, some deliberate, others accidental. Willie Ferns came into both categories; a tall Scot, who, legend had it, once played for Liverpool, though no doubt for their Central League side. A great chuckle ran around the ground as Ferns lined up a direct free kick to one side of the centre circle. This turned to gasps of disbelief and then a roar of acclaim as the thunderbolt shot crashed into the far corner of the net. Don Gapper was the only right back with a built-in slice. His touch kicking was immaculate and would have won him many honours in the game with the funny shaped ball.

The side did contain one player of genuine class. Nigel Page-Jones, despite his rather poncy name, was a star, an overlapping left back with a strong tackle, far too good both for City and for the Southern League. He eventually married a French girl and moved to Brittany where he played for the local Second Division club, Brest, and, in true, 'Nige Of The Rovers' fashion was their player of the year as the club swept to promotion. His stylish play attracted the attention of top French clubs, but he refused to leave Brest.

Prior to Page Jones was a full-back who went on to become one of the best defenders of his era. The Welsh international, Rod Thomas, started his career at City in the early Sixties, joining them from local junior club Longlevens, for whom your correspondent used to perform as midfield dynamo for the reserves, although not at the same time. The same club was also the starting point for Bristol City winger, Gerry Sharpe, who was tipped for full England honours until a Nobby Stiles tackle broke his leg in three places and he never played again.

Alas, the Tea End is no more. City declined even further than the rock bottom of my youth and were rescued by the ubiquitous and largely unwelcome breed of football angels, the property developer. Westbury Homes arrived with their money and eyes on Horton Road's lush acres. Damn them, they even changed the club strip from its traditional red and white to the company colours of yellow and black. It won't be long, we said, before they sell the ground for housing. It wasn't long. Surprisingly, the deal included a new ground on the other side of town, Meadow Park (turn right at the docks, you can't miss it).

A new manager, Brian Godfrey, had City playing some delightful, attractive football — too subtle for the cloggers of the Midland Division. Another successful season and we could be soon renewing rivalry in the Conference with our old enemies, the Robins of Cheltenham Town. The present side's success owes a lot more to the twin strike force of Chris Townsend and Shaun Penny, who between them rattled in 57 goals as City finished 5 points clear at the top. Townsend is the undoubted star and showed his current form in frightening the life out of Coventry in a pre-season friendly (then again, who doesn't?).

One story sums up the City for me. Recently, Arsenal came to Meadow Park for a friendly which doubled as a testimonial for Barrie Vassallo, an ex-Arsenal apprentice who wandered around the lower reaches of the League before going semi-professional. An injury had brought early retirement and Vassallo turned up a couple of days after the Arsenal game to collect his testimonial cheque. Due to a shortage of players, he had to turn out that night in a league match…

Steve Corbett

Tommy Hutchison began his career in Junior football

The weather was well-suited to the first day of the Scottish Junior football season at Newlandsfield Park, Pollokshaws; glowering skies, sporadic, but vicious, showers and a mid-August cold to chill the bones nicely.

Pollok are one of the most successful of Junior clubs with attendances hovering around the 1,000 mark. This may not seem much of an average, but the ground sits within the shadow of Pollokshaws East station, from where all of Glasgow's senior grounds are well within an hour's travel.

The Juniors, however, possess attractions which the Scottish League lacks. Whereas the slightest whiff of alcohol about the person of a senior football supporter can be enough to prevent entry to a match, at Junior level, *"bevvying"* appears to be positively encouraged. Fifteen minutes before the start of this Tartan Special Sectional League Cup tie against East Kilbride Thistle, the terraces are deserted apart from a 100 or so spectators. Have the faithful suddenly decided to take up some of the many alternatives on offer in Glasgow's South Side?

The answer is provided at five to three as the trickle of bodies from the Social Club turns into a flood and a horde of wee grey men, well-fortified against the cold, take up their positions. Even at this early stage of the season, heavy overcoats and anoraks are already out in force.

The relationship between social and football club is vital to the well being of the game at this level. Junior football can be placed somewhere between Senior Professional and Amateur. Despite the name, there's no age restriction on the players and there is a pay structure together with a national association and competition. Funds are essential. With admission at £1, it would be difficult for the smaller clubs to survive on gate receipts alone, with some getting regular crowds as low as 50. Under Scottish law, a social club cannot exist for the sole purpose of consuming alcohol. In the case of the Juniors, the social set-up provides an annual donation to the football club with which it is associated. This acts as a lifeline in many cases.

Its importance can be measured by the fact that a number of the clubs which have folded in the last decade (eg Lochore Welfare, Lochgelly Albert and Corrie Colliery) were based around the mining industry in Fife where unemployment is now as high as anywhere in the UK.

Port Glasgow are presently struggling in tandem with the area's shipyards, and after a dreadful start to this season, put out a public

As did Pat Stanton

appeal for help. Ex-Morton centre-half, George Anderson promptly offered his coaching talents. Some ex-professionals, however, aren't so magnanimous. A charitable group of former pro's, including Joe Harper, Willie Garner and Jocky Scott, stepped in when Aberdeen Rosemount fell on hard times. Much needed sponsorship was provided, but with Harper and Garner both ex-Aberdeen stalwarts, it seemed surprising that they should rename the club Rosslyn Rosemount...and then move out of Aberdeen to the prosperous suburb of Dyce.

After a year, the new name still didn't sound right and was therefore changed to the aesthetically pleasing Rosslyn Sports, which, coincidentally, happens to be the name of a sportswear company owned by the ex-footballers...

But back to Pollok v East Kilbride Thistle. The facilities at Newlandsfield are certainly basic, though far from decrepit. There are no seats but the terracing is well maintained and the ground could safely hold 10,000. The home club go out of their way to involve spectators who arrive early. Unlike senior teams who spend the warm up period passing to each other in neatly-formed triangles, the Juniors keep the *spectators* at either end warmed up and on the move. A series of shots rain in on goal with some venom, and with roughly one in five on target. As the terracing is about three foot high behind the goal, six steps deep and backed by a brick wall, the punters resemble plastic ducks in a shooting gallery as they pass by on their way to the covered terrace.

Child's Play

After this, the 5 minutes when the teams return to the dressing rooms to prepare are filled in by some wee boys taking over the goalmouth and practising their own skills with a 'ball' formed from a rolled up scarf. A tired monotone issues from the tannoy, exhorting them to leave the pitch, and casually announces that there will be a minute's silence for Jack Currie, who died *"earlier."* Choked on a lunchtime pie, maybe?

The next announcement is equally mysterious, made with practised lassitude: *"Wednesday's game against St Anthony's will be here at Newlandsfield. It was due to be away but St Anthony's have given up their ground rights."* Conversations continue without interruption. St Anthony's situation stemmed from the fact their ground, Moore Park, sited only 100 yards from Ibrox, received an unwelcome Summer visitation from some of the more fanatical Glasgow Rangers followers.

Another hundred yards from Moore Park sits the home of Benburb. Known as the 'Wee 'Gers', they're the only Junior club to fly the Union Jack on matchdays. Benburb isn't a part of Glasgow. Strangely, it's the name of a village in Northern Ireland which was the venue of a battle victory for William Of Orange. Keen to develop ties with the

or   Showtime

senior clubs, Benburb arranged for Rangers to train at their ground for a suitable fee. Despite this kind offer being taken up for a year, no money changed hands. With the bill standing at £5,000, Benburb (blue shirts, white shorts, red socks) decided to take Rangers to court. Sad days for the club which nurtured the talents of Ron McKinnon.

Even the smaller Scottish League clubs aren't above reproach. The big Junior tournament of the season is their national cup, where all 174 clubs go into an open draw. Fifty seven different sides have won the competition in its 102-year history and any team is in with a realistic chance of winning the trophy if they reach the last sixteen.

One such team, last season, was Blantyre Victoria. A few minutes before midnight on the Friday before their tie, they received a call from Stirling Albion, who wanted to recall their on-loan keeper, Mark McGeown to play for them the next day. Normally, there is an unwritten agreement that a loan player will stay with the Junior club until the end of the season, or at least until they are eliminated from the Scottish Junior Cup. Blantyre coach Tommy Coggill was left with the pleasant task of making numerous midnight phone calls in an attempt to sign an amateur keeper for his club. Vics lost the tie 2-0.

Back to our featured game. East Kilbride have in their line-up a new signing, Bruce Clelland, just off the plane after 18 months in the USA. His last game in Scotland had been for Stranraer in a Scottish Cup tie when he missed both a penalty and a open goal in a 1-0 defeat at Parkhead…

He seems to have discovered a predilection for American fast food. Barely mobile to begin with, the match is only a

…And Martin Buchan, too. Blimey.

minute or two old before he has fallen flat on his face in the centre circle with no potential culprit near him. High farce threatens, but with the rest of the players in good condition the game settles into an entertaining struggle which wouldn't seem out of place in the Scottish Second, or even First, Division. Pollok run out 5-2 winners after a lethal Junior cocktail of clever skill, monstrous errors and a spirit of healthy 'competition'.

Brief details of a couple of East Kilbride's opening matches this year may give a hint of what the Juniors is all about. For the Pollok game, EK started with ten outfield players who hadn't belonged to the club at the end of last season. All nine squad members who had re-signed were injured, suspended or…on holiday.

In the second match, against Cambuslang Rangers, substitute John Nelson took the field in the 70th minute. Three minutes later, he crossed the touchline in the opposite direction after 'stiffing' an opponent. A club record. On to Benburb, where a 5-4 victory established another club record of a first ever win in a nine-goal match. Gerry Allen was the main man, grabbing a couple of goals — and a sending off.

Many players have 'stepped up' from the Juniors over the years, including Gordon Durie, Martin Buchan, Jimmy Johnstone, Alan Gilzean and Tommy Hutchison. Sean Connery was a winger with Bonnyrigg Rose during the late '50s, while Scottish miners' leader, Mick McGahey would have needed his full communicative powers as a goalkeeper for Vale Of Clyde. The Juniors were also represented at the first World Cup. Jock Coll, formerly with Parkhead Juniors, coached the USA side which included some ex-Juniors among its half-a-dozen Scots.

Despite these heady connections with

fame and fortune, perhaps the best thing about the Juniors is the unlikelihood of this brand of football ever outgrowing its basic links with the people who support it. The biggest clubs, such as Pollok, Petershill and Auchinleck Talbot barely average four figure attendances, so this particular strain of football is unlikely to be tainted by some of the financial excesses of the senior game. This is despite the efforts of the man in the souvenir hut at Newlandsfield, where T-shirts are touted with the enticing selling point of the sponsors' name being prominently emblazoned on them. If you have ever dreamt of owning a shirt with 'Central Car Auctions' stamped on the chest, send off to Pollok now.

Expense Account

For many clubs, the only way to attract promising young talent is to negotiate set 'expenses', similar to Maradona's stipulated annual number of flights home to Argentina from Naples. It s more likely, though, to be the price of a peak BR return, even if the individual in question, plus four team mates, shares a lift to matches and training and parks outside the Match Secretary's office.

The Junior game is no Platonic footballing haven, certainly, but the clubs still seem to belong to the supporters in a way which is often no longer the case with bigger outfits.

At the Pollok match, East Kilbride's injured captain took in the game standing amidst the non-segregated supporters of both teams, who were able to barrack each other before heading for the Social Club and a drink and a laugh with the players. Just like Ibrox.

…And Jimmy Johnstone

Graham McColl

SOCCERPRINTS

How would you like to wake up every morning to see Terry McDermott or Niall Quinn on your bedroom wall?! They are just two of the top footballers featured in our range of magnificent, full-colour (limited edition) portraits! Also available - Dick Krzywicki, Eric Skeels, Dudley Tyler, Mike Stringfellow, Ted Hemsley, Hugh Fisher and many more! Write for catalogue: Dept WSC; 2-4 Av. Andre Duclos, Differdange, Luxembourg.

Tender Moments From The Life Of Kevin Keegan...

I'm earning this much!

Embarrassing Moments As A Teen Supporter Part One

From Nathan Denison who says *"Even at the age of 17, I have already amassed several..."*

1. Individually kissing each post following a 1986 promotion pitch invasion.
2. Became an academic outcast by shunning my 5th year presentation evening in favour of Argyle v Brighton.
3. Ran up a bill of £5.00 by photocopying 100 PAFC 1987-88 posters and distributing them throughout the school, which completely failed to amuse the headmaster.
4. Arrived two hours early at a match v Sunderland, lying my way in as a pasty seller, then staked a claim as the first fan there.
5. Flicked numerous 'V's from the safety of a coach on the M6 passing Watford, Villa and Southampton fans.
6. Took great pride in starting the *"We will win"* chant whilst we were losing 6-1 at Arsenal.
7. Made a meal of the fact that I got struck by a stray 2p at Man City, much to the annoyance of my friends.
8. Skipped Double Physics to walk 2 miles to a hospital where an Argyle player was in bed, thanks to a 'Graeme Sharp Special'. Then lied my way in to see him by claiming to be a cousin!

Pompey & Circumstance

Portsmouth fans rather lived on their nerves last season, as our man-in-Hampshire-with-the-curious-name reveals.

And it all started so well. The season opened with three victories. It was 11th September, and a large army of dockers, fishermen, tractor drivers and nuclear warhead assemblers travelled the short way up to Swindon. The game had been conveniently timed to allow for the traditional Sunday lunchtime hair-of-the-dog recovery from Saturday night.

Everything was going to plan. Chamberlain had spent the best part of an hour and a half seeing who could kick the ball the furthest; one long shot had rebounded from a post; another win bonus was imminent. And then it happened. Just when you knew they couldn't score, even if we put Bobby Park in goal, the bastards did.

That 86th minute equaliser set the scene for the whole season. Nine days later, Pompey go 2-1 up at Stoke after 85 minutes. But, as John Motson would say in such situations, *"Stoke City are at their most dangerous when they're behind"*, and they equalised in the last minute.

Just seven more days gone, and the massed international might of Scarborough face a possible giant-killing at Fratton in the Littlewoods Cup. Pompey, the brave underdogs, lead 2-1 until the last minute, when a penalty is awarded, and Scarborough send the travelling thousands delirious. Acute embarrassment follows in the second leg.

More embarrassment as Walsall score an 84th minute equaliser at Fellows Park (they pick up one point from the next 16 games). Then Blackburn score in the 89th minute to win 3-1, and it's back to Swindon. Or more precisely, at home to Swindon in the FA Cup. They'd won at Fratton in the League the week before, and it was a delight to welcome back such an imaginative side so soon (sour grapes!). They equalise with two minutes to go, and I'll leave you to guess who wins the replay.

So to Oldham, the 14th March, and an incredible change in luck. 86 minutes...Aspinall scores (a miracle in itself), 87 minutes....Quinn scores, 89 minutes....Quinn scores again. Hang on a minute. Are we kicking the right way? Pompey score three in the last four minutes. It's a bit of a shame that Oldham had managed five in the previous 86 minutes, but it took us that long to get used to the pitch.

If the season had produced some exciting five minute conclusions so far, the last two

Warren Aspinall heading for that early bath

months produced a hat-trick of finishes even the most cynical of 'North Terrace Critics' could not have predicted. First to Brighton for a midweek game, apparently played on the beach with the tide in from what I could see through the Iron Curtain. The rain made Pompey frisky, they must have thought they were all back in the showers, and Fillery, in a brief moment of enthusiasm, put us 1-0 up.

Then, after 85 minutes, all the Pompey players hear an imaginary final whistle and decide it's home time. Brighton equalise, and this is followed by the rare sight of a Pompey player making his way to the dressing room before the final whistle. Gary Nelson then kicks the ball straight for the first time in the 90th minute, scoring in the process.

A few weeks on, and Blackburn come to Fratton chasing a play-off place. To be honest they were absolute toilet. They trailed 1-0 with five minutes to go, when the ball was lobbed to Colin Hendry standing on the edge of the Pompey area, and offside by even more than Bobby Stokes was in 1976. Everybody stops, waiting for the whistle, but the linesman is examining his pubic hair.

Now, Hendry is not quite what you'd call a touch player. In the time it takes him to cover the two yards into the penalty area, Hogg has managed to cover about 10 yards, (a conservative estimate for this to happen would be about 3/4 of an hour), and the inevitable penalty results. However, to many people's surprise, Hogg is not dismissed. A couple of minutes later, Sandford handles in the area, Gayle scores his second penalty, and the Blackburn players hand over their win bonuses as agreed before the match.

Surely nothing could surpass these two matches. But the final act is yet to come. The last away fixture of the season is at Barnsley. The match is generally quite entertaining, but everyone on the away terrace is looking at their watches, waiting for 4.40 and the real action to begin. Lee Sandford commits a rather innocuous foul, and everyone looks at him. Martin Kuhl feels a bit left out. Quite what he did or said is a bit of a mystery, but the longest running farce in British football continues as the red card appears once more, and he strolls towards the dressing room.

At this point, a flippant comment is made by the Man In Front Of Me (I sense a new feature here). It was something along the lines of *"they'll get a penalty now."* And God said, *"Let there be a penalty"* and there was. To be honest, my thoughts were directed more towards whether the off-licence would still be open in Crawley when I got back.

The entertainment continued as Currie put the ball into the net. But we're not finished yet. Gavin Maguire decides he wants to get in the bath with Martin Kuhl, and starts walking towards the referee. The look on his face suggests that he's not going to invite the official out for a drink after the game. The St. John Ambulancemen quickly swot up on how to remove an inflated leather ball from beyond a middle-aged man's sphincter; should they try and deflate it first? Luckily one of the other players guides Maguire towards the tunnel, the red card wasn't really needed, everyone knew he was on his way. The remaining minute or so passed without incident, and it was time to head for Crawley.

I hereby propose that football matches be reduced to 40 minutes each way.

'The Illegitimate Offspring of Colin Sullivan'

Quinn of the South

Spotless Kitchen

The Positive Touch

For a young lad growing up in the late Sixties, all that really mattered was the Great Game. Snooker was for old men, there was none of that American rubbish, and after all, England were World Champions.

They were days of discipline. Your Dad took you to see your local League team and you jolly well supported them through thick and thin. As my father took me to see Leyton Orient v Swindon, a 0-0 draw on 1st April 1967, some may say that what followed amounts to a deprived childhood. In fact it wasn't so much the lack of trophies that I missed through supporting the O's - after all, we had our moments, the Third Division Championship in 1970, the final of the Anglo-Scottish in 1976 and, of course, the London Challenge Cup in 1972, but oh how I begged for a goalscoring hero; an Osgood, Hurst or Greaves to worship like the other boys in the playground

Kitch Culture

Over the years shirts 7 to 11 seem to have been filled with some of the great non marksmen of the era. The early Seventies were dreadful. We hit the target 29 times in the 1970-71 campaign, top scorer Lazarus with six (he could have got eight but had Jewish holidays off) and the malaise continued throughout most of the decade. Twenty eight scored in 74-75 (with twelve nil nils), thirty seven in 75-76, and again a year later. In those days there seemed more chance of England reaching the World Cup finals or the Tories winning an election than an Orient player hitting fifteen or twenty a season, or of the lads averaging even a goal a game. That's why 77-78 became so special.

It was the second home game of the season with Oldham the visitors; arriving five minutes late I smelt a rat immediately. The O's one up? A goal in the first minute? Unheard of at Brisbane Road. The scorer? Some new bloke who'd come down from Doncaster though by the look of his silly moustache he could have come from Mexico City. He scored again that afternoon and we went on to score five for the first time in years. And so a Leyton legend was born. Peter Kitchen was short, fat, lazy, couldn't defend, liked his pint and knew where the goal was. At long last we had a hero.

By the turn of the year he'd got over half of our 29 goals in League and Cup. I used to sit and stare for hours on end at the 'Leading League Scorers' list in the Sundays, unable to believe that one of our boys was up there with the Latchfords, Dalglishs and Hankins of the world. None of those present at Brisbane Road on December 3rd 1977 will ever forget the first hat-trick scored by an O's player for six years, against Mansfield.

More memorable than any of the goals that day, however, was his attempt at a somersault after the third. After nearly breaking his back in the process, Kitch never attempted the feat again, abandoning the idea of being a Sanchez of the Seventies. After all, Hugo didn't have to train on Yorkshire bitter.

Our man had come South for a small fee in the close season. Lawrie McMenemy had introduced him at Doncaster as an 18 year old. He scored after two minutes of his debut at Shrewsbury, and repeated this feat within two minutes of his first home game against Swansea. He came to Orient with a good record of scoring against higher division clubs (including a goal at Anfield when Doncaster were in the Fourth, to secure a 2-2 draw). This re-emerged during our Cup run of 1977-8, making him a Leyton folk hero.

It would be unfair on the rest of the team that season to say that he was 100% responsible for us getting to the FA Cup Semi Finals for the first and only time in our history. But in scoring seven of our nine goals along the way he was at least seven ninths responsible. Most memorable was the Fifth Round replay when Kitch beat fifteen Chelsea defenders (including Micky Droy eight times) before slotting the ball under 'The Cat' for a memorable equalizer.

In the next match, he scored from a spectacular bicycle kick 25 yards out against Middlesbrough. He said at the time it was the best goal he ever scored. In fact it was the only one he ever got from more than two yards out.

We never talk about the Semi Final. The 'Kitchen Fries Rice' banners were sadly misguided as Arsenal sneaked home 3-0. The dream was over and it was back to fighting relegation. Kitch kept plugging away, but it came to the last game and a win at Cardiff was needed to stay up. Only one goal was scored in the ninety minutes. Only one guess who scored it. Of the forty three League goals we scored that season Kitch

got twenty one. We even managed to average more than a goal a game because of him.

Sadly things started to turn sour in the Summer. There were rumours our man wanted First Division football. Eventually, in pursuit of this, he moved to Fulham for £150,000. Unfortunately for him however they had just paid £2,000 to Merthyr for Gordon Davies. Peter always took second place and soon moved on to Cardiff. Without Kitch, Orient slipped out of the Second and to the bottom of the Third.

Then in December 1983 the news came. Kitch, who had moved to, of all places, Hong Kong, was coming home. His comeback game was a wet Friday, with the attendance just about outnumbering the Sally Army band that played before the match. The game was set for 1-1 before Kitch intervened five minutes from time to round the keeper and notch the winner.

We won six of our next seven (we were one from bottom when Kitch came) when disaster struck and PK broke his toe.'He returned late in the season in time to play in Orient's customary win to stay up last game against Sheffield United, and duly scored the second in a 4-1 win.

Special K

The following season he helped the O's to Third Division mid table, becoming the first Orient player to score four goals in one of his last games, against Millwall. He returned north to finish his days at Sealand Road.

He may not have been a Worthington, Rush or MacDougall but his strike rate of 49 in 114 League games was truly amazing in Orient terms. Getting us into the Semis in 1978 was the equivalent of Liverpool doing ten doubles, England winning three World Cups. OK, so we score more regularly now (85 last season and an annual 8-0 win). However, six years on, I still miss that dreadful moustache, his beer gut in the supporters club post match on a Saturday and, even, all those 'Kitchen Sinks 'Em' headlines on a Sunday morning. For me he will never be replaced. A true Brisbane Road superstar.

Martin Strong

Ten Football Figures Who Are Media Stars And Shouldn't Be

1. Denis Law
2. Jimmy Greaves
3. Emlyn Hughes
4. Trevor Brooking
5. Mick Channon
6. Ian St John
7. Bob Wilson
8. Emlyn Hughes again
9. Terry Venables
10. Elton John

A Dozen Football Figures Who Aren't Media Stars And Should Be

1. Chris Kelly ('Leatherhead Lip')
2. Uncle Joe Mercer (visionary)
3. Ray Wilson (happy undertaker — give him a quiz programme)
4. Tengiz Sulakvelidze (big Georgian)
5. Tommy Lawton (shiny hair)
6. Arthur Horsefield (it's the name)
7. Willington Ortiz (Bobby Charlton of Colombia. Best first name ever)
8. Jack Rollin (Renaissance Man)
9. Duncan McKenzie (for describing Keegan as *"the Julie Andrews of football"*)
10. Jimmy Sirrel (the teeth)
11 & 12. Ray Lugg and Ron Wigg (because *Luggy & Wiggy* sounds better than *Saint & Greavsie*)

Tender Moments From The Lives Of The Stars...

Bobby wants to testify (woo yeah)

On The Touchline

We sat in the dug-out with Jock Wallace and Alan Ball the other Saturday. Jock wore a tired blue suit and a badminton club tie. He looked like a Clydeside ship worker dressed for a wedding.

Alan wore an old SPALL sweater and a paunch. Both men have the sort of hair that is called 'luxuriant': Alan's red, thick, wavy copper. Jock, who (it turned out later) has no respect for bald men, has hair like steel.

Alan's famous rasping, rancid counter-tenor has dropped half an octave. Perhaps he matured late, and his voice only broke when he was 35. *"Hook it! Hook it!"* he yells. He says most things twice: *"Play it down the line. Play it down the line."* Or *"Switch it. Switch it"*. Then, with a poignant, more-in-sorrow-than-in-anger tone: *"Oh, Hicksy"*...

The youth team, in smart jackets and United blazers, are Jock's servants. Alan nods backwards to one of them and Jock shuffles his arms into the anorak held for him without turning round.

Of course, we weren't actually in the dug-out, but it feels like it when you're in C Block, Row A, seats 4, 5 and 6 at Layer Road. Jock and Alan are a Rolls and a Bentley at Colchester: easily the most impressive vehicles in a car park otherwise full of beat-up Ford Escorts, Robin Reliants, and Capris that have had one joyride too many. The locals reckon Jock and Alan saved United from the Conference last year, and they will win promotion to the Third this season.

One of the beat-up Escorts, right back Stuart Hicks, made a bid for a Great Own Goal Of Our Time just after the interval. The first half had been packed with centre circle action and silky-skilled offside trap play, and the score was still 0-0. Inside his own goal area, Stuart dived at a speculative shot that was going wide and nodded it home. *"Nice one Stuart, nice one son"* sang the twenty-seven Halifax supporters behind the goal. *"Nice one Stuart, let's have another one"*.

Stuart is a classic enactment of what is wrong with the Protestant work ethic. He has to be doing something. I bet his garden fence is perfect. No re-pointing problems on his walls. On the field, sweat that looks like spittle lodges along the tops of his eyebrows, and escapes down his cheeks. Even Stuart's hair stands to attention. Long-ball player or short passer, you wouldn't know with him, you're just gazing in admiration at his work-rate. He makes getting booked look exhausting. The programme notes said once he'd been a computer programmer, but I'm sure he had several jobs all at once before he turned pro at Colchester, and is still feeling guilty about having any spare time.

Insult To Injury

After the own goal, he knelt on the field holding his head, and then limped back to the halfway line. *"What's the matter with him?"* shouted Alan, a few minutes later. *"Knee I think"* said Ian Allinson, one of the Capris, our experienced professional, who once came on as a substitute for Arsenal. Stuart hobbled as long as it took him to get a minimum of self-respect back, and then charged back into battle, missing one clearance with such venomous energy that the opposition was unsighted anyway, holding their hands over their faces and genitals in case it came their way.

Then another clearance startled, in rapid succession, the front row of the family enclosure; seven old Essex codgers who remember beating Leeds here some time in 1971, and who've always liked being rained on twenty steps up; a man working on the broken fence at the top of the home supporters' end (whom Stuart has probably noticed has just stopped for a cigarette); and three pigeons.

Alan was holding the spare ball ready: a necessary thing in a ground as small as Layer Road, where high balls frequently clear the 'Welcome To Colchester United' sign over the terracing. Occasionally they re-appear, bobbing down through holes in the roof, then on and off girders, like pin balls.

Sometimes Alan holds two balls simultaneously - a comment, perhaps, on the play, or (one muses during one of the many less than exciting moments in a United home game) a demonstration of the family coat of arms.

A decision by Mr Pawley went the wrong way for Jock, and he commented *"Pawley by name, poorly by nature"*. Then, more trenchantly, he shouted, just about quietly enough for the ref not to hear *"You bald-headed old..."* using an noun that even *The Guardian* prints with a * in the second place. *"What did he say Mum?"* said our eight-year-old, Daniel. *"I don't know"* said his mother. *"It was something about him being bald, I think"*.

But ten minutes later, Colchester equalised: a good-looking goal, but not as classy as Stuart's. Gary Bennett ('Benno' to Alan, a Mini with a sticker in the back window saying *"My other car is a Porsche"* to me) got his rhythm perfect as he tore in from the right, passing handsome but statuesque left back called Mitch Cook, to drive the ball into the far corner without, as the *Green 'Un* said, felicitously for a change, *"breaking his stride"*.

Jock and Alan took this coolly, but when Halifax went ahead again, six minutes later, the visitors' dug-out exploded like shrapnel: Manager, physio and subs leaped about and hugged each other.

I felt sorry for Stuart and his mate, and thought of a story about Jock chasing a player round the field at Ibrox with a pick-axe, and of another of him throwing an entire defence in the bath before they's stripped. The back of his neck worried me.

Probably, though, the worst excesses of his fury were turned away in the last minute, when Colchester got a penalty and scored it twice, the first time being disallowed for encroachment: probably by Stuart, who was worried about having nothing to do for a few minutes.

Mark Radford took it with stylish ease: unforgivable, that, to a man like Stuart, who thinks everything should not only be work, but should look like it.

Fred Sedgwick

Tommy Trinder? Dennis Waterman? Johnny Haynes? Yes you've guessed. Neil Hurden reveals the pitfalls of supporting a club that were quite good a few years ago...

In the space of a dark, unforgiving week in June, European civilization lost three of its great twentieth-century cultural icons. One was an eccentric Shakespearean actor, prone to tears on public occasions, another a distinctly temperamental Austrian composer, with a slightly dubious political background; the third was a Fulham fan.

For all I know, Laurence Olivier may have had a soft spot for Exeter City, and von Karajan a lifetime's allegiance to Wacker Innsbruck. Only Tommy Trinder's obituaries, however, concentrated as much on the football team he supported as they did on the principal reason for his fame. Part of the explanation for this is clear — Trinder did not quite scale the artistic heights achieved by his two near contemporaries, although I would have like to have seen them try to tell a good mother-in-law joke, followed by a roistering music-hall anthem.

The main reason, though, is that a vital part of the Trinder character was his personification of the Fulham myth and tradition. He was instrumental in creating this, and we are still lumbered with it today. Obviously it's a bit too easy to categorize Fulham as *"The Friendly Club"*. There are a good many other teams which take a perverse pleasure in their eccentric image, — at a higher level, Man City, Leicester and, perhaps, Chelsea spring to mind. For a club of its size and recent 'achievements', however, Fulham has a remarkably well-defined character. With the (therapeutic) exception of Brentford supporters, it's incredible how many people feel positively about Fulham. It's rare to hear anyone saying, *"I really hate Shrewsbury"* but then again, few would have anything particularly

positive to say about them either. With Fulham, though, sentiments are almost always favourable.

Since the sad departure, in an opposite direction, of our two traditional rivals Chelsea and QPR, there's been little proper derby feeling in the area. Although we still like to think of Chelsea as the main rivals, it is only in the distant West of the capital that Fulham fans are looked upon as representatives of a dangerous footballing threat. Usually, we are greeted with a patronizing chorus of *"Oh, yes, you used to have a useful team a few years ago, didn't you?"* This piercing remark is traditionally answered by a wailing sound, and a bitter recounting of the transfer fees received for Paul Parker and Ray Houghton — without doubt the footballing equivalent of the World Bank's policies towards the Third World in the 1970s.

On The Merger

We have always revelled in the image of unpredictability, and, indeed, it could be said that this was vital in helping us survive the attempted merger in 1987. Bulstrode's dastardly design would have destroyed the identity of QPR almost as successfully as that of Fulham , and at the same time, Palace, Wimbledon and Chelsea were also threatened with drastic changes. Yet the bulk of the media attention focused on the lowest placed of all these clubs. We still hold that position today, nobly determined not to

let popularity sweep us off our feet.

Apocryphal tales are of vital importance for Fulham fans. Not surprisingly, these tend to be the preserve of the Haynes and pre-Haynes generations. For those of us who narrowly missed out on seeing Haynes play, it's rather like slipping away just before half-time and then missing the best goal of the season, only to be reminded about it, in intricate detail, throughout the second-half — only this goes on for your whole lifetime...

The older, pampered generation all have a story of a certain pass — the one that transcended all others for its length, and depth of imagination. Perversely, these were often unsuccessful, as the stories are meant to illustrate the fact that the man's distribution skills were so inspired that the rest of the team were as outfoxed as the opposition. Most of the moves seem to have ended with Tosh Chamberlain, Bedford Jezzard or some other unfortunate running into a corner flag, while the maestro's pass sailed majestically towards the empty goal mouth. This would cause him to stand, hands on hips, directing a withering glance from the half-way line. There are the many goals too, but mercifully for we members of the 'Lost Generation', the living legend, Gordon Davies, has just surpassed Haynes' League goals record.

Although he was a great loyalist — helped, perhaps, by the League's first £100 a week contract — Haynes was a bit too tetchy to appeal to the true spirit of a club chaired by such a cheeky Cockney chappy as Tommy Trinder. Other faces were needed, therefore, to provide some more basic entertainment, and their stories are still bounced off the walls of the Enclosure,

tage Industry

when today's Third Division going gets a bit boring — ie between offside decisions. The great performer of that era was another one-club loyalist, Tosh Chamberlain. When he wasn't running into corner flags, he seemed to have spent most of his time talking to the crowd, and is also strongly rumoured to have taken more than an occasional cigarette break by the touchline, while waiting for the ball to be cleared.

All this and a hatful of goals too in the late '50s, including three in the *"Greatest game of all-time"*, which, of course, we lost 5-4 at home to Newcastle in the 1956 FA Cup. With Jimmy Hill up front too; the gloriously unorthodox Tony Macedo in goal; and Jim Langley at left-back (who had stranger legs than Malcolm Macdonald and one of the great original flat-top hair cuts), it is not surprising that even Bobby Robson looked happy and relaxed in the team photos of the time.

As with the Nordic sagas, there are plenty of fairly improbable stories handed down as well. Ronnie Rooke, the archetypal craggy, 1940s centre-forward with reinforced steel toe-caps, seems to have regularly scored from distances that would sorely strain most Olympic javelin throwers. My favourite, though, is the one about Eddie Lowe's headed clearance which soared 75 yards right into the opposition net.

The First Division days of the Sixties were characterised on the pitch by increasingly desperate lunges for the security of twentieth place — in 1966 we took this escape route to ridiculous lengths, by relying on a linesman falling over in the mud at Northampton, so missing a probable goal which may have kept the home team up in our place.

Off the pitch, the excitement value of all

this attracted a whole host of actors and musicians to the Cottage, cementing the club's close associations with show-business, begun by Trinder and another Director, the bandleader Noel 'Chappie' D'Amato. A good many 'celebrity' fans still exist but it was significant that as the crowds fell away in the Seventies, the archetype of the 'famous' Fulham fan tended to be transferred to TV fiction. After *Budgie* and *Citizen Smith*, *Minder* gained some valuable mileage out of the Fulham trademark, and, although I'm not quite sure where this fits in, there was even talk about the Pope having a sneaking affinity for the team...

Final Fling

The standard of entertainment has remained generally high since we surrendered our First Division status — we've seen a few great players come through (and usually out of !) the ranks, and there's always been Les Strong to laugh at. In many ways, though, the Seventies witnessed the end of the club's earlier vibrancy. Even the greatest moment in Fulham's history — the FA Cup Final of 1975, was based around an ageing team and there was an air of resignation on the day, which certainly didn't make for an adventurous approach.

We weren't disgraced *on* the pitch — (at least not by numbers 3 to 11!) — but this was not the case off it, as the club was let down by the worst Wembley record ever released — the sub-Chas & Dave *"Viva El Fulham"*, with that hauntingly embarrassing chorus: *"Well Bobby, need we all say Moore?"*

If the old man's team of 1975 had ultimately failed, little was learned from the experience. Shortly afterwards, the management again opted for pure entertainment rather than long term development, with the arrival of George Best and return of Rodney Marsh at the start of 1976-77. Crowds boomed 21,000 for Bristol Rovers and 18,000 for Hereford!; the team played in neat triangular movements; Brian Moore got all excitable; and we finished 17th! At one stage it seemed that we would surpass all records by playing the most attractive relegation football witnessed in League history. The boring pragmatists among us breathed a huge sigh of relief when a 6-1 win over Orient, in Bobby Moore's last Cottage appearance, saved us from this dubious honour.

The Eighties have represented a fairly subdued period for the club, on the pitch, at least. Our recent signings of 'experienced pros' is a response to the increasingly desperate urge to see the back of the Third Division, rather than a quest for flamboyance. Doug Rougvie and Des Bremner are unlikely to attract 21,000 for a game against Bristol Rovers. Nevertheless, the potential for future excitement is there, particularly now the emphasis has switched back to building a team from the foundations of a strong youth policy. After all, we did have a useful side a few years back. Oh God, did I say that....?

Neil Hurden

OK, so Italy have some fairly handy football clubs. But what about the supporters? Phil Gibbins fills us in on what it's like to be a tifosi (look it up).

The first thing to be said about Italian football fans is that they are not treated with the same contempt by the police, the government and the press as their English counterparts.

Compared to Britain, there is a greater range of ages and types on the terraces, and rich, fashionable people frequent the ludicrously expensive Main Stand seats (up to £100 per match). Giovanni Agnelli, who calls the shots in Italy no matter who the Prime Minister might be that week is, of course, Juventus' No1 fan and paymaster. And he's not just on a Maxwell style publicity kick; he never misses a home match and he knows nearly as much about Calcio as he does about cars, giving informed interviews on the games he has seen.

Another big difference at Italian matches is that the heavy smell of alcohol is absent. Italians generally drink far less than northern Europeans, and as games are played on Sunday afternoons, after the traditional enormous family dinner, anyone seen throwing up would be more likely to be suffering from an excessive intake of cannelloni than cans of lager. On the whole the atmosphere in and around grounds is less threatening than in Britain and both sets of supporters cross paths before and after the games without too many problems. This is quite impressive given that 90% of the fans wear scarves, hats, wrist bands and all the other tacky regalia of the 70 s.

Before this begins to sound as if watching football here is an oasis of peace and sanity, it must be said that violence here is probably at a higher level than in Britain nowadays,

though in a more organised and less random manner. There have been two murders this season outside grounds and an end of season clash between Fiorentina and Bologna was marred by a Molotov attack on a train carrying Bologna supporters to the game; one teenage fan suffered burns to three quarters of his body and a dozen other fans were injured.

This extreme violence comes from a very small fanatic minority. The clubs from Milan and Rome are the worst offenders, though all clubs have their nutters. One notable exception is Napoli; in the past they had a fearsome reputation for soccer violence and the city itself is no place for the timid. These days, however, the fans get involved in almost no trouble, despite their huge away following. They seem to have changed much along the lines of Scotland fans in the last decade, and (might we dare to hope?) England fans in the next.

War Stories

Italians, not surprisingly, regard English fans much as the Romans regarded the Visigoths. They imagine English matches to be full scale urban warfare; something like Beirut without the sunshine. My attempts to enlighten them as to the improvements in recent years were given short shrift after Hillsborough which was too similar to Brussels for them to react logically to and,

more recently, the Birmingham fans' end of season stupidity, which was given wide coverage here.

Committed Italian hooligans seem to dream of being English, often bedecking themselves in Union Jacks and carrying banners written in English. Fans at one game that I attended showed their unfamiliarity with the delicate nuances of Shakespeare's tongue, as they puzzled over a large 'Fuck Off' banner being held aloft. They have been similarly puzzled about the plastic inflatables craze. They made a brief appearance here among Inter fans but they were brandished in an aggressive rather than playful manner. As there are fewer things less threatening than a giant banana they were soon abandoned and placed in that category marked 'English Eccentricity'.

The Ruud Gullit wigs that you must have all seen on *Saint and Greavsie* have been less evident this season, but Atalanta fans have responded with a bright yellow version in honour of their Swedish footballing hippie, Stromberg.

One strange phenomenon is the twinning of rival cities' fans. For example, the followers of Genoan club Sampdoria detest Lazio and Milan but get on fine with Roma and Inter. Correspondingly, fans of the rival Genoan team, inventively named Genoa, have no great quarrel with Lazio or Milan, reserving their hatred for Roma and Inter. Juventus are an exception to all this alliance forming, as they are disliked by everyone. The club are resented for being too successful and generally too Fiat, while their fans are perceived as armchair supporters who can't stomach defeat.

The level of optimism among most Italian

stful Of Lira

fans is remarkable. Losing is never really considered until it becomes a painful reality. They will start to celebrate before the final whistle even when their lead is slender, where a British crowd would be screaming for the ref to blow. This year I was taken aback at the serene confidence of Napoli fans as they prepared to take a shaky 2-1 lead away to Stuttgart in the UEFA Cup Final. They were, of course, justified, and kept city centres across the nation awake with their jubilant horn tooting.

No Great Rush

Fans are also very optimistic about the foreign players that arrive; though those who don't come up to scratch are in for a rough ride. In the last two seasons Juventus fans have hailed Rush and Zavorov as the second coming of the Messiah (Platini being the first). Neither player settled and their biblical status soon diminished to that of the leper.

The press also judge foreign players on completely different grounds to home players. Each week the papers give the players marks out of ten for performance, and foreigners are invariably either up in the genius seven to seven and a half range, or down in the four (donkey) section.

Italian fans are justly famous for their noisy and colourful displays. A match cannot start until the ritual has been duly completed. They arrive on the terraces very early and self appointed corporals scamper

around checking everything is ready as kick off time approaches. Torino fans have even set up their own PA system so that their leader (a chubby bloke in his early 30's who stands, Pope-like, on a raised platform) can co-ordinate the songs and call for silences, raised hands etc at the appropriate times.

The official club tannoys play their parts as well, with a theatrical reading of the team line ups which is accompanied by huge cheers and large amounts of confetti at one end and by deafening whistles at the other. The stage is then set for the simultaneous entrance of the players; at both ends fireworks are let off, banners waved and unfurled, balloons released and general mayhem enacted. After this, the match can be something of an anti climax, as the noise level dips appreciably and rarely reaches such a crescendo again. The goalmouth oohs and aahs are certainly not as clamourous as in Britain and neither is the roar that greets a goal.

There is a steady level of singing throughout the game, though, similar to England nowadays, the lyrics are somewhat dull and uninspiring. They have even imported some crap English songs, which they manage to follow for about the first ten words, eg *"Oh when the saeents, go marcheen een, na na na na na na na na."* Torino fans do have a witty retort to all that 'Juve Magica' graffiti that festoons their city. *"If Juventus are magic then Cicciolina's a virgin,"* they cry in unison. Not Oscar Wilde admittedly but it's a start.

Napoli tend to have the most inventive and tuneful songs, though they have a

worrying obsession with Signor Maradona as the following lyrics clearly show. *"Ma ma ma ma ma mamma, Ma ma ma ma mamma/ Do you know why my heart is thumping?/ I've just seen Maradona. I've just seen Maradona./ And Mamma I know I am in love."*

No British players have yet wrought this level of devotion; fans here haven't been too impressed by the performance of the Anglo Saxon imports. Generally they don't think much of British football, saying that it is too rushed and too physical. It's a shame that they haven't had a chance to see at close quarters the skilled displays of Liverpool and Forest in recent seasons. The standard of football offered in the Italian league is higher than that offered in Britain, though (as it should , be given the gathering of world talent assembled here). And if you consider that some of the pre match displays are worth the price of the ticket, there's a lot to be said for taking your soccer fix south of the Alps.

Home Thoughts

However , at times I can't help looking affectionately back at a rain diluted Bovril on a Friday night at Barnsley, or the discovery of a new freeze bonding process involving the Gallowgate End terracing and my feet. The Bloke Behind Me isn't half as witty here, but I suppose you can't have everything.

Phil Gibbins

Ghana Tell You A Story

Horsey Park, Obuasi, Ghana, is a bizarre excuse for a football stadium. From the outside, surrounded by a rusty corrugated iron fence, it looks like a disused latrine. Inside, terraces made out of planks teeter on the verge of collapse under the swaying weight of an excitable crowd. Along one side runs a slab of concrete covered by a low tin roof. For the spectators who've handed over their cedis for a seat here, the next two hours will be a tense, sweaty experience — a bit like being microwaved alive.

Behind this stand, on a tiny patch of ground the size of a suitcase, the players limber up. Because of the limited space, this involves standing erect and shaking intensely. Everyone knows that over the next ninety minutes anything can happen, the outcome depending on a combination of the bone-hard pitch, eccentric refereeing, volatile crowd, trigger-happy police, bribery and magic.

The pitch is the stuff of players' nightmares. Sections of grass alternate with undulating patches of dirt. An ill-advised sliding tackle could put a player in hospital with third degree burns. Controlling a bouncing ball is virtually impossible.

Yet to Goldfields — perennial first division strugglers, despite representing the local gold mine — Horsey Park is home. To the mighty Asante Kotoko, the Liverpool of Ghana, it must seem like hell — a far cry from their own 100,000 capacity stadium, 30 miles up the road in Kumasi. A bad pitch can be a great leveller, but this one is awful. It would need to be levelled just to achieve badness.

Strike Farce

For ten minutes it was typical stuff: the ball bouncing all over the place, some neat touches in midfield, but a total lack of co-ordination in the opposition penalty area. Goals are usually few and far between in Ghanaian football, forwards get a rush of blood to the head or find their feet freezing over as soon as they get anywhere near goal.

But Goldfields' goalie must have read another script. Faced with an innocuous Kotoko attack down the left wing, he inexplicably raced from his area in a vain attempt to intercept a cross-field pass and, completely stranded, could only watch as a disbelieving Kotoko forward easily lobbed him.

Nil-one and, Liverpool style, Kotoko settled down to sit on their lead and kill the game. However, they had not reckoned with the Horsey Park crowd, who were getting restless, and the referee, who was looking increasingly edgy. Perhaps he'd been bribed; perhaps he feared a lynching. Either way, a Goldfields forward aimlessly hoofed a ball over the Kotoko goal, and the ref gave a corner.

The cross came over, and up went Goldfields' number six, a sort of Frank Bruno on steroids. He casually swatted the ball down with an outstretched hand, and a team mate scrambled it into the net, watched by an incredulous Kotoko defence.

The ref promptly gave a goal, and just as promptly turned tail and ran — pursued by a pack of Kotoko players. They caught him at the half way line and proceeded to prod and harangue him until the Kotoko goalie, sneaking up on the blind side, settled the debate with an excellent over-arm punch to the head.

Down went the ref. On rushed the police. Up bobbed the ref. Away ran the ref. On came the crowd. Pandemonium. Only after five minutes of arm waving, baton yielding, and rifle brandishing was order restored, the pitch cleared, and play resumed — the goal standing, but the ref avoiding a further beating by keeping his red card firmly in his pocket.

Both sides proceeded to play out a scrappy and bad tempered draw, the man in black wisely keeping a low profile until the inevitable armed escort could whisk him to safety at the end of the match.

He probably had a sore chin, but got off lightly, all things considered. At a previous match at Horsey Park, a strong-willed — some might say foolhardy — referee had awarded the away side a penalty with two minutes to go and Goldfields leading 1-0. The spotkick was converted and the match ended in a draw. The crowd went for the ref, who was protected by the police and soldiers until an armoured car arrived to rescue him. Enraged fans proceeded to bombard the vehicle with rocks until they were dispersed by a few warning rifle rounds.

This time, against the mighty Kotoko (motto: 'A thousand will come, and then a thousand more'), a 1-1 draw was good enough. Honour was shared; the crowd were placated. They didn't even seem to mind when, late in the second half, the Kotoko keeper drop-kicked a Goldfields forward in the head on the edge of the penalty area, and the ref, having learned his lesson, waved play on.

After that incident, Kotoko could hardly complain either. When Cornerstone, the 'other' team from Kumasi, played at Horsey Park, their left back unwisely took issue with some heartless barracking by the home fans. A few of them decided enough was enough, came on to the pitch and trashed him. If the Kotoko keeper hadn't been such a headcase, apparently willing to take on the whole crowd (and clearly confident of his chances), the same could have happened to him.

Maybe, after all is said and done, this match ended 1-1 because a draw had been predicted by ju-ju. They don't mess about with all that superstitious 'last man out of the tunnel' rubbish in Ghana: this is serious stuff. At one game the mischievous Horsey Park crowd nicked the opposition's team bag from the touchline and passed it over their heads and out of the ground. It had 25,000 cedis in it — the visitors match fee and share of the gate — but the money was returned untouched after the match. The crowd just wanted to get the other team's magic symbol (ju-ju) out of the ground.

Whenever the ju-ju doesn't work, you can always rely on plain, honest bribery. It was the power of the cedi that distinguished the relegation battle at the end of last season, and led to a finale that made Arsenal's victory at Anfield look like playtime at Sesame Street.

On The Level?

On the last day of the season, Hassacas were tied on points with Brong Ahafo United. Whichever team lost or ended up with the worst goal difference would be relegated, along with the already doomed (wait for it) Manchester United. Brong Ahafo were at home to the hapless Man Utd.; Hassacas were taking on Eleven Wise.

Both Brong Ahafo and Hassacas had bribed their opponents to let in as many goals as were necessary; both were keeping tabs on the other's score through radio contact with the other ground. Consequently, at the end of a nail biting afternoon, the final scores were Hassacas 19, Eleven Wise 0; and Brong Ahafo United 21, Manchester United 0. All four teams were afterwards suspended indefinitely.

Perhaps this goes to prove that you can't buy your way out of trouble. Nonetheless, in Ghana, almost anything goes. Try two hours of non-stop sweating in the furnace of Horsey Park, Obuasi, home of Goldfields, and see.

Alastair Whitson

Les Bence's
Xmas Carol

Looking back, that momentous year of 1939 conjures up memories of a cherished boyhood defiantly oblivious to the dark foreboding awaiting us around the bend.

Fondly I recall a time when 1/6d was 2/8d, when people said *"please"* and *"thank you"* and gentlemen laid their jackets over dog poop in the park if a lady passed by, when thirty people choked on 2 inch lead models of Newcastle United stars as they tumbled down their throats in a mouthful of Runcie's 'Sugar Coated Rice Footers', and when Athletico Whaddon went on an ill timed tour of Poland.

What hangs on the wall of my memory more than anything else from '39 however was a strange event, now passed into local folklore, that occurred on Christmas Eve.

Snow lay thick with smog as smoke bellowed from the toppling chimneys behind the sulphur works. Chimneys that topped a small ramshackle row of 19th Century losers' cottages, that tilted like a drunk at the bar - Docherty Terrace.

Here at number five there was no fire in the grate, for the family were too poor to waste their meagre income on life's essentials. Around a lump of coal painted bright orange huddled 'Mr and Mrs B' and their young son 'LB'.

Though desperately poor, 'Mr B' was a proud man for he was the first, the only, footballer to sign professional terms with Athletico. Sadly, his signature was on the contract before he spotted the small print two rooms away on another piece of paper. He discovered that he had to pay them if he wanted a game! To satisfy his lust for the sport, he would take any job, however menial or degrading just to raise the cash to get out there on the park. He suffered for his art, while his family just suffered.

Cruelly, injury and loss of form cost him his place and all the family furniture in compensation to the club. So here they were on Christmas Eve, a family in the pit of despair. For however much 'Mr B' loved his soccer, he loved his son even more. He would gladly sacrifice his team place and a hat-trick per week just to give the lad a decent present, but he knew that wrapped in a mildewed strip of wallpaper was all he would get; an old shoelace and a lemon.

Little 'LB' went up to his bed of sackcloth and wire wool knowing that for him tomorrow would be just another day. Though cold, hungry and unhappy he soon fell asleep.

Suddenly, nothing happened. But later, deep in the night, he awoke and saw a strange light shining through a hole in the roof. Slowly the light grew bigger and brighter. Soon it was in the room with him! It took on strange shapes, until, unaccustomed to the glare, 'LB' could make out the outline of a tall handsome man in an England football strip, in one hand a football, in the other a turnip. It was Mick Channon.

"I be the Ghost of Football Future, like." he said. *"Oh sir"*, quivered little 'LB', for he was sorely afraid, *"what do you want with me?"*

"Well kid," says the ghost *"Your Dad's been having a run of bad luck recently but I do reckon 'ee's a useful little player, like, so I do want you to give 'im these boots of mine, 'cos they are real magic. Ee'll become a brilliant player, and when 'is playin' days is over I do reckon that if he gives them to you your name will be up there with the greats of the day like Marrydonner and Lineacre. But remember, whoever these boots do fit will become the greatest player ever!"*

Off The Bedpost

With that he neatly sidestepped the bedpost, headed the turnip against the upright of the open door and vanished into the night. Bursting with excitement, 'LB' ran to the gap in the wall where his parents slept and breathlessly related all that had happened. His father was sceptical, but on seeing the boots knew his son must be telling the truth.

"Oh, Papa!" cried 'LB' *"You're going to be a great footballer and we will be rich and happy. This is going to be the best Christmas ever!"*

As the Yuletide dawn broke 'Mr B' collected up the boots and went out saying that he had to see a man urgently. Little 'LB' knew where he must be going; he was off to see Mr Plumb, the Athletico Whaddon manager, to tell him he was quitting his rotten club and with his magic boots was off to Bolton Wanderers for a trial.

A frightening vision

That morning the young boy and his Mother played contented with his shoelace and lemon, eagerly awaiting his father's return and the tale of Mr Plumb's come-uppance. At midday the door fell in to reveal Father. *"Merry Christmas, my darlings, Merry Christmas!"* His arms were full of brightly wrapped parcels of all shapes and sizes and nestling on top was the biggest plucked turkey that young 'LB' had ever seen.

"You were right son.", grinned his father *"these boots have made this our happiest Christmas ever. Look, presents for everyone and a turkey."* *"But where are the boots Papa?"* 'LB' enquired. *"I swopped them for all these goodies. Great isn't it? Mr Hughes down the road was only too happy because his young son Emlyn had wanted football boots for Christmas but Mr Hughes had left it too late. So wasn't it lucky that they fitted his son perfectly?"* *"You sodding prat!"* wailed 'LB' *"For the sake of one sodding Christmas Emlyn Hughes is going to become the greatest footballer in the world one day instead of me!"*

Then poor little 'LB' cried and cried and did not stop crying until March 26th 1942.

But as we all know, he had the last laugh because it turned out that these boots were not magical at all.

The caption beneath a photo of the late Don Revie's frowning, lantern-jawed face and alongside a perfunctory tabloid account of his momentous career seemed to sum up the Great Leeds United Debate:

"Revie: revered and reviled." revealing a penchant for alliteration and not a little perception. Even now, twenty five years after 'Dirty Leeds' came kicking and snarling into the First Division, it is difficult to remain ambivalent about the club that Revie built.

On the surface there is little to get steamed up about. The records show that Leeds United AFC were formed in 1919 after the old Leeds City were expelled (portentously, cynics claim) from the League eight matches into the 1919-20 season because of illegal payments made to players.

Big John

They record too, that up to the 1960s, Leeds bobbed between the top two divisions, never falling lower but winning the Second Division title only once. In the FA Cup the furthest they went was the sixth round, on one occasion.

Such a history would be deemed glorious at Lincoln or Leyton, but the truth is that Leeds, with the exception of John Charles' prolific scoring achievements, had been through four decades of sustained mediocrity.

When I was first taken to Elland Road as an eight year old I had already been to watch rugby league at Leeds and Hunslet (and cricket at Headingley and Bradford Park Avenue). Leeds was very much a rugby city, after Charles left for Juventus in 1957, United had no-one of the crowd pulling charisma of his compatriot Lewis Jones over at Headingley.

Indeed, Leeds looked to be Third Division bound for the first time when, they lost 4-1 at Southampton (the 16 year old Gary Sprake's debut, another portent) in March 1962, leaving them second from bottom with barely a month of the season left.

Relegation was avoided in the last game and promotion achieved two years later. The rest, as they say, is history. The epic matches, the cup runs, international honours, Continental conquest and endless near misses. Oh, and the nastiness.

Nasty? Leeds, to teenage believers like me were 'professional', hard but fair, brave and unlucky, as much kicked against as kicking. But in the back of my mind was the nagging feeling that fortune favours the decent and honest.

My partisanship was exaggerated by a family move away from Yorkshire which set me down among Stoke City and Manchester United supporters. It suddenly became the most important thing in my life that the city of my birth now had a team that could beat the best of Merseyside and Manchester and the namby pamby Londoners. (It was an article of faith that Norman Hunter was unjustly kept out of the England side by Bobby Moore, whose sexual preferences were the subject of loud terrace speculation and who *never* played well at Elland Road).

We went to Wembley regularly. Into Europe annually. For that we had to thank Don Revie. He had almost singlehandedly transformed the club, forced the city and county to learn to love it, and achieved it in a satisfyingly 'Yorkshire' way. He rarely bought players. Mention Giles, O'Grady, Jones, Clarke and Cherry and you have practically the sum total of signings between promotion in 1964 and Revie's departure for the England job 10 years later.

He did not tolerate (long haired) prima donnas. He was reknowned for his (god)fatherly way with the apprentices, and only the best landladies were good enough for Revie's young players. If they had 'problems' there was always the club chaplain.

But Revie was a paradoxical figure. His nickname was 'Don Readies'. He was allegedly motivated by money, even obsessed with it. Of all the criticisms laid against him this is surely the weakest. Consider his background: he was born in 1927, a year after the general strike, his father was a joiner, often unemployed

Dynamic duo? — 22 —

Revie, Reveren

Lovely movers

during hard times, in Middlesbrough; his mother died when he was twelve; he left school at fourteen to become an apprentice bricklayer.

As David Miller, now chief sports writer of the *Times* and hardly a Revie supporter put it in 1978: *"It is easy to see why he grew up to place a disproportionate value on money, why he should be obsessed in his tactical attitudes by insecurity."*

The tactical aspect is another matter, but let the 'greedy Revie' jibe be laid to rest. Most of those who actually served under him, with Leeds *and* England, actually point to his generosity. And there are many in the higher managerial ranks who have capitulated to Mammon while maintaining a pious and popular public profile.

No, those who revile Leeds because of the Revie legacy invoke his defection from the England job to the United Arab Emirates (he believed that he was about to be sacked) as the reason they are on shaky ground.

But if they claim that his Leeds sides were often dirty that they were masters at time wasting, feigning injury and manipulating referees, it would be hard to argue. For this bad example, and as a successful side Leeds were influential, Revie cannot escape responsibility.

He is also criticised for his superstition (remember the 'lucky' suits?) the theory being that it put fear and doubt into the minds of players who had enough class to beat most teams without the need for good luck charms. And he has been attacked for his over emphasis on the opposition in the form of his legendary dossiers. Though not irrelevant these are flimsy accusations when set against the charge that Revie's tolerance of the 'physical' approach (he was not alone in that, Alf Ramsey come on down) set the tone for the next decade.

Long before he put them in Admiral shirts with smiley badges (proving that

And Revulsion

Leeds *were* the first acid house team) Revie had changed the club colours from blue and gold to all white, after Real Madrid. Deep down though he wanted them to be universally loved, like Manchester United. Revie felt that they had comparable skills (if you doubt that buy the BBC *Glory Years* video), but he did not give them free rein until the early Seventies.

For most of the Revie years, the team had a worse name for hooliganism than its supporters. When Merseyside 'fans' were smashing up soccer specials in the mid Sixties, Leeds followers had almost a 'cissy' reputation. Self-styled experts on the 'ends' and the hooligan subculture, like Chris Lightbown of the *Sunday Times* never rated them.

Almost as if they were trying to maintain the reputation of Leeds United as 'top dogs' (something that the teams of the 1980s have signally failed to do) elements in the Elland Road support have sought to establish their adherence to the instruction on the dressing room door in Revie's time; 'Keep Fighting'.

They had fought at Elland Road in 1971 when Mr Ray Tinkler operated a little known rule that a West Brom player cannot be offside when scoring against Leeds. That decision, like a high number of others in big matches, merely strengthened the 'everyone is against us' mentality of the lads on the Gelderd End.

They fought at West Brom and practically tore down the ground on the night that the First Division said good riddance as Leeds were relegated. They fought at Grimsby on the return to the Second. They fought at Birmingham on the day of the Bradford fire. Eighteen months later they set alight a chip van at Odsal, Bradford City's temporary home.

Some of them made life unbearable for black players wherever Leeds played, an unbelievable state of affairs for those who remember the affection bestowed upon Albert Johanneson and, later, Terry Connor. Fascist 'literature' was on sale outside the ground and a forest of arms would make sieg heil salutes. The club seemed unwilling to confront the problem.

The nadir was reached in the mid 1980s. One scribe dubbed those who had made Leeds United's name synonymous with loutishness *"Revie's children"* — the fans, like his team were bad losers. Simply put they were spoilt by success, though that does not explain the vicious racism. Ultra right politics have long had a foothold in Yorkshire, an insular parochial county where, it has been said, *"Wogs begin at Todmorden"*.

Things began to improve, paradoxically, when the club hit rock bottom. United were £2.5 million in debt (thank you Allan Clarke, Peter Barnes, Kenny Burns) and repeated outbreaks of violence were testing the FA's patience. In desperation the club struck a deal with the Labour controlled city council, sold them the stadium and leased it back.

The council wanted a supporters' club official on the board and one of a number of community based initiatives was an anti-racist campaign. Coinciding roughly with the arrival of Vince Hilaire and Noel Blake, as well as the emergence of young black players like Steve Mulrain and Kevin Noteman, it helped to bring the matter out into the open.

The feeling that Leeds return to their rightful place was imminent, encouraged by 1987's near miss in the play offs and a marvellous FA Cup Semi Final and sustained by Howard Wilkinson's imitation of Viv 'Spend Spend Spend' Nicholson also provided a more wholesome focus for

Striking Terry in their hearts

interest. That does not mean that the problem will not return if beauty and the beast (Gordon Strachan and Vinny Jones) do not deliver promotion.

Leeds, like Manchester United, Rangers and the rest now have supporters all over the world. Don Revie would have liked that. Their name still antagonises followers of other clubs; a Sheffield Wednesday fan writing to the *Green 'Un* sniped at *"Moneybags"* Wilkinson (rich, that) while Bradford City's *City Gent* enviously derides the *"onion heads"* of Elland Road (a reference to the latest Leeds badge). Still, it's better than indifference.

Little Gordon

I'm stuck with them for better or for worse (if Robin Day can 'come out' as a Liberal, then I can declare my colours). Having been born and brought up in the city and suffered the swings and roundabouts of outrageous fortune of the post Revie era, I don't intend to give up now that the good times are just around the corner.

Before you scream *"Nazi!"* there are actually signs from Leeds supporters that the 1990s may not be as embarrassing as the past decade. There was a priceless moment when United trailed 7-1 at Stoke, instead of dismantling the stand 2,000 conga-ing youths took up the park footy chant, *"Next goal wins it!"*

There's also a good fanzine called the *Hanging Sheep* devoted not only to the white, blue and gold but also carrying that symbol of hope and fraternity, the Football Supporters Association logo.

And there is also a group of supporters with more bottle than David Batty or Vinny will ever have, Leeds Fans United Against Racism and Fascism. They leaflet the ground, produce a mag called *Marching Altogether* and are trying to reclaim the club from the poison pushers.

If they do not succeed I will not be the only one withdrawing my critical reverence.

Phil Shaw
of *The Independent*

YOU ARE THE REF

The USA Invades Libya: Do you

a) **Award an indirect free-kick?**

YES☐ NO☐

b) **Consult with your linesman to see if an infringement has occurred?**

YES☐ NO☐

c) **Address an emergency session of the United Nations and urge them to arbitrate?**

YES☐ NO☐

d) **Wave play on?**

A Dozen Over-Used Football Facts

1. Football needs to rid itself of its 'cloth-cap image'.
2. The formbook goes out of the window in derby games
3. Off the pitch, John Fashanu is a really nice bloke
4. With the exception of Ibrox, British football stadia are appalling
5. Alan Smith took a year to settle in at Arsenal, but now he has 'come good'
6. It's good to see that Wolves, one of football's sleeping giants, are on their way back
7. Football fans could learn a lot from rugby supporters, who are always well-behaved
8. Billy Wright was one of football's gentlemen
9. In pre-War times the game was 'hard but fair'
10. Burnley are a famous old club, now 'languishing' in Division Four
11. Players' boots didn't used to come off in the old days
12. The only foreign players to have been succesful in English football are Muhren, Thijssen, Ardiles and Villa. Oh, and Molby, before he went to prison.

And Ten More....

1. Newly-promoted sides are 'rampant'.
2. Forwards lob advancing goalkeepers.
3. It's bad for the game if one side gets too far ahead in the First Division.
4. The football season seems to start earlier and earlier each year.
5. Large attendances are always 'bumper'
6. Steve Perryman is sure to go on to better things.
7. Ron Atkinson's champagne + jewellery image is not a fair reflection of his image.
8. Peter Shilton hates conceding goals — even in training.
9. Goalkeepers play out of their skins in front of the Kop.
10. You can never rule out Brian Clough's young side for the title.

Football Un-Funnies

"He's the new striker"

Tender Moments From The Lives Of The Stars...

Malcolm has a steamy relationship with Glyn and Colin

Broken Biscuits

Great Own Goals Of Our Time *Reading FC, 1970-71*

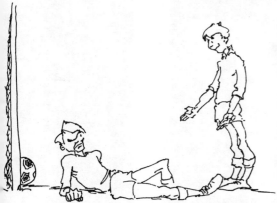

Christmas is generally regarded as the season of goodwill to all men, but as far as Reading defenders are concerned the season of goodwill lasted throughout 1970-71. The team were many experts' favourites for promotion that season (a tremendous handicap for any club), a view based on the fact that they had been the League's highest scorers in the previous season. Unfortunately, while they attacked like Brazil (Jimmy Hill said that, not me), they defended like girl guides.

Clearly, manager Jack Mansell's task was simple — get the attack and defence operating at the same level and Reading would celebrate their centenary by getting out of Division Three. However, Mansell never did anything simply and while he succeeded on both counts it was not quite what the Elm Park faithful had in mind.

Reading had difficulty scoring at the start of the new season. By the time they travelled to Doncaster in October any goal would be welcome, or so they thought. With a minute of the first half left, Barry Wagstaff headed the ball past goalie John Pratt — into the wrong net. In doing so, he started a craze that had reached epidemic proportions by the end of the season.

Within a month, Reading's own goal total was up to four. Club captain Fred 'Iron Man' Sharpe, and full back Dennis Butler both got their insubstantial frames between opposition forwards intent on doing serious damage to members of the crowd, only to deflect wayward shots into the Reading net. By now, John Pratt had had enough and was replaced by the diminutive Steve Death. He

did not prevent any more goals, but at least he made things easier for sub-editors who came up with their usual imaginative headlines — "*Steve's Death-defying Display*" etc.

Not that Deathie was given any preferential treatment — in his first game back, Fred Sharpe scored from a spectacular diving header that must have been Torquay's goal of the season. Sharpe had, therefore, scored twice in a month, double what he managed for Reading in two seasons.

Reading could not let Christmas pass without the gift of a goal, Walsall being the lucky recipients from Santa Wagstaff. The club New Year's resolution survived six minutes of play when Steve Death decided to join in the fun by juggling a shot over his shoulder and into the net at Watford.

An own goal a month for the last four months was bound to be extended when Reading started off February with a trip to Gigg Lane. Bury hold such a jinx over Reading that they would probably win without even turning up. In fact, they would have won without playing that day since both Dennis Butler (again) and Barry Wagstaff (yet again) scored for them. The final score was 5-1 and the two own goals were enough for Chairman Frank Waller. In a typically inspired move, he decided that if the team wanted to score for everyone, they could play for everyone and promptly declared that the entire playing squad were up for sale.

This obviously put the fear of God into the players, who immediately stopped scoring own goals. Unfortunately, they stopped scoring at the other end as well, going a club record of 515 minutes without a goal. March was free of 'oggie's, but this was of little comfort to the fans since our opponents managed 19 of their own. Remarkably, April slipped by without a similar indiscretion and supporters began to wonder if the players were saving themselves for something special. They were!

On May 4th 1971, Reading travelled to Villa Park, needing a draw to avoid relegation to the Fourth. With just 25 minutes of the season remaining, they had

Done to Death

the point they needed with the score at 1-1. Then, John Pratt was bundled onto the running track by Villa's McMahon. It would normally have been a goal kick or a foul but the referee was Leo Callaghan, the biggest 'Homer' since the *Odyssey* was written. From his vantage point in the centre circle, he awarded Villa a corner and with the threat of relegation at last apparent, Reading did something unheard of for them; they pulled back forwards to help out. Terry Bell, presumably there to mark Barry Wagstaff, outjumped the rest and was just about to head clear when Geoff Vowden gave him a mighty shove. The ball sailed into the net. Mr. Callaghan wasn't going to spoil his last League game by annoying a lot of noisy Midlanders, so Reading went down.

Nine own goals in a season is a lot to take, especially when you consider that if they had one in the right net, Reading would have finished 15th. The only person in the club who attempted to keep the number of goals down was secretary Fred May — wherever possible he credited them to an opposing forward, so the *Rothmans* shows us as only having scored six. Did I say *only*?

Kerry Senior

Some Footballers With Criminal Records (Really)

1. Kevin Keegan — *"It Ain't Easy"*
2. Brian Clough — *"You Can't Win 'Em All"*
3. Justin Fashanu — *"Do It Cos You Like It"*
4. Bobby Moore — *"Sugar, Sugar"*
5. Brian Labone & Francis Lee — *"Cinammon Stick"*
6. Gordon Banks — *"Lovey Dovey"*
7. Johann Cruyff — *"Oei, Oei, Oei"*
8. Jeff Astle — *"Sweetwater"*
9. Kevin Keegan (he was *unstoppable*) — *"Oh To Be In England"*
10. Terry Venables — *"What Do You Wanna Make Those Eyes At Me For?"*

Books That Should Have Been Written By Footballers

1. *100 Years Of Solitude* — David Evans
2. *The Age Of Reason* — Ken Bates
3. *My Brilliant Career* — John Farmer
4. *Grapes Of Wrath* — George Best
5. *The Secret Agent* — Mo Johnston
6. *Bring On The Empty Horses* — Alan Ball
7. *Hard Times* — Ron Atkinson
8. *The Power Of Lateral Thinking* — Ray Wilkins

Ten Embarassing Celebrity Fans

1. Freddie Starr (Everton)
2. Rod Stewart (Scotland)
3. Eddie Large (Manchester City)
4. Ted Rogers (Chelsea)
5. Stan Boardman (Liverpool)
6. Nick Owen (Luton)
7. Irving Scholar (Tottenham)
8. June Whitfield (Wimbledon)
9. Vince Hill (Coventry)
10. Roy Castle (Leeds)

Alt

The Ten Worst NASL Team Names

Jacksonville Tea Men

The New England Tea Men was stupid enough, but at least there was some vague connection between that area and a famous 18th Century tea party. What the connection was between tea and Jacksonville, Florida, or even what a Tea Man was supposed to be, nobody could fathom.

Connecticut (nee Hartford) Bicentennials

Proof positive, if it were needed, that when Americans celebrate, they just don't know where to draw the line. The nickname was sometimes abbreviated to the 'Bi's', which undoubtedly offended a great many in the organisation.

The Caribous Of Colorado

Not merely the Colorado Caribous, which would have been bad enough. No, this was Designer Soccer at its most excessive, with a kit believed to be the only on planet earth to feature a Western-style fringe across the chest. The club logo was a caribou with a soccer ball stuck in its antlers. It summed up the team rather nicely.

Toronto Metros-Croatia

"Come on you Metros-Croatia"? Once, they were simply the Toronto Metros, but Croatian interest in the club reached executive level and the NASL, against all it's principles, begrudgingly allowed this very silly hyphenated nickname for a few seasons before new owners renamed it the Blizzard.

Oakland Stompers

Despite the owners' facile attempt at honouring the area's vineyards, one couldn't help but imagine the players running about the pitch in over-sized Doc Martens, gleefully squashing everything underfoot.

Golden Bay Earthquakes

Better known as the San Jose Earthquakes, they decide to confuse us all in 1983 by mysteriously changing the front-end of their name without the obligatory franchise relocation. This was presumably an effort to gain greater regional interest by attracting more fans from nearby San Francisco and Oakland. The 'Golden Bay' moniker, though, didn't seem appropriate next to the word 'Earthquakes'.

San Diego Sockers

An oh-so-clever play on words, this. The original club logo featured a mascot called Socko, but club officials admitted they didn't really know what a Socker was supposed to be. Whatever it was, it's lasted to this very day; the club currently plays in the Major Indoor Soccer League, the birthplace of (would you believe?) even sillier nicknames.

San Diego Jaws

The predecessor to the Sockers (naturally), here was the only NASL nickname to feature a part of the human anatomy. The Jaws in question, though, owed more to a certain motion picture than to mandibles, as the club's only season of existence was at the height of killer shark mania, 1976.

Team Hawaii

It must have taken months of careful thought and research to come up with this one. Most definitely one of the strangest team names in the history of American professional sport, and much more appropriate for something like Grand Prix racing.

Minnesota Kicks

Well, at least it's better than the Minnesota Throw-Ins. The management obviously felt it was important to convey the message of what soccer involved, regardless of how inanely it came across.

Five Commonly Heard Phrases During NASL Telecasts

"For those of you who may be new to the rules of soccer...."
"We've played over ten minutes, and there is still no score here..."
"During that commercial break, a goal was scored..."
"He's quite a celebrity in his native country..."
"Remember, there are no time-outs in soccer..."

The NASL's Four Most Important American Players

Bob Rigby

Perhaps the first American soccer 'star' of the NASL, the Pennsylvania-born Rigby was, not surprisingly, never a household name, even in soccer circles, but he kept goal for the Philadelphia Atoms in 1973, at a time when American soccer players, let alone stars, were virtually non-existent. Rigby was capped seven times by the USA and played with four other NASL clubs, finishing with Golden Bay in 1984.

Kyle Rote Jr.

The only American soccer player most Americans have ever heard of. This is largely because of his winning performance in an early 'Superstars' competition on US TV, which showed the American Public At

red States

Large that, son of a gun, them soccer players are athletes. Played five seasons for the Dallas Tornado and one for the Houston Hurricane before turning his attention to the indoor game, even owning part of a franchise in Memphis at one point. Helped *Subbuteo* get off the ground in America through his endorsements.

Shep Messing

Controversial Brooklyn-born goalkeeper. Among other things, he graduated from Harvard, wrote his autobiography, posed nude for a magazine centrefold, and was alleged to have instigated a match-fixing incident, which he later dismissed as a joke between opposing goalkeepers. Served as player-coach of the Oakland Stompers for a few months in 1978 (well, somebody had to). Never capped — a rather surprising fact, given his relative fame. Wound up concentrating on the indoor game, where he excelled. Has done some television commentary of what little soccer is shown in America.

Rick Davis

The New York Cosmos' only bona fide American 'star', Davis, born in Colorado, is currently the best known and most capped of American players. He came to the Cosmos after a distinguished college career, and was one of the few Yanks to play regularly for the NASL's best known team. In recent season his career has been hampered by participating in indoor soccer to the exclusion of the outdoor game. A commentator during NBC-TV's ill-fated 1986 telecasts, he is tipped by many to be a future national team manager.

Five NASL Innovations

The 35-Yard Offside Line

Here was the rule, which perhaps more than any other kept aging imports from wheezing under the sun after half an hour of running back to the halfway line. It supposedly encouraged 'open, attacking soccer' but plenty of clubs discovered it was just as easy to set up the offside trap a little closer to goal.

The Shootout

In 1975 and 1976, the NASL decided it s drawn matches on FIFA-style penalties. Those didn't prove dramatic enough, though, and in 1977 'The Shootout' replaced them. For this exercise, the 'shooter' started at the 35-yard line, the goalkeeper on his goal line, and once the linesman dropped his flag *a la* motor racing, there were five seconds for a goal to be scored. A bit fairer than penalties, perhaps, and hilarious when a newly acquired striker didn't have a clue about what he was supposed to do.

'Sudden Death' Overtime

Perhaps the most laudable of all NASL innovations, this, like many of the league's ideas, was culled from professional gridiron football, where the first team to score on overtime (extra time) won. It forced teams to attack from the start and goalkeepers to bite their nails as best they could through their gloves.

The Mini-Game

In two-legged play-off matches, aggregate scores counted for nothing. If each team had won once, a 'mini-game' was held immediately after overtime of the second match to decide who would advance. This meant a possible two and a half hours of football in one game; a rather daunting

prospect for 35-year old Englishmen on a muggy Summer afternoon in Florida. The Minnesota Kicks grew to loathe it when, after having dismantled the mighty Cosmos 9-2 in the first game of their 1978 playoff series, they lost 4-0 in the second game and went out after losing 1-0 in the ensuing mini-game.

Names And Numbers

In the NASL's early days, players wore huge numbers both on the front and the back of their shirts, for better identification on TV. This practice, making players viewed from the front appear as if they had their jerseys on backwards, was discontinued once television interest waned. In the mid-Seventies, the league adopted the habit of other American sports by plastering players' surnames across the backs of their shirts. Of course, this proved difficult in some cases, particularly those of Eastern European players with five-syllable last names, who wound up with their name curved halfway around their back, rendering it impossible to read. Considering that smaller numbers were also required for sleeves, shorts and chests, there was a crying need for a club seamstress.

The Ten Most Colourfully Named NASL Players (in alphabetical order)

Ogun Altiparmak
Chud Ben-Tovin
Manfred Bundschoks
Austin Cumberbatch
Sandje Ivanchukov
Trakoon Jirasuradet
Enes Mamaledzija
Stanko Mrduljas
Chaka Ngcobo
Ace Ntsoelengoe

P. T. O.

Five Unique Problems At NASL Grounds

Organ Music

A baseball tradition, this regrettably spilled over to selected NASL grounds, with repetitious, clap-your-hands-to-the-beat stuff during play, or perhaps some vapid rendition of *"Happy Days Are Here Again"* after the home team scored. This may explain why the NASL had attendance problems.

Artificial Surfaces

In 1967, the Houston Astrodome hosted a National Professional Soccer League match between Houston Stars and The Los Angeles Wolves, believed to be the first league soccer match on an artificial pitch. The NASL had its share of plastic pitches, some with a camber so severe, players on one touchline could see players on the other only from the ankles up.

Baseball Infields

Many NASL grounds were shared with those of major league baseball teams, which often meant playing in the dirt of the infield at certain places on the pitch. Clouds of dust during a goalmouth melee were possible in the right weather conditions, and when it rained...ugh.

More Than One Pitch Marking

After American football's pre-season began, NASL pitches often contained a myriad of lines and markings, especially on artificial pitches, where gridiron logos and three foot wide sidelines were too much to erase every other week. As a result, players on the touchline resembled ballboys, or would make fools of themselves trying frantically to play within the confines of the smaller gridiron field.

Ball Retrieval

Time-consuming delays in play, which could be split up into two categories: a) the crowd would fail to throw the ball back, thinking they could keep it, like in baseball. b) the ball would wind up in a barren section of the deserted stadium, half a mile from the nearest human being.

Four Untimely Franchise Deaths

Philadelphia Atoms, 1973

League champions in their very first season, the Atoms initially attracted five-figure crowds on a regular basis. They were also the only team of their day, and one of the few in NASL history, to feature a conspicuous number of American players. What is more, their head coach, Al Miller, was also American. Near the end of a disappointing 1975 season, though, crowds had thinned to 3,000, and the owners, fearing a collapse, bailed out, selling the franchise to a Mexican group. Out went most of the American players, to be replaced by 18 Mexicans.

This did not particularly perk up the Philadelphia soccer community, which wasn't very large to begin with. Crowds fell to even more depressing levels, the team lost it's last six matches of the season, and, only three seasons after winning the league, the Atoms went out of business.

Montreal Manic, 1983

Le Manic de Montreal, as they were known by the city's French, were a big hit among the ethnic community, with crowds of up to 50,000 in the team's first season (1981). In 1983, however, the owners, Molson Breweries announced that the Manic would become more or less a Canadians-only team, releasing most of its star players, who were anything but Canadian. League gates

thereafter plummeted to around 8,000. After one season of Manic depression (ugh), the club folded.

Seattle Sounders, 1983

Long regarded as one of the NASL's most viable franchises, the Sounders' management acquired a bad case of xenophobia as the league approached its final seasons. One of the club's new owners pronounced his dislike of long-serving head coach Alan Hinton. He said he was tired of hearing him call the players 'lads', and the playing surface 'the pitch'. *"Lad, is what I call my dog, and pitch is something I get on my hands when I put up the Christmas tree,"* he said. (Why an Englishman, Laurie Calloway, replaced Hinton is not clear but nothing was at this stage of the NASL).

On the pitch, er, field, the Sounders, who once attracted nearly 60,000 for a pre-season friendly were now struggling to attract even 10,000 for a league match. One season of this proved enough for the new owners, who disbanded the franchise, perhaps in order to spend more time walking their lads.

Team America, 1983

Here was supposedly a panacea for dwindling interest in NASL soccer. Ostensibly this was the US national team, playing as a league entity out of Washington, DC, which would give flag-waving Yanks a reason to follow soccer. As it turned out, many of the top American players in the league refused to leave their current clubs, because of their salaries or whatever, and Team America wound up with ten foreign-born players, most of whom were first team regulars. Fan interest in DC was low, and the whole idea was abandoned after just one season. Oh yes, and that man Alkis Panagoulias was the head coach.

David Wangerin

Football Fans From The Fifth Dimension

1. Despair At An Awkward Cup Draw.

2. Poor Facilities Are A Cause Of Disquiet.

3. Left At the Mercy Of The Elements.

4. Playing Standards Vary Enormously.

Nasty Jackets In the Lives Of The Stars...

Pat is a slave to fashion

Footballers With Famous Names

1. Dean Martin (Halifax Town)
2. Tom Watson (Grimsby)
3. Neville Chamberlain (Port Vale etc)
4. Jimmy Carter (Millwall)
5. Tony Hancock (Stockport County)
6. David Puttnam (Leicester City)
7. David Coleman (Bournemouth)
8. Steve Davis (Burnley)
9. Tom Jones (Swindon)
10. David McNiven (almost David Niven — Leeds & Bradford)

Two Austrian International Players Who Have Publicly Supported Their Country's Social Democratic Party

1. Hans Krankl
2. Herbert Prohaska (Well, it's a list isn't it?)

"His expression may often be called bald.....but it is bald as the bare mountain tops are bald, with a baldness full of grandeur."
(Matthew Arnold on William Wordsworth, the Dickie Rooks of the Lakeland Poets XI)

There are some great questions of the age that remain unanswered: whatever happened to the Blue Peter baby? Why is there always a woman's shoe on top of a bus shelter? Who finances the Gideons? And, more importantly, where have all the bald footballers gone?

Take a look through a collection of Barrat's bubblegum cards, fuzzy coloured portraits of soccer stars of the Sixties and Seventies still emitting the chemical sweet smell of white powder the gumsticks were dusted with. There they are; Hennessey, Gilzean, Coates, 'Pop' Robson, Stiles, Charlton, Springett, Mancini. Practically every other player looks as if the head's been sprayed with Agent Orange.

A glance through some back issues of *World Soccer* shows that the Football League was not alone in producing players who were, in the nicest possible sense, a little bit lacking on top. Uwe Seeler was as bald as a doodlebug. Lato's cranium glistened like a Wyborowa label, Gerson's pate was as bronzed and hairless as the Girl From Ipanema's thighs. In those not so far off days, defences were dominated by depilated centre backs; midfields masterminded by thatchless passers and tonsured tacklers; and goals banged in by forwards whose foreheads began at their eyebrows and didn't stop until they reached the back of their necks.

Then, in the early Eighties, the moulting maestro began to disappear. Some explain the phenomenon by pointing to the overall improvement in medicated shampoos. Others argue that Mrs Thatcher's economic policies are responsible. Many seek consolation in the philosophy of Pascal, seeing the demise of the shiny scalp as yet another example of how an infinite series of random events can generate a result which is at once improbable and implausible and yet remains as likely as any other. *"Reason can decide nothing here"* they mutter as they gaze wistfully at video tapes of Archie Gemmill.

Unsatisfied by any of these explanations I decided to carry out my own investigation. What follows is a true story, only the names have been change to protect the innocent. My first action was to check the obvious. It seemed possible that the bald players were still out there, but that someone was supplying them with hair pieces. In short, I suspected a cover up.

Prunella Prefab has been wigmaker to the stars for over thirty years. At her workshop in London's West End I asked her if it was possible that British football's top talents were wearing toupees. The answer was an emphatic no. Why? Would a player have problems heading the ball? *"That wouldn't be a difficulty. The fixatives we use hold the hair piece firmly in place. I supplied all those worn by Sean in his later Bond films and he was forever jumping out of planes and having punch ups. It's not the rough and tumble that cause slippage, it's the damp. The glues we use are modified PVAs which means that they are water soluble. If you suffer*

from excessive scalp perspiration, or it rains, then you're heading for all sorts of trouble. And that's the problem a soccer player would face. After half an hour in the pouring rain running around sweating, every time he fell over his toupee would dislodge."

Perhaps that's why Trevor Francis spends so much time crawling round on the edge of the penalty area. But if the toupee wouldn't work did she have any ideas of what might? *"I should think that the most likely thing is hair transplants."* What would that involve? *"An operation. Hair is surgically removed from another part of the body and inserted into the empty follicles in the bald patch of scalp."* Another part of the body? *"That's correct."* Which might explain Peter Shilton's curls, and the late Seventies fashion for bubble perms. Prunella Prefab gave me the name of the country's leading hair transplant specialist. The plot was thickening. And so was the hair.

"Good news for bald men." You've seen the advert. I phoned them. A woman answered. *"Hello."*, I said, *"I'm carrying out some research into the disappearance of the bum topped footballer. Can you tell me if any of Britain's top players have recently undergone hair transplant operations?"* *"I'm afraid that information is strictly confidential."*

A scene from *All The President's Men* flashed through my mind. I was Robert Redford. The woman at the other end of the line was 'Deepthroat'. *"OK, OK."* I snapped *"If you haven't called me back in two minutes I'll take that as an affirmative. Right, have you carried out any hair transplants on*

aldy!

British footballers in the last six years?" I slammed down the receiver. I waited. The seconds ticked away. The woman from the clinic didn't call back. I had my answer.

It wasn't until two weeks later that I realised that I hadn't given her my phone number. I was back at square one. I had to take a risk. I decided to go straight to the top. I phoned the FA. *"I'm inquiring about the mysterious demise of the napless soccer player"*, I said *"You know, at one time every team, had a …"*.

"We have every confidence in Bobby Robson" the man at the other end of the line said. *"I don't think that you understand. I'm investigating the whereabouts of today's Terry Hennessys. You see…"* *"We firmly believe that Bobby Robson is the man best equipped for the job of leading England to the World Cup Finals and we intend to support him fully during the current qualifying competition."* *"I'm not getting through to you. What I'm asking about is the men with proceeding foreheads. Where have…"* *"Mr Robson has the backing of the FA, the backing of the players and…"*

I rang off. Expecting a straight answer from the FA was like expecting a decent cross from an England winger. I was at a dead end. I thought of phoning the Football League, but somehow I knew that they would blame the disappearance of the shiny pate on a tiny lunatic fringe. This was the end of the trail. I gave up the search for explanations. So what if Ruud Gullit had discovered a revolutionary new way to prevent hair loss by wearing a macrame plant holder on his head, I didn't care.

Then some months later, a chance remark made me reopen the investigation. I was sitting at breakfast with my girlfriend. She was reading *Le Monde*. (Actually she isn't French, but we're mature adults and sometimes we like to bring an element of fantasy into our private life. On other occasions I put on a seventies Crystal Palace shirt — the white one with the diagonal red and blue stripe — a false moustache and a fright wig and pretend that I'm Don Rogers. But that's another story.)

"What do you make of this, mon petit chou?", she said looking up from her paper, *"It says here that according to research carried out at L'Institut D'Hygiene de la Nouriture et des Cheveux in Chauve, certain E numbered preservatives, flavourings and colourings can cause the release of pectin producing histamines in the scalp. Apparently the relevant numbers, 435 and 728, are most commonly found in salad cream, prawn cocktail sauce, frozen breadcrumbed dishes such as scampi, and steaks which have been tenderised for flash frying.*

The news, coming just days after the University of Idaho's report on the gelling agents released by body cells treated with carbohydrate emulsifiers of the type sprayed onto potatoes during the process by which the reconstituted pulp which is turned into French Fries is produced, points to a correlation between the increasingly wide distribution and consumption of convenience foods and an as yet marginal, but by no means unnoticeable

decrease in the number of…"

I wasn't listening. I had dashed upstairs and was flicking through a pile of back issues of *Shoot!* There it was, just as I had expected; favourite food — Scampi n' chips, favourite food — Steak n' salad; favourite food — Roast Aardvark and sweet potatoes. (No wonder Bruce Grobbelaar's hair is coming out in handfuls.)

In the months that followed I carried out an exhaustive investigation. They confirmed my first impression that the demise of the egghead is the result of soccer players eating habits, habits so unique, so stultifyingly unvaried that the devastating effect of E435, E728 and starch modifiers of the diamectone type can only be fully appreciated by gazing upon the lushly carpeted craniums of the worlds footballing superstars.

The gradual disappearance of the baldy from the soccer pitches of the globe has come about at a pace directly proportional to the increase of sales of food containing the pectin-producing chemicals. The extinction of Gilzean and Co occurred within months of the first frozen pizza hitting the plate in a motorway service station. Whether the increase in public awareness of the side effects of preservatives and the growing popularity of the Greens will lead to their return only time will tell. One thing though is certain. Were it not for his fondness for prawn cocktails and butterscotch Angel Delight, Carlos Valderrama would be the new Terry Mancini.

Harry Pearson

Personally I blame the parents. Or in this case my father. Not content with inculcating several addictions bound to cause endless angst in later life — voting Labour and supporting Glamorgan among them, he chose to pass on to me an incurable passion for Swansea Town, as they then were.

Still, he got it from his father, who'd been watching since the mid 1920's, when centre forward Jack Fowler was the local hero, and the favoured terrace chant was *"Fow-Fow-Fow-Fow Fowler, score a little goal for me."* Given the widespread musicality and literacy in South Wales at the time you wonder how there were no riots.

From a first sight of Ivor Allchurch and the Vetch Field at Christmas 1965, I was hooked. But while enjoying paternal anecdotes about the likes of Trevor Ford (a sort of 1940s Steve Bull), Mel Charles and other stars of the Second Division days, I couldn't help noticing that the team I was watching was rather less impressive.

Ivor Allchurch or not they lost that first match 2 - 0 to Millwall. Eighteen months later they were relegated to the Fourth Division for the first time in spite of scoring 85 goals, and still having the inimitable and ageless Ivor.

And that was the pattern for the next decade. Never a dull moment but precious few winning ones. Unfulfilled class, eg Geoff Thomas, whose dissipation of a great talent was welcomed by nobody except Swansea publicans, mixed with less talented performers like the alarming Carl Slee, a centre half with timing modelled on Italian railways and tackling techniques popularised by JCB.

The nadir was 1975. Harry Gregg built a side whose disciplinary record suggested that the back four carried machetes, but whose goal against tally proved that they didn't. Jewel of the team was Micky Evans — a full back too psychopathic even for Walsall's taste, whose transfer to the Vetch was followed by landslide selection as Young Clogger of the Year for 1974-5. Any future chairman scrambling through the fence for the sake of their biographers can only have been trying to get out as the Swans headed unstoppably for re-election.

Panegyrics published at the height of Toshack's success would have it that this was the club he inherited. In fact, the next three years saw a considerable revival under

Alan Curtis stares in disbelief across at the opposite page

Harry Griffiths, one of the most popular players of the 1950's.

Attacking with an abandon that would have caused adverse comment in the Light Brigade, they scored 92 goals in 1977-8, missing out on promotion because they conceded 68, notably four at home to Watford on the penultimate weekend of the season.

But by February 1978 chairman Malcolm Struel was afraid they'd miss out again. After Eddie McCreadie turned down the manager's job, it was offered to John Toshack. The North Bank weren't that impressed. Griffiths was a popular local hero while Toshack suffered from the almost terminal handicap of coming from Cardiff. Furthermore, returning Welsh internationals had been among the numerous disasters of the previous decade. Barry Hole (£20,000) and Ronnie Rees (£28,000) were overpriced at 1989 figures, never mind the early Seventies.

We should have known better. Anyone with the sheer chutzpah to call his autobiography *Tosh*, an excellent description of the entire genre, has to be reckoned with.

Legend, always preferred to reality by Fleet Street when the subject is outside London or the top five of the First Division, claims his subsequent success was built on acquiring the whole Liverpool team.

In fact a nucleus for the subsequent climb already existed. Alan Curtis was testing the contortionist abilities of Fourth Division defenders. Robbie James, already past 200 League games, interspersed 30 yard rockets with wing passes that Carl Lewis couldn't have caught, while Jeremy Charles' hereditary talent was yet to be eroded by a psychosematic makeup reminiscent of Chris Old. Centre half Nigel Stevenson was still giving coltish impersonations of the hero of *Gregory's Girl*, but Toshack presciently refused him a free transfer.

Wyndham Assisted

At full back Danny Bartley jinked and sidestepped in a manner that recalled Phil Bennett, and was certainly far too good for anyone rejected by Bristol City. And Wyndham Evans' hold on the crowd's affections was a reminder that artistry is not always the way to folkhero status.

Wyndham's musculature and Llanelli origins convinced many a nervous winger that he was an escaped Scarlets second row. The timing of his ferocious tackles occasionally deserted him against quicker opponents — one memorable series of challenges on Brentford's nippy Steve Phillips would have excited the professional admiration of a Qualcast technician and earned an early visit to the Griffin Park baths. But the fans loved him for his work rate commitment and integrity, and for being local.

The Liverpool gang, however, were very much a passing phase in the lower leagues. Ian Callaghan injected restraint and control into the Whirling Dervish, while Tommy Smith showed more discretion than valour

History may record John To golden fortnght, but the voic

Robbie only wanted to be a dancer

in choosing Osvaldo Ardiles for a League Cup demonstration of his low opinion of the masculinity of Spurs newly acquired Argentinians.

Beating Spurs, by the way, was a rare cup triumph. Even at their best the Swans could be counted on to make total prats of themselves in a range of cup competitions, even their Welsh Cup victories being accompanied by indignities such as a home draw against Colwyn Bay.

Phil Boersma and Colin Irwin, the only ex Red to play regularly in the First, saw their careers cut short by injury, while my memory has mercifully erased all recall of Emlyn Hughes' short stay.

Of all the unlikely people it was Alan Waddle who made the greatest impact. Scorer, some time in the early Jurassic Period of a goal in a Liverpool derby, he had subsequently joined the long list of strikers who had failed at Leicester and looked a decidedly dodgy use of £20,000. But his large amiable, lumbering presence (can Chris really be his kid cousin?) made a massive impression as the fans again adopted a limited trier as their hero. We even forgave him for his finest goal, an unstoppable diving header which unfortunately counted for Bristol Rovers.

Toshack's role in the first promotion deciders confirmed local suspicions that someone up there was looking out for him (although Gareth Edwards denied ever being more than a fan). Against Halifax Town, he ingeniously bent a free kick off their centre half's head, although credit for this victory has to be shared with the club official, who calmed the paranoid fears of a half time crowd by announcing that rivals Aldershot were 2-0 down. In fact they won 3-1.

If that wasn't theatrical enough, a year

ing Tosh

*...as the architect of Swansea's
...e Vetch knows different.*

later, Toshack emerged as substitute against Chesterfield and headed the winner from Danny Bartley's cross with seven minutes to go. Mrs Thatcher had been elected eight days earlier. At the time it seemed like a fair exchange.

Two more years and Jeremy Charles was settling it with three minutes left at Deepdale after the sort of mass panic associated with bank crashes as Preston pulled back to 2-1 with ten minutes to go. Our only regret was that their loss kept Cardiff up. The wooden away terrace shook after 90 minutes under the crazed mass of 10,000 Swans. Days of miracle and wonder indeed. They were still singing when I got off the train at Birmingham, and doubtless went on all the way back to Wales.

The nucleus was still there but other personnel had changed dramatically. Full back Dzemal Hadziabdic arrived from Velez Mostar as a test for radio reporters unable to avail themselves of the North Bank's expedient of renaming him Jimmy.

His headlong dashes across crowded penalty areas were regarded as pretty daring until his compatriot Ante Rajkovic arrived to play in the First Division. Ante's favourite method of launching attacks was to take the ball on the edge of his own area, wait until surrounded by four attackers then beat them in sequence. The effect this had on other defenders nerves is recounted in Dai 'Teflon' Davies excellent memoirs, translated from the Welsh. But Ante lost possession very rarely. Any existing film of his systematic humiliation of Kevin Keegan — show him the ball, take it round him, take it back, repeated several times — would surely sell well among the righteous thousands who detested the unctuous little git. I can't confirm for certain that Ante is the only sent off Yugoslav to have received the Welsh Cup, but it seems a fairly safe bet.

Both Yugoslavs are strangely forgotten by Fleet Street scribes who tell you that continental imports hardly ever succeed, or hail Trevor Francis and Terry Venables for continental inspired innovation in the British game whenever they play a sweeper. Rajkovic did it brilliantly for a year, impressing Brian Glanville (and even he has to be right sometimes) in the 2 - 0 win at Arsenal.

First leg of that peculiarly satisfying double had been secured by a staggering volley from Maxwell Thompson, a centre half acquired from Blackpool, whose mingled ecstasy and disbelief were expressed in a manic run towards the other end mercifully stopped around half way by a scrum of team mates. Maxwell never moved as fast again, and gave his name to a sofa in my flat in, er, Cardiff, which was also large, ugly and virtually impossible to shift.

Most successful sides get a quota of goals nudged in from the three yards, or deflected off the backside of someone facing the wrong way past an unsighted keeper. There were a lot like that from Bob Latchford, but the archetypal Swans goal seemed to be a 25 yard shot following a seven man move started on their own goal line. And once they dried up.....

Nor was any defence built around the erratic Davies, (whose exploits were feelingly celebrated by fans erecting a massive set of cardboard hands in front of the new grandstand) going to be much more stable than the Yugoslav dinar. To be fair to Dai most of his alleged defenders spent most of their time in the opposition penalty area.

Five defeats out of six as the season ended should have been a warning, but the expectation of success had been ingrained by seven consecutive years of progress. Swansea had used up their luck, and the next year exposed limited reserves as an horrific series of injuries wrecked the squad. The transfer market collapsed, meaning inflated prices paid for the likes of Irwin and Ray Kennedy were impossible to recoup.

Factor Life

Toshack's omnipotence deserted him in a matter of months, some pointing to the loss of erstwhile advisor, Bill Shankly, as a key factor. For some fans Toshack was never quite the same hero again following the trip to Anfield days after Shankly died.

Wearing a Liverpool shirt and going to the Kop afterwards may have been natural emotional reactions to the loss of Shankly, but many crammed into Anfield's excuse for an away end felt he might have remembered whose manager he was. After all, we were six places ahead of Liverpool at the time.

In a time of recession Swansea had benefitted from an upward spiral. Better results meant better gates, more money to buy better players, and in turn better gates and better players. Once in the First Division they gambled on long term success; expensive players, long term contracts and a new stand complete with hideous floodlight pylon. But once their luck ran out, the

downward spiral asserted itself; poorer results mean lower gates and less income, so players have to be sold, weakening the side further.

Short of real alternatives Toshack hurled the youngsters in. It did them little long term good. Only Dudley Lewis survived for a long term career with the club, and he suffered badly in their decline, failing to fulfil promise that made him a mature First Division centre half at the age of 19. There was also a lad called Dean Saunders who got a few goals in the Second, but they gave him a free transfer. No idea what happened to him.

Unhappy with his players and the board, Toshack resigned with Swansea near the bottom of the Second, saved from the ultimate ignominy by Cambridge United's record breaking incompetence that year. But there was to be one last bizarre hurrah.

Changing his mind two months later, he returned not only to his job but also to the team. Now slightly less mobile than the average listed building he still scored in the Boxing Day visit to Cardiff, where League points are fortunately not subject to the Druidical conduct of the National Eisteddfoddau, under which awards can be withheld for lack of quality.

Yes, that really is Dai Davies keeping hold of the ball

A few weeks later he was fired, went off to Spain and now manages some rather less distinguished bunch of All Whites. Two years later to the day the collecting boxes were out at Ninian Park, and the bailiffs in at the Vetch after the clubs winding up order in the High Court.

It was a time of endless tension, nervous exhaustion and all the other things that cause coronaries. We finished where we'd started, broke and in the Fourth. A repeat would kill most of us. But offered the choice between our last ten years and Brentford's decade of Third Division solidity there's no contest. Bliss was it in that dawn to be alive, but to be young and the owner of a student railcard was very heaven.

Huw Richards

Embarrassing Moments Part Two

Newcastle fan Paul Hanson bares his soul...

1. Blue-tacking all my programmes to the bedroom wall - and listening to them fall off one at a time.

2. Keeping a small piece of carpet for three years after being assured by a fitter that he had just laid Malcolm MacDonald's living room carpet. (And giving some of it to a friend).

3. Having my left hand, shoulder and ear on the front of Newcastle's programme for half a season.

4. Playing centre forward for my cub scout team in two 10-goal victories and failing to score in either of them.

5. Losing to Paul Gascoigne at *Space Invaders*.

6. Asking David Barton for Mark McGhee's autograph.

7. Being asked for Peter Beardsley's autograph by a myopic adolescent.

8. Getting very drunk in the Tollbooth Bar, Edinburgh, and telling the proprietor, Pat Stanton, how I had worshipped him as a small boy (aaaaargh!!!).

9. In a quiet moment at St James's shouting *"Newcastle, these short corners are crap!"*, whereupon Beardsley passed his marker and put his shot in the top right hand corner.

10. Chasing Mirandinha down Market Street and asking him to sign my mate's birthday card.

...And anybody else who knows me.

The Footballing Kama Sutra

Tony warms up with a chum

① Archie Holmes
Leicester City F.C.
1921 - 1929

Skillful wing-half who made 259 appearances for the Midlands team. Might well have gone on to gain full international honours had his left leg not been some 6¼ inches shorter than his right.
Before becoming a footballer, Holmes worked as a steward on a cruise liner, but was dismissed as his lopsided gait made passengers sea-sick.

PLAYERS

PLAYERS

ALMOST FAMOUS

② George Spratt
Huddersfield Town F.C.
1933 - 1935

Heaviest man ever to have played in the English Football League (that is, up until Jan Molbys League debut for Liverpool F.C.) Spratt weighed in at 26st, 10lbs (28st. in his woolly roll-neck goal-keepers jersey).
Played 59 games for Town in two seasons before leaving the sport for a career in stand-up comedy.

PLAYERS

ALMOST FAMOUS

PLAYERS

ALMOST FAMOUS

PLAYERS

ALMOST FAMOUS

③ Dick 'Shorty' Hobbs
West Bromwich Albion F.C.
1927 - 1939

At 4ft 9¾in, Hobbs remains the smallest centre-half in the history of the beautiful game.
Made up for his lack of height with an extraordinary athletic ability, and a very personal interpretation of the FIFA rule-book.
Represented Britain in the 1936 Olympic Wrestling competition.
League + cup appearances = 321
Bookings = 104 Sendings off = 41
(No-one ever called him "shorty" to his face...)

PLAYERS

Dear Jimmy

You've got a big football problem. Who do you turn to? Yes, but after them, who else? Yes, OK, but after all them, what about Jimmy Hill? Well, it was only a suggestion…

Dear Jimmy,

The professional foul is ruining the game! What can be done about it? Do you have a daring, well thought-out solution to this problem?

**Mia Farrow
Manhattan**

Jimmy Says:

As a matter of fact, yes. Radical measures are obviously required to rid the game of this abomination. I have long argued for the introduction of capital punishment for every footballer who commits a cynical, pre-meditated foul against an opponent. At the very least, we should set up a committee to look into the possibility of cutting off the limbs of regular transgressors. I know the PFA would have some objections to this, but they can be made to see reason. I used to be a player, you know. Some of the great old characters who were around in my playing days (and where are they today?) would not have uttered a word of complaint had they been required to surrender a leg after a particularly hard tackle on a fellow professional.

Dear Jimmy,

Why should cricket fans be alone in enjoying the best weather when us football supporters have to suffer through the worst indignities of the English Winter? Let's have Summer soccer!

**Bob Wilson
Chesterfield**

Jimmy Says:

I entirely endorse your cogently expressed views. I have been a lone voice in the wilderness, football-wise, in calling for a radical rearranging of the Football League timetable. It seems so obvious, doesn't it? If football were to be played throughout the Summer, it would give supporters plenty of free time in the Winter months, enabling them to jet out to the Southern hemisphere to look after their various business interests while that half part of the world is enjoying its own Summer!

Furthermore, what better place for a family picnic than the cool shade of a football stand? Club restaurants, many of which are constructed along the lines of the revolutionary Sky Blues Bar And Grill which I initiated during my time at Coventry, would welcome an opportunity to widen the (already excellent!) range of food they have on offer. It is not enough to simply put our own house in order. It must also have a split-level bar, and those sort of amenities.

Dear Jimmy,

The offside trap is killing football! They might as well re-christen the game Association Offside Trap and have done with it! I was wondering if you happen to have strong, hard-hitting, and, possibly, radical, opinions on this matter?

**Anthony Burgess
Monte Carlo**

Jimmy Says:

Indeed I do. I have prepared a series of recommendations to be put before a football think-tank, which I hope to organise, at a top hotel in a pleasant rural setting with a good golf course, at some point in the near future. As a temporary measure, I think we should instigate legal action against any team who persistently operate an offside trap in League or Cup matches, as they have quite clearly failed to provide the customer with the entertainment for which he has paid. Players' assets could be seized and their children taken into care. A few hundred hours spent working on Community Service schemes or in helping to build modern extensions to the well-appointed holiday homes of various radical, highly regarded football thinkers should soon bring them to their senses!

Dear Jimmy,

I prefer to stand at a match rather than pay exhorbitant prices to sit. Let's have more consideration for the terrace spectator!

**Doris Lessing
London**

Jimmy Says:

It's people like you who are ruining our sport and dragging the name of English soccer through the mud. For years, I have been arguing that the backward old stick-in-the-muds at the FA and the League should sit up, take notice and start doing what I tell them. I have been trying to revolutionise the game through improving facilities for everyone and all I hear is grumbling. If it hadn't been for thankless people like you and other spectators, and players, and the press, I would have become the most influential figure in English football by now, and would be well on the way to being offered a job as some sort of problem-solving trouble shooter for the United Nations…I might even have had a chat show, you bastards….

Brace yourselves. Manchester City describe ther new away strip thus: *"Alternate maroon and white striped shirts with fine blue line between, England neckline with button down neck, integral shadow diamond weave, maroon shorts with 1 1/2 blue stripe and white stripe, maroon stockings with sky blue diamond on turnover."*

Long, long ago, when little boys used to run around muddy school fields in long sleeved, round necked, plain shirts, no one gave much thought to football kits.

Any seven year old worth his salt could recite the club colours of at least the top two divisions and they seldom changed if ever. Even the club themselves would hang on to a set of shirts until they were faded and tatty.

The huge club badges (often city/town crests) which had adorned football shirts for eons were dropped by many teams in the late Sixties. Many (most?) fans who can recall this period generally seem to regard it as the pinnacle of football fashion, simple, effective... and taken for granted at the time.

But then it happened. Someone somewhere, let's call him Mr Bastard for the sake of argument, decided it was a shame that no one was making a vast profit out of the kiddies' love of their local side.

There was a brief period of transition around 1972 when clubs began to incorporate hideous '70s fashion into shirts with the 'filled in' V-necks, which invariably accompanied long, straggly hair and bushy sideburns. This wasn't too bad until a little badge appeared on the Leeds strip around 1973. It was composed of a few stripes with a circle on the top and it bore the word Admiral. Innocuous enough, but experts agree that this was the start of the 'The Great Kit Caper'.

Rare Admiral

The next year Don Revie became the new England manager and one of his first actions was to sign another contract with Admiral. This time though, they were given a licence to completely bugger about with tradition. The garish red, white and blue apparition, complete with Admiral badges on the shirt and shorts, was greeted with horror by the older fans and many journalists. The kiddies though, who could name every ground in the league but had never heard of commercial exploitation or subtlety, were delighted to a man (or a kiddie).

The strip sold like hot cakes and a divide appeared in under-10 team training sessions and Soccer Summer Schools between those that could afford and those who.....

Fortunately, however, the scruffiest kids were usually the best players. (In true Nipper-style *Tiger* readers!). Admiral's advertising campaign in *Shoot!* included a dishonourable attempt to instill unsportsman-like behaviour into gullible minds by insinuating that England players would be loath to swop their shirts for those of the dull opposition at the end of the match.

After the national team had sold their soul the clubs rapidly fell in behind them. Norwich, Southampton, Manchester United, Coventry et al began sporting the Admiral logo. Coventry's kit deserves an article on its own. Mere words can't express the horror...

West Ham also dismayed long-standing followers with a strip which debuted in the 1976 Cup Winners' Cup Final. Bringing out a kit for the major final at the end of the season proved to be another money-spinner, the ploy repeated as recently as this year's Cup Final with Everton's new Umbro number.

Umbro, a well established firm producing similar but always slightly more tasteful goods, signed up Scotland, Derby, Everton, Manchester City, Arsenal and Liverpool. Around 1976-77, no self-respecting 11-year old would be seen without his baggy pinstripe flares with five buttoned-waistbands topped off with an Admiral shirt. Any team would do. One of the authors amassed a personal collection of five, one for each day of the week, with Leicester City, West Ham, Sheffield United, 'Leeds Away' and Wales.

This was the high water mark for Admiral's profit margin as we went on to big school the next year where school uniform did not include sporting attire, therefore limiting its use to the playing fields. At this point, the German giants Adidas weighed in with their famous three stripes and signed up Ipswich, Forest, QPR and others. This

rp Shock

started a battle with Admiral which Adidas eventually won.

The turn of the decade saw a change of design for England, which, remarkably, was even worse than Admiral's first effort, with the white shirt again defaced by preposterous bits of blue and red. The company deservedly suffered a dent in their popularity from which they were never to recover.

Adidas were a huge multinational company and already dominated Europe. (Today the only competition offered to them in West Germany comes from Puma, the firm set-up by the brother of Adidas's founder. Perhaps both organisations' obsession with kitting out their Bundesliga clients in either red or white started out as a private joke between siblings). Admiral's set-up was tiny by comparison and its days as top dog were numbered.

Many teams changed their kits around the turn of the decade. The two great trends were for pinstripes (the legacy of which can be seen on any Sunday morning council pitch) with almost every team in the League adding thin white lines to previously plain shirts, and 'contra-shadow', the latter devised by the French firm, Le Coq Sportif. Football strips were becoming impossibly complicated.

By the mid-Eighties, Admiral were in financial trouble and had even lost the prized England contract to Umbro, who opted for a much simpler design. Prices were soaring with shirts at over £15 and

shirts over £5. Umbro lost the Liverpool and Arsenal contracts to Adidas who were pursuing the biggest teams, having already scooped up Man Utd.

Hummel from Scandinavia sneaked their way up the League, kitting out smaller teams like Middlesbrough, Darlington, Swansea and Palace before dispensing with them to concentrate on Tottenham, Wales, Southampton, Coventry and Villa, some of whom were clothed in the dreaded 'Test Card' monstrosity previously worn by the otherwise impeccably stylish Danes.

Kit turnover was now down to two years, with some being changed every season. Some clubs opted for the unscrupulous practice of bringing out a new strip when a firm had only one year of a contract left.

Nothing To Adidas

And so to the present. Admiral, a shadow of their former selves, have only Charlton in the top flight. Their grey (sorry, silver) kit is widely regarded as appalling. Adidas are responsible for Liverpool's new shirt, which has a peculiar splattered-white effect which looks like the Liver Bird has relieved itself in a particularly forceful manner.

Umbro seem to be the most honourable party in a shark-infested business. Their new penchant for baggy sleeves and button down collars, as worn by Leeds, Watford, Celtic, Man City and many more appear to be widely popular. Rangers have just entered their third year wearing the same kit.

Scoreline, a new company promising (threatening?) to revolutionise the kit industry, seem to have had little effect among top clubs although they lay claim to 20 lower division teams. Their products seem to be of questionable quality, though, with sports shops' carpets and lower division pitches littered with the trademark little arrows which have peeled off shirts. They hardly distinguished themselves during 1988-89 either, with Norwich's shorts becoming a lighter shade of green with each match played, while Leicester's shorts took on a bluey-whiteness as colours ran.

What of the future? Contra-shadow has made some kits harder to counterfeit than a twenty pound note, but it is being used to saturation point. An awful scenario presents itself. It runs something like this. There are some horrific kits on public display in the French League at present, baggy-sleeved shirts which hang limply around the elbow, huge shorts which obscure most of the lower leg and are inching ever nearer to the wearers' ankles. Due to the presence of Glenn, Chris et al, there is a sudden and entirely superficial interest in French football among media types over here. They probably play squash with kit manufacturers. Talk is bound to turn to football strips....

The worst is yet to come. Where will it end????

Gary Silke & Gerry Conway

Promised

Remember 1970? Bonetti instead of Banks in Leon, Tostao, Jairzinho and Pele turning it on in style, and also that epic Italy-West Germany Semi-Final? One of the also rans in that tourney were Israel, at that time representing the grit and bravery of what was still the fledgling Jewish state.

Then, Israel could do little wrong in the eyes of the world, having overcome the might of the Soviet backed Arab bloc three years earlier in the '67 war, and the lads who made their way to Mexico were either in the middle of, or had just completed, their three years national service.

That squad included the greats of Israel's short footballing history. Motty Spiegler — whose goal in the 1-1 draw with Sweden was voted into the tournament's top six — Giora Spiegel, dubbed 'the golden boy' of Israeli football and Yitzhak Vissoker the keeper who drove a bus for a living, were the stars. Having won the Oceania group, they went to Mexico on a hiding to nothing and came back with two draws, (Sweden and Italy), and a 2-0 defeat by Uruguay. More important still, they were paid nothing. They collected a token of pocket money.

At that time football mirrored the state itself — it was life or death. Crowds flocked to the league games despite the one day weekend and the problem of getting to games in a country where all public transport stops for the Sabbath.

In twenty years, the football, not to mention the state, has gone from crisis to crisis, with current gates either pathetically low or charged down by irate fans who don't want to pay £15 to see second rate football. In short, money don't buy goals in Israel, but it seems to buy political favours.

The game, like all sports in Israel, is administered and financed by the political parties. Most teams, including the Arab-Israeli clubs, have the name Hapoel (Labour), Maccabi (Liberal), or Betar (Likud right wing bloc) preceding their name. Thus, a Hapoel-Maccabi Tel Aviv derby is more than a tense local struggle, it's a kind of football hustings where Hapoel players are called 'communist maniacs' and the Maccabi fans come from the opulent north Tel Aviv suburbs to taunt the 'reds'.

What seems to have happened over the last fifteen years is that this political influence has been less than scrupulous, resulting in a kind of hyper-inflation in players' salaries which is not nearly matched by takings at the gate. There are at least ten players pulling in over £40,000 a season and playing before less than 5,000 punters each week. Apart from the obvious financial repercussions of such economic madness, there is a psychological spin-off with players assuming an unrealistic superstar status on and off the field.

Instead of accepting the standard as low and trying to build for the future, teams continue to compare themselves with European and even South American set ups. This myth was exploded in no uncertain terms three seasons ago, when the champions Maccabi Haifa pulled off a real coup in signing Daniel Barilowski from the Mexican club America.

Argentina Turner

Billed as the greatest Jewish player ever (sorry Barry Silkman!), Barilowski brought a very impressive CV with him. Originally from Argentina, he had played alongside Diego for Boca Juniors and was in the national squad for the warm up games before the 1982 World Cup.

All that happened at Haifa was that he sprayed superb balls around the pitch which no team-mate could comprehend and left in a huff after two seasons due to the incessant arguing over money and conditions.

The two main reasons for the disintegration of the football are greed and basketball. Players these days reflect a country which is strong militaristically, resulting in an 'everything is possible' attitude.

One need look no further than last season's champions Hapoel Tel Aviv, the pride of the Labour Party and trade union

The Hammer that could have been - Mo[...]

movement. Despite massive debts to the income tax incurred over the years by corrupt officials, they continued to pay huge salaries until the courts stopped the cheques, the players went on strike, the league deducted points and Hapoel were relegated. The whole dirty business came to a head when one player went on television proudly displaying his bounced cheque for £10,000.

As for basketball, the authorities seem to have developed the game the right way and are now enjoying the fruits of success. Champions Maccabi Tel Aviv are one of the strongest teams in Europe having taken the European Cup twice and been runners-up four times. The league is said to be the strongest in Europe, behind Italy, and top ex-NBA pros are lured here, which raises the standard.

To reach this level, basketball had to serve a long apprenticeship which football still needs. The problems of the game are well reflected in the performances of the national team. Due to political circumstances beyond Israel's control all World Cup and Olympic qualifying games involve games with Australia and New Zealand, both of which should be beatable on paper. However, it was only in the recent World Cup qualifiers that Israel overcame them after nearly 20 years. To reach Italy, the team now has to beat Paraguay, Colombia or Ecuador.

Of course, there are some fine players developed here. Eli Ohana, Ronnie Rosenthal, Shalom Tikva and David Pizanti are competing well in Europe but Ohana

Betar Tel Aviv, with their British fan club

League

Spiegler

appears to have taken some of Israel with him after failing to agree terms with Udinese in a $1million deal, saying it wasn't enough for him to leave Mechelen of Belgium! It was enough for Rosenthal who signed instead.

To lure the fans back, the Israeli FA have opened the way for foreign players to play in the league and some East Europeans, tempted by the bucks, have expressed interest. However, the truth is that unless admission is reduced by at least 50% and players get into the game for the football, rather than easy money, Israeli soccer will never be able to recapture its past.

One issue beyond the players' control is the religious parties' influence on the game here. Following their success in the November 1988 election, they have a strong presence in the coalition government and have threatened more than once to rock the boat if football continues to be played on the Shabbat.

Gone To Lunch

One prominent rabbi wrote in a sports column of a national paper that *"football fans really prefer to spend their Saturdays around Grandma's lunch table,"* and that *"all games should be played on Tuesdays."*

Given the current quality of the football that is served up here, he may be right, but Saturday just ain't Saturday unless it comes with a professional football match.

But it's by no means all gloom. In the typical tradition of Jewish humour, Israeli football has thrown up incidents and characters over the years to match even the great Tommy Docherty's infamous bacon and eggs in a breakfast caravan on the A1. The boys on Israel TV who deal with the game would give Bernard Bresslaw a run for his money any time. Pride of place for banalities and lack of insight, not to mention innacuracies which would make even Private Eye gasp, must go to Nissim Kaviti. With his bald head, snazzy shirts and thin leather ties, he's a real hit with the test card boys. His famous *"Barcelona United 1, Dundee 1"* was excusable, *"I won't tell you the result but stay with us to the last minute for an amazing finish."* (Liverpool v Arsenal), was understandable, but his *"so it's Brazil 1, Spain 0,"* 10 minutes after the Brazilian effort was disallowed was really his finest moment.

Tel A Story

It doesn't end there. Israel TV, void of it's own idea, (or funding), grabs its ideas from GB. *Mastermind* is a real hit here with four professors from various universities usually battling it out over nuclear physics. Imagine our surprise to find Yossi from Tel Aviv answering questions on Liverpool Football Club in Hebrew. Even *This is Your Life* gets the occasional airing. Occasional, because the programme is an agonising six hours long, in two parts. Tired of wheeling out the ubiquitous concert pianists, writers and other intellectuals, the sports department was given room to flex its muscles as the great Yakov Hodorov was awarded the yellow jersey last May.

Smooth as Silkman (well, you know)

Hodorov, as any discerning fan knows, was the great Israeli goalkeeper of the Fifties and Sixties, the man who kept the Soviets down to 6-1 in '52, and only let in four against Wales in a World Cup qualifier. Rivetting viewing. We were glued to the set and had just reached the bottom layer of the Milk Tray, when who should be wheeled on as *"a great friend of Yakov's"* but John Charles, looking four months pregnant and a bit the worse for wear.

In his less than fluent Hebrew, the great Welshman recounted the famous World Cup struggles of '58, when poor old Yakov had his nose broken by an *"accidental knock when me and him went up for the ball."* Next, we were treated to a caption photo of John visiting Yakov in Cardiff General, *"I knew a lot of Jews in Leeds,"* he said. So did I, John.

As for dolce in Israel football vita, one has to look no further than the legendary Ronnie Calderon, currently turning out for Sao Paulo's main prison XI where he is chalking the walls for various narcotics misdemeanours. A real star of Israeli football in the late Sixties and Seventies, he actually had trials with Ajax in 1972, but said he wasn't interested and came home. He is best remembered as the innocent victim of an incident so bizarre it would undoubtedly have had Greavsie saying, *"cor blimey, Saint, what are these front wheels up to?"*

The celebrated game was in the 1969-70 season, when Calderon was at his height, masterminding Hapoel Tel Aviv to a 4-1 thrashing over Betar Jerusalem before an ecstatic home crowd. With Hapoel 3-1 up, Calderon took the ball, beat five Betar defenders, rounded the goalie and was about to slot the ball home, when out of the crowd stepped a soldier, tackled him and booted the ball away. This was the signal for action for hundreds of disgruntled Betar fans, who stormed the pitch and set fire to the goal.

Ordinary Joe

Another local hero is Yosef Mirimovitch, the former national team supremo, known to most visiting British managers as 'Joe'. Underneath his tough hombre exterior, Yosef is really a shy man at heart, so when a New Zealand sports magazine accused him of selling Israel's soccer secrets to the Socceroos he didn't follow the advice of the local press and *"take the Kiwi bastards for all they've got."*

Always ready to lend a hand, Yosef, when managing club sides here, would take his players to training. Rumour has it that when his car broke down on one such occasion, two players in the back gave him a push, with Yosef driving off to the training ground without them, and subsequently fining them two weeks' wages for being late.

And if you think Vinny Jones' extra curricular activities on the field are confined to Blighty, spare a thought for Maccabi Natanya's Ronnie Levi, who had his you-know-what tugged by Betar Jerusalem's Ehud Ashash three years ago. Only difference being that with Gascoigne, there was more to hold on to.

Mark Rivlin

Stoke supporters are dismayed by the departure of talent from the Potteries, as Tony Maddox reveals...

"Given the chance, anyone else would have done the same."

That chance is to earn in the region of a million pounds, for playing football in the South of France. The logic of Terry Venables' message to supporters upset at the loss of Chris Waddle is obvious. But I'm afraid he's rather missed the point. None of those supporters are ever going to get that sort of chance. Ever. In football few things hurt more than the sale of a favourite player. To the committed it's comparable to losing a lover. It can be even worse, because you have to watch the target of your affections out with their new suitors. If their relationship is a success, that's bloody well unbearable.

Spurs should complain. Down at the Victoria Ground we've said goodbye to so many of our favourites that the average Potter has more stories of lost love than Leonard Cohen.

When we are on the wrong end of a good hiding from the likes of some crack outfit like Walsall, memories drift back to happier days. Of course, Stoke are not the only club to go through this. But for some, admittedly bizarre reason, the Stoke fan feels the club's rightful place is up there with the contenders.

The sad fact is that Stoke's best young players have won every domestic honour in the game in recent years — after they have left the club. Even more painful is the fact that most of our best have been truly local lads.

Attitudes towards the departed vary enormously. Some supporters can manage a

"good luck to them", others settle for chants of *"Judas!"* The latest ex-Potters, to rapidly sample glory following their departure are Arsenal's Lee Dixon and Steve Bould. I'll come to these likely lads later, but first let's see where the recent haemorrhage of talent began.

Some of the club's older rifles will say the trend began with the sale of Sir Stanley Matthews, but if these people had their way the world's greatest would still be beetling up and down the right wing today. As far as most of the younger supporters are concerned, things really began to hit the fan with the sale of Jimmy Greenhoff. In the Bootham End the mention of the man's name must be followed by, *"the greatest player never to play for England."*

Waddington's Games

He was sold to Tommy Docherty's Manchester United, where he linked up with his gormless looking brother Brian, and soon went on to win an FA Cup medal. The sale marked the beginning of the end for Tony Waddington. The club enjoyed its only successful spell with him at the helm. He also sold a couple of our other stars from the Seventies, Alan Hudson and Peter Shilton, but everyone was more or less resigned to seeing the back of the glamour boys. Selling Jimmy was like Roy Rogers flogging Trigger to the glue factory.

Things were made worse because everyone had convinced themselves that the

player didn't really want to go. Why he shouldn't want to join one of the biggest clubs in Europe, who were putting together an exciting side, is something of a mystery, but love is blind.

He was soon replaced in the forward line by young Garth Crooks. The story goes that he had been playing with a few school friends on the club car park when he hoofed the ball through the window of Tony Waddington's office. *"Sign the lad up,"* said Tone, and the next thing anyone knows he's an under-21 international.

Sadly, young Garth failed to see eye to eye with Waddington's successor, Alan Durban, who had more teeth than a box of combs. We did have a couple of acting managers in between, but it was pretty poor acting. Anyway, the Golden Haired One sold Garth to Tottenham, and as we all expected, he soon went on to FA Cup glory.

I recall one of his visits to the Victoria Ground, when he scored a couple of goals in a sound thrashing. Because of a broken leg I was sitting in the stand behind the visitors terrace. After cracking one in he ran over to salute his supporters beneath me. Talk about rubbing it in, but I swallowed manfully, and kept a brave face. His second came from Stoke's weekly defensive cock-up, one of the few habits religiously maintained through to the present day. Garth scored, punched the air and then laughed. He laughed. It was all I could do to keep from throwing my crutches at him.

Still, we did have another home grown talent in the forward line, although it must be said that many were slow to see the talents of Lee Chapman. By now Richie Barker was holding the reins of power, and

tery Lottery

tery

he had introduced what he clearly thought was a revolutionary coaching innovation. He would happily spend hours describing the science involved, but from the terraces it seemed to consist entirely of whoever had the ball toeing it up the park to big Lee, who was fifteen feet tall.

Despite what the critics said, Lee did score quite a few goals, and this obviously persuaded Arsenal to stump up a big fee for him. This meant Barker's system fell apart, and so did big Lee, who was despised by the North Bank, much to the delight of the Stoke fans. As we all know he eventually moved on to Sheffield Wednesday, where Howard Wilkinson was assembling the world's tallest team. After rediscovering the scoring touch, he linked up with the Cloughs, and has inevitably started to accumulate the silver.

Heath Service

Back at the Victoria, our next out was Adrian Heath. He was truly a local boy made good. Too good for Stoke, who sold him for a club record to Everton. He repaid them by banging in their goal against Oxford that kept them in the cup, and is widely thought to have saved Howard Kendall from getting the sack. 'Inchy' was then at the centre of the glory days that followed, before his ill-fated move to Espanol. He has prepared for his triumphant return to the Potteries by opening a wine bar (what else) in the area.

Of this vintage is Paul Bracewell, a

Shropshire lad, who was made one of the youngest captains we've had. Sadly this couldn't prevent him from linking up with Alan Durban, who had gone 'to sort things out' at Sunderland. Paul was many things, but he wasn't stupid, and he wisely moved on to Everton.

This was also about the time Stoke temporarily abandoned the red and white stripes. No consultation of course, the club had just turned it's back on more than one hundred years of tradition, and opted for an outfit that looked suspiciously like Arsenal's. Fairly or otherwise, manager Richie Barker had his card marked after this episode. He was a traitor. He didn't last much longer.

Many of us will remember Steve Bould's early appearances for the club as a full back. He was like one of those gangly young giraffes featured in *Wildlife On One*, that clambers to its feet for the first time only to crumple to the floor seconds later. Eventually Mick Mills, who had by now taken over from the wretched Bill Asprey, listened to young Steve's plea that he wasn't a natural full back. As statements of the bleeding obvious go, this would rank alongside Kylie Minogue saying she isn't Ella Fitzgerald. The Boothen Boys remained unconvinced he had got what it takes, but 'Bouldy' went on to form an unpromising partnership with club captain, 'Whoo' Georgie Berry.

True, both were hitting some spectacular own goals, but there was a feeling they could provide a platform for better times. We now also had young Lee Dixon haring up and

down at full back, God was in his heaven, and with a bit of luck, Stoke would soon be back in the First Division. Some hope.

Despite winning every supporters' award going, 'Dicko' was promptly sold to Arsenal, at a whacking profit, admittedly. He was soon reunited with 'Bouldy', who also went to the Gunners, despite being offered a five hundred year contract at Stoke. (For all their virtues, The Potters fans have never been very good with nicknames. If the club signed a one-legged shi-ite Muslim, called Mustapha Smith, they would call him 'Smithy').

In fairness to Mills, he hasn't really wanted to let any of the young players go, but it seems a wider power is at work. The irony is that the one big sale who hasn't gone on to greater things has more natural talent than any of the others.

Making A Mark

Mark Chamberlain spent last season in and out of the Portsmouth side. He left to Stoke to join Sheffield Wednesday, but Howard Wilkinson obviously thought he looked bigger in the catalogue. Mark spent most of the time getting a bad neck, watching the ball skim the clouds.

At 21 he had broken into the England team, at the same time as John Barnes, and with a similar level of ability. Don't ask me what he's doing at Fratton Park, but at Stoke, he's one who we are prepared to forgive, and don't want to forget.

Tony Maddox

It's not easy being a Derby supporter, especially when your faith is tested by a demanding job...

I think that I am a fairly typical football supporter. I am a season ticket holder at my club (Derby County), a shareholder (of absurdly modest proportions) and I generally make virtually all home matches and a smattering of aways during the season. But do many people realise the efforts we have to make sometimes to get to matches, the torments we endure when we are forced to miss them or the vilifications we suffer in the pursuit of sporting happiness?

For the nineteen years I have been attending football matches, I have tried to impress upon family and friends that if they want me to attend some event of minor importance on a Saturday afternoon (such as a wedding) then they have only to consult the Rams home fixture list to gauge my availability. The problem has always been made worse by my ability to play the organ and invitations to nuptial celebrations usually take the form of expecting me to play the wretched instrument or to function as Best Man.

It always causes some quite unreasonable resentment. The worst occasion was when the girl next door got married in November 1979 - on the day that Derby were home to Forest. Those in the East Midlands will know that the desertion of one's post for that game makes you about as popular as Colin Moynihan in a crowd of football supporters (or anyone else for that matter). I regret to say that emotional blackmail was applied and for once I surrendered. It is, of course, Sod's Law that states that such a marriage will be joined at 3pm and 60 miles away from the Baseball Ground so that any attempt at escape is useless.

Derby Day

However even if I had to miss the game in person I was damned if I was going to ignore it completely. The second that I had played the last note of the Voluntary, I shot out of the church and ran to the car to discover with delight that we were 3-0 up over the forces of darkness from the City Ground. Learning that it was to be the second half

commentary I settled down with a will.

I didn't know that the father of the bride was going to publicly thank me and gesture in my direction (or try to) during the reception. I was not there, of course, and my mother nearly passed away in shame. Anyway, Derby won, which was the main thing, and I can suffer any amount of indignity when we beat the enemy. I knew we would win the minute I couldn't go, and I have to pretend that I was there if the subject ever comes up in a pub.

When I was organist at a church in my sixth form days I earned valuable pocket money playing at weddings. There was one couple who actually got married at 3 pm on Cup Final Day (1974 Liverpool 3 Newcastle United 0). It's hard to believe that some people are so ignorant. I had no alternative but to have radio in my cassock pocket with an earphone in the ear which was not facing the congregation, but it was difficult to concentrate on whichever hymn I was supposed to be playing with Keegan bearing down on goal.

However, despite having missed the now legendary 4-1 thrashing of Forest, I was there that glorious night in October 1975

ate Ramblings

when we stuffed Real Madrid by the same score. I was at boarding school some fifty miles away and was desperate to get away for the game, but the Housemaster would never have let me out in midweek even if there had been some way to travel to Derby.

I was forced to bribe a colleague by saying that I would pay for petrol and his admission (and virtually anything else) if he would drive me there. Fortunately he was a good sort (by the name of Nicholson, inevitably christened 'Bill' by those of us with a football bent and once called that to his face by my mother who thought it was his real name) and by the time a Classics master and one of my friends came as well it cost me very little. (I can remember pacing the grounds of the school during the second leg and the agony when that elegant defender Rod Thomas gave away a penalty in the last few minutes, thus condemning us to defeat in extra time.

After Derby's last European match, in which they lay down and let AEK Athens walk all over them in one of the most spineless performances I have ever seen (made worse by having taken a Chelsea supporter with a stutter who witnessed my

humiliation), I was so shaking with wrath (and almost as incoherent as him) one and a half hours later that I missed my train stop and had to walk the two and a half miles back to the University.

Play As You Learn

For six years I was in teaching exile in Devon while Derby went on their grand tour of the minor divisions. They rarely came close enough for me to see a game, but I decided to nip up the M5 to watch them at Cardiff. The problem was that my last lesson finished only two hours before kick off, the time it would take me to get there in my ancient Mini. The answer was to tell my class that I just had to pop out to fetch something. Like Captain Oates I added that I might be some time, and, like him, I never returned. It was then just a matter of avoiding the Headmaster on the way to my car. In the event there was such a jam on the

Severn Bridge that I was late for the game anyway.

When normality returned and I applied for a job in Leicestershire the interview was conveniently on a Saturday morning on the day when Derby were at home to Darlington (in the event a miserable 1-1 draw). I thought that I would never get the job after asking the headmaster what time we would finish because I had a game to attend, especially as the school plays rugby.

But I did. And at the right time. When I went down to Devon in 1980, Derby immediately sank out of the First Division and respectability and proceeded to mess about. I said at the time that the club would not revert to its rightful status until I returned to the Midlands and I was right. Immediately I got the job in Leicestershire in 1986, the Rams went up to the Second and then to the First in consecutive seasons. It is not everybody who is unselfish enough to change their job in the pursuit of footballing success. Who really understands the sacrifices of the football supporter?

David Whittle

Lee At Sea

The pitch invasion

I wonder how easy lies the conscience of Bradford defender Lee Sinnott in these troubled days of membership schemes and identity cards. As he tucks into his pre-match steak and chips at Valley Parade does he ever let his mind drift back to Vicarage Road on the evening of March 6th 1985? Does this cultured defender with the prodigious throw ever think about what he did that night, and what it led to?

Seventy five minutes had been played and Watford were deservedly 2-0 up against local rivals Luton, when the ball was played to Nwajiobi who had taken a position nearer to the Watford goal than anyone save the home keeper. As the ball bounced past the aforementioned Sinnott, he thought better of hoofing it clear and chose instead to stand petrified, arm aloft, and throw himself on the mercy of the officials.

The linesman was far too busy watching the match to be in line and to Sinnott's mortification kept his flag by his side. Luton scored and went on to equalize four minutes later through Ricky Hill, precipitating extra time and a second replay which Luton won by the odd goal in one. The game of football and its genuine supporters have suffered ever since. Those supporters not affiliated to either of the two sides involved will obviously not remember that the prize for winning this thrice played Fifth Round tie was the honour of hosting Millwall in the Quarter Finals.

Watford might have the least atmospheric ground in football, but what the club does have is organisation. All ticket matches are a regular feature at Vicarage Road, with ample policing, clear segregation and a special matchday British Rail station for visiting supporters. Tickets were already in hand in case Watford won the tie. They did not. Luton did. The rest is, as they say, history.

Those of us not in the first flush of youth who travel to away matches remember only too well Luton's attitude to visiting supporters. Treat them like lepers and they might not come back. It is true that Luton town centre has suffered badly from visiting hoodlums travelling out by train from London. This does not, however, apply to Watford supporters, with the M1 being such a short link between the two towns. After more than a dozen visits to Luton I still don't know where the town centre *is*, so am unlikely to run amok up and down it.

The last time I visited Kenilworth Road was for a Boxing Day game. As is always the case the lack of seating meant that many older and usually sedentary Watford supporters were on the terraces. I suppose we were rather provocative when the 'lads' emerged onto the pitch, emitting the odd *"Come on you Hornets!"* along with a festive burst of clapping.

The game was not all ticket and our spontaneous burst of applause was greeted by a posse of incognito Luton louts, charging down the terracing, scattering the mobile and knocking down the less fleet of foot. I was glad that I was nearer forty than twenty, or I might have had my collar felt for aggressively throwing myself to safety to avoid going under a flailing Doc Marten. To my surprise and their credit the Luton Constabulary quickly rounded up the considerable number of infiltrators and pushed them into the tunnelled cage in the middle of the away end. I expected that an ejection (too lenient) or a totally warranted night in the cells would follow, but this was not the way they dealt with troublemakers in Bedfordshire — especially home supporters.

The 100 or so perpetrators were led down the cage to the touchline, around the perimeter of the pitch to the fence by the penalty area, where home supporters who had been in position for hours were pushed aside to allow them to re-assemble. For the rest of the game they barely looked at the pitch, just spending their time jeering at the Watford supporters and their team. Hypocrites do not deserve sympathy and Luton never 'kept their house in order' prior to their ban on away fans and much of their problems were self inflicted.

I digress. Following the Fifth Round win previously mentioned, Luton received Millwall with the same disorganization as always. When the Metropolitan Police informed their Luton counterparts that a large number of 'supporters' were leaving London for the game, and asked if they wanted any help, the Luton police declined saying that they could handle any trouble. They couldn't! We all remember the scenes from that evening. It signalled the revival of the media's interest in the hooligan.

Publicity for this unwelcome phenomenon had been quietening down, but the Kenilworth Road pitch invasion gave the press and television the sort of sensational news they thrive on. Who knows how much influence the publicity had on events at Heysel — another disorganised stadium? Do the media, having so publicised the hooligan element who attend matches not deserve some blame for the state of mind of Liverpool supporters that night and also for the armed readiness of the Italians?

It's a Sinnott

I take my hat off to the group of Luton supporters who provide tickets for visiting supporters during the present ban. Their club does not deserve them. I grind my teeth every time I see the former Luton chairman/MP on the television telling us that they have got it right and we should all follow.

So we now face membership cards, queues to get into grounds and perhaps worse. Would the situation have evolved if that night four years ago Lee Sinnott had whacked the ball into the crowd?

Malcolm Paice

ALMOST FAMOUS

④

Vernon Taggart

Blackburn Rovers F.C.
1924

Talented Scot whose career in England was cut short when he was banned from the game by the FA for life, apparently the result of his consistent refusal to tuck his jersey respectfully into his shorts during league and cup matches.

League + cup apps. = 17
League + cup goals = 20
Scottish caps = 2

PLAYERS

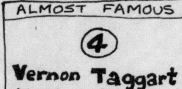

ALMOST FAMOUS

PLAYERS

"He's the new winger"

ALMOST FAMOUS

PLAYERS

ALMOST FAMOUS

⑤

Charles Kripps

Nottingham Forest F.C.
1952 - 1956

Ex-sideshow hypnotist Kripps played 172 times for Forest in the mid-fifties. Famed for refusing to remove his spectacles to play, and his frantic, some-would-say-reckless midfield performances, he was diagnosed criminally insane in 1954, but retained his first-team place until 1956, when he was arrested following a lengthy investigation of offences committed both on and off the pitch.

PLAYERS

Embarrassing Moments Part Three

Confessions from Peter Gutteridge who…

1. Explained to fellow Rams fans that I liked and admired Forest.

2. Made enquiries at the Baseball Ground about FA Cup Semi Final tickets before the Quarter Final tie with Plymouth Argyle in 1984.

3. Bought a lurid green anorak so I could be readily identified on *Match Of The Day; Mid Week Sports Special* etc

4. Stood in front of a TV camera at Newcastle v Wrexham Cup tie wearing said anorak. Later seen on *Match Of The Day* creating havoc with the colour balance.

5. Seen on *Mid Week Sports Special* by my parents while throwing the ball back to Peter Lorimer whilst wearing anorak (myself, not Peter Lorimer)

6. Enjoyed going to Partick Thistle home matches whilst I lived in Glasgow.

7. Ditto Cambridge United now I live in Cambridge.

8. Asked a policeman in Cardiff for directions to Ninian Park at 2 30 pm for the Boxing Day match v Swansea which kicked off at 11 30 am.

9. Spent one and a half hours trying to find Dundee's football grounds only to discover that both teams were playing away.

ALMOST FAMOUS

⑥

P. J. Wickerstaff

Aston Villa F.C.
1899 - 1933

The most loyal servant in the history of Association Football (making Billy Bonds look like Mo Johnston), Wickerstaff played 1,403 reserve team games during his 34-year spell with the club, also making 4 first-team appearances (in 1904, 1911, 1921 and 1932)

Wickerstaff made one full international appearance, in 1913, which was later discovered to be the result of a clerical error.

PLAYERS

ALMOST FAMOUS

PLAYERS

Ten Dutch Footballers' Names That Sound Great To Us (although we're not Dutch, admittedly...)

1. Addick Koot (PSV Eindhoven)
2. Ruud Brood (Willem II Tilburg)
3. Fred Grim (SC Cambuur)
4. Erik Ten Hag (FC Twente)
5. Gerrie Slagboom (VV Venlo)
6. Orlando Trustfull (Haarlem)
7. Albert Plugboer (SVV Schiedam)
8. Walter Smak (Telstar Velsen)
9. Gerrit Plomp (Vfl Bochum, W. Germany)
10. Peter Pot (SC Heerenveen)

Marine Biology

I'm an Evertonian. But OK, I'll admit it: I didn't watch them much in the dismal Darracott days of the 70s. For one thing, I could never afford the extortionate admission fees (at 14, would you have paid to watch Mick Buckley?) and for another I was tiny in those days and couldn't have seen a thing when I got in there. But there was another reason for my prolonged absence from Goodison. The truth must out — I confess — I was a teenage Marine supporter.

If you follow Non League football in the North, you'll know about Marine: the little men of the Northern Prem with a ground so small they only managed to fit three sides of terracing around it. They boast the longest serving manager in the whole world — Roly Howard, Merseyside's most revered window cleaner — and since joining the NPL ten years ago, they've finished in consistently high positions, the best being 2nd in 1985-86.

Not bad for a side which, it is rumoured, began life as a bunch of drunken sailors off the North Liverpool docks (hence the name) and worked their way up via such infamous local leagues as the Liverpool County Combination and the mysteriously-named I-Zingari League. I started to watch them in 1974 when the suburb of Crosby was gripped with Cup fever. Marine drew Rochdale in the First Round of the FA Cup and record truancy levels were recorded in the area on the Wednesday afternoon of the replay, which had to kick off at 3.00 as they had no floodlights at the time. Mighty Rochdale managed to struggle to a single-goal victory, but my pre-pubescent appetite was whetted.

Marine won the Cheshire League three times in six years, putting in some memorable performances such as the time they were 1-0 down to Stalybridge Celtic, but came back to stick eight past them in the last half-hour. That was glory and bliss but the 1975-76 Cup run was sheer ecstasy. In November 1975, we trounced Barnsley 3-1 at a packed Rosset Park (capacity 4,000) in a game which featured one of the best Cup goals I've ever seen. Winger Billy Morrey stampeded straight up the left touchline

Wally Bennett (left) gives a toss

with the ball and from what was virtually the corner flag, curled an unstoppable shot into the far top corner of the Barnsley net.

The national papers saw fit to record this event by reproducing photographs of balding midfielder Gerry Glover, who'd followed up the shot just to make sure, swinging wildly on the back netting with the crowd behind the goal going equally ape. In the next round, Hartlepool visited the cauldron of Rosset Park and added to the temperature by attempting to set alight the tiny wooden stand. This was worse than any away day at Chorley where the yobs were fat, middle-aged women with foul mouths and a penchant for throwing scalding tea at opposing supporters when riled. We were eventually trounced 6-1 in a replay, with Hartlepool losing by the same score to Manchester City in the next round.

In normal Non League fashion, the Marine team of the Seventies was full of characters. Goalkeeper Terry Crosbie looked and played like he modelled himself on Gordon West and was wisely replaced by the solid, if unpronounceable Ken Skupski. There was the lynchpin of the defence, Wally Bennett, who played exactly like you would expect a central defender called Wally Bennett to play. He was partnered by dark, moustachioed Peter Smith who is still there. His speciality is vicious, rocketing, spot-kicks, most of them scored past trembling goalies like Droylsden's Rupert Leggett who knew from long experience the trauma of being caught in the firing line of a Smith special.

Ironically, Smith's major moment of fame concerned a penalty incident in which he was the villain, which got him on *News At Ten*. While on a Summer spell with Los Angeles Aztecs, he was captured on film scything down Pele in true Non League style inside his own penalty area.

There were other heroes, but the best of all was the aforementioned Billy Morrey, a devil of a winger who only went in one

Peter Smith (right) surprised by a back-flick

direction — straight up the touchline, despatching any obstacles (opposing defenders, linesmen, stray dogs) at right angles as he hit them on the way. There were only two things that could stop him reaching the goalline and putting in the most perfect of (second-rate) crosses: Chorley's George Telfer and the weather.

Telfer and Morrey always fought and generally got sent off together in their Cheshire League grudge matches. As for the weather, Marine's pitch had an unfortunate rut right along one side. When it rained the rut became one huge puddle and Morrey was in trouble. It meant a choice between aquaplaning, and probably losing the ball, or moving infield into areas that were uncharted. It was his undoing. Morrey emigrated to Australia where no doubt he's still making perfect touchline runs safe in the knowledge that he's not going to hit any water further upfield.

Looking back I recognise, of course, that the football was probably pretty dire, although Roly's teams have always attempted to keep the ball down and knock it around through midfield. It was probably the fans that made it for me. There was the lad with the trumpet who used to play the battle charge as Morrey stormed off upfield, and led us in renditions of the anthem borrowed from the Beatles - *"We all live to support the great Marine."* There was also the qualified referee who'd turn purple abusing his fellow official on the pitch throughout every game.

It's still the same today. The superfan who, when asked if he was going to get married, replied *"I'm married already - to Marine"* is still there and there was a second generation trumpeter, too, last season. They'll never make it big because they haven't got the resources, but they'll be good at their own level for a while yet. Now Everton are falling under the Darracott influence again, it's not half tempting to jack them in and get back to the Northern Prem.

John Davies

Game Of Two Halves

You play each match by throwing twice; first for the home team's score, then for the away team.

england No.2-type dash...

After each game write down the result and the number of points gained.

Equipment: counters, dice, pencils, scarves, rattles, klaxon horns

Number of players: one to infinity

The story so far: because of your fans' exemplary behaviour your team has been invited to compete in a European Super League

For each match you will have landed on one of the three match squares printed with instructions which affect the result, eg if your team loses to Ajax 3-2, but you have landed on the square that says 'Emlyn Hughes tips you to lose, score two early goals' the result will be 4-3 to you.

Arsenal No.6 in typical pose...

(There's only one Bobby Mimms...)

You start in the centre circle & throw the dice to travel round the board twice, in either direction, but following the arrows, playing each European opponent in turn, at home on the first circuit, away on the second.

When throwing in a match 1 to 5 count as the number of goals, while 6 counts as nil.

If you land on a square marked X throw again to enter the adjacent game. Your score (1/4, 2/5, 3/6) will determine which match square you land on.

When throwing to leave a game always start counting from the X square.

The winner is the player whose team has the highest points total after everyone has completed two circuits of the board. Alternatively, you can agree in advance how many points are required to win the league, & play until that number is achieved.

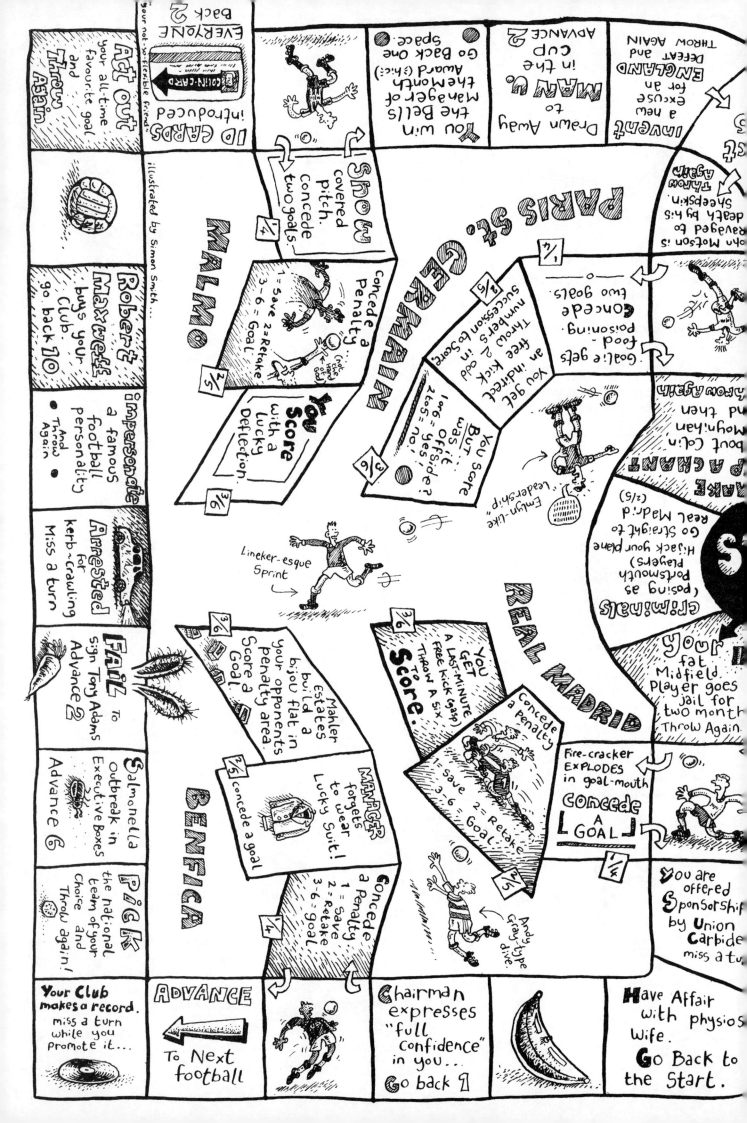

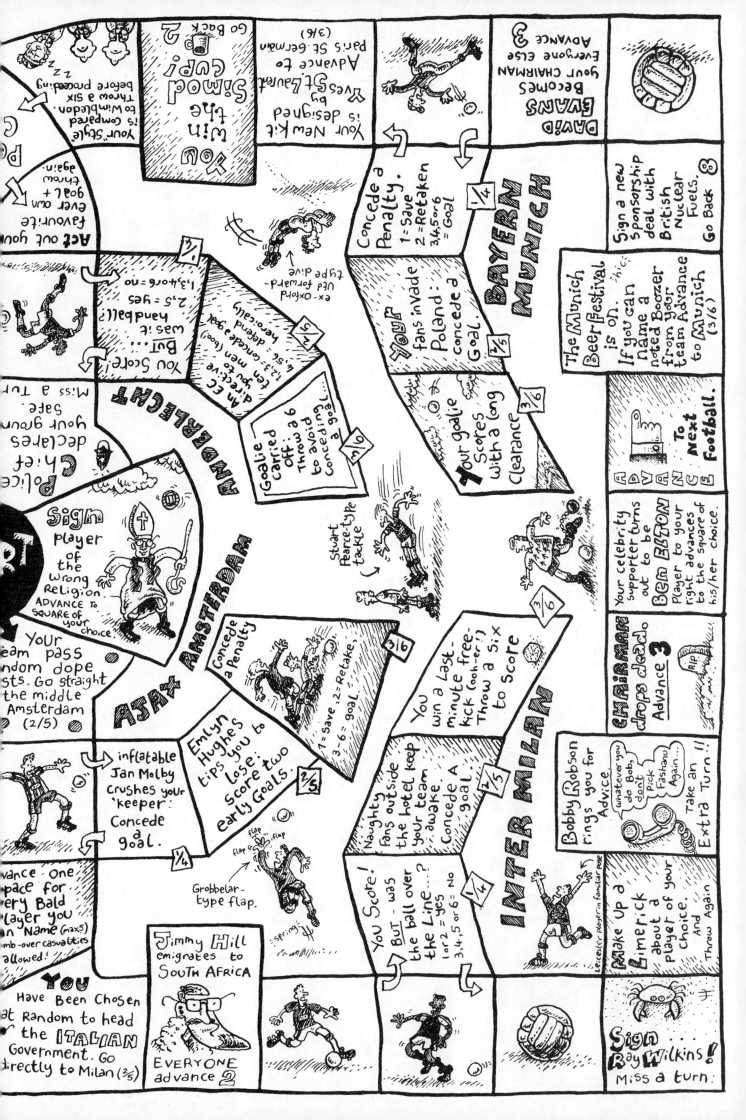

The boy scout performs many useful functions. The football scout also does a variety of jobs for his club. He makes reports on individual players as requested by his manager of chief scout; he writes match reports on games involving teams which are shortly to provide the opposition for his club; on other occasions he follows up tips, hunches, intuitions, or just simply selects a game within his locality and goes window shopping.

It is tempting, of course, to watch locality play Liverpool but in practice he chooses Mansfield v. Notts County, hoping all the time he'll spot some talent everyone else has overlooked. He can't hope to have the same expertise and judgement as men like Tommy Docherty and Ron Atkinson, who only to turn up at Old Trafford, Anfield or Highbury to spot a promising player.

The boy scout is always prepared and diligent. The football scout should be. He should do his homework on teams and players and he should double-check any information he receives. I didn't always manage that. Once I spotted a midfield player with a modest Northern club and was sufficiently impressed to take a second look and recommend him to my club.

When nothing happened and a few weeks later the player was transferred to a club on the South Coast for what I considered a ridiculously low figure I asked my chief scout how they could let such a bargain slip by. I really fancied that player — what I hadn't realised was the same player really fancied his chairman's daughter (in fact, anyone's daughter) and he was banished to the 'Deep South' for the good of Northern society at large. But my biggest mistake concerned a visit to Bath City.

Newcastle United has asked me to report on Bath's midfielder, a young man called Roger Swift. I travelled to Twerton Park to watch Bath play Bexleyheath. After ten minutes it was painfully obvious that Mr Swift was very inappropriately named. Not only was he the slowest man on the park but he hadn't the faintest idea what wings were

You can't judge a Book...

for. But my attention was taken by Bath City's right back. He had spindly legs, baggy shorts, rounded shoulders, grizzled hair, and you saw hundreds like him on cigarette cards before the Second World War. Could he play, though! His tackling was crisp and incisive, his interceptions positive, his kicking clean, his passing deadly accurate, and his brief surges down the wing suggested he would have made an excellent winger. I marvelled at the man and decided to investigate.

I moved into a group of gnarled veteran Bath supporters and asked my questions. Had he come from a League club? *"No"*, I was told, *"but he's the best back in the Southern League"*. *"Why hasn't he joined a League club"*, I asked, *"has he got a super job outside the game"*? the supporters didn't think so. *"How old is he"*? I asked. *"37"* said the first supporter; *"No, 38"*, said supporter number two. I was frankly amazed and concluded that somebody, years previously, had missed their way.

Shortly afterwards I read in the papers that Bath City's manager, Mr Malcolm Allison, had been appointed manager of Plymouth Argyle. His first signing was the Bath full back, 27 year old Tony Book. The scout who mad missed his way was me.

Vanishing Point

The boy scout is always conscientious. I can truthfully say that out of three thousand matches covered in my career, I left early on only a handful of occasions. I have always been contemptuous of the scout who turns up late, and leaves fifteen minutes before the end of the game. Such men are not all that rare in football. However, I recall an occasion when I was less than conscientious — and very embarrassing it proved to be.

Late one Friday afternoon Nottingham Forest's chief scout asked me to report on Bill Garner of Bedford Town. Having ascertained that Bedford were due to meet Gravesend & Northfleet away and that Mr Garner was playing I set off on the long train journey from the Midlands. I arrived in plenty of time at Gravesend only to find the ground was at Northfleet. Still, I got there early and was entertained by the home team's chairman. I took my seat in the director's box, the game kicked off and then the chairman remarked, *"There's a scout from Villa coming today as well"*. My heart sank when I saw who it was — a man who spent most of the time talking about his favourite subject, namely himself. Sure enough he chatted incessantly, pausing only for a lengthy refreshment period at half-time. In the second half the monologue continued.

An alright Jack

My head was splitting and when my companion suggested I share his taxi to the station- *"there's an excellent connection if we leave early"* — I was too exhausted to argue. We left at 4.30 , there was no score and Mr. Garner, apparently famed for being good with the outside of his head, had done nothing of note.

The following day I wrote my report and popped it in the village pillar-box. I read through the Sunday papers and glanced idly at the Southern League results - Gravesend 0 Bedford 4. Worse was to follow. A small item remarked that not only had Bill Garner scored all four goals in the last six minutes but each had been headed in. I raced to the pillar box, waited for my friendly village postman to arrive and I reclaimed my report. I rewrote it. My opinions hadn't changed but the facts had.

Staff And Nonsense

The boy scout respects his elders and superiors. Here I differ. I have never understood why managers will disregard the advice of their own staff but hang on to every word of their fellow managers. I was scouting for Carlisle United when I received a call from the late Dick Young. *"I've just had a long chat with John Harris* (assistant manager at Wednesday). *He says they've got a surplus of good centre halves and he recommends we take a look. Go and watch Wednesday reserves on Saturday, will you, and tell us what you think of Dave Cusack".* I

— 50 —

or Mr Right

already knew Cusack; left footed, left sided and one to be left alone. I said so, but Dick Young was adamant. *"John Harris says he's good"*. We ll, I've never yet been in a market and heard a man shouting *"Rotten fish for sale"* but mine is not to reason why.

However, I received this call on the Tuesday morning and there was a game at Huddersfield that evening against Bournemouth. The latter had a substitute called Kevin Reeves I rather admired so it was off to Leeds Road that evening. There I was astounded to see not one, not two, but three Sheffield Wednesday scouts present. I went over to them. *"Something important here, or are you just lonely"*? I asked, *"We've had a right rollicking today"*, said one of them. *"The Boss* (Jack Charlton) *had all his scouts in and told us Wednesday are managed by two men who had a reputation for being good centre halves. And yet we haven't got one good centre half on our books. Go out and find one"*!

The boy scout is encouraged always to be positive. A football scout should be positive, too. Billy Coulson is a name few have heard of. Jackie Milburn is well known. Billy Coulson spotted Milburn. He didn't comment on Jackie's heading ability — he had very little. Jackie was no tackler. But Billy saw the tremendous pace, the power, the control, the great finishing ability, and recommended Milburn to Newcastle United.

Early in my scouting career I noted Frank Barton of Scunthorpe. I watched him several times and on the last occasion before Carlisle signed him, I watched Frank play at Oxford. In goal for Scunthorpe was a name new to me. A spidery youngster, he made

some astonishing saves; his agility was exceptional, his bravery unquestioned. Scunthorpe won 3-2 but Oxford's two goals were the direct result of mistakes by the young goalkeeper. Foolishly, in my report, I concentrated on those errors. I should have been mesmerised by the youngster's obvious positive qualities. I do hope that Ray Clemence never made the big time.

One aspect of scouting I heartily detested was schoolboy football. The really talented schoolboy footballer isn't spotted — he selects his own big club, and they in turn have the prodigy in their sights when he is no more than 11 years old. The vast majority of schoolboy internationals fade from the scene when their superior physical maturity at fifteen no longer exists in their late teens. But how I hated the schoolboy football scene, watching these prima donnas strutting round the stadiums with scouts and sometimes even managers carrying their boots and fawning over the prodigies' parents.

Teenage Lament

One Sunday, when I was a Forest scout, I was asked to travel to Stoke to persuade a schoolboy international trialist to sign schoolboy forms. I was met by the boy's father who asked how much he (the father) would be paid. I told him that Forest did not pay anyone anything and that it was illegal anyway. Unimpressed, he told me the others weren't so mean. I asked if I could talk to the son and was ushered in to his presence. The boy lay on the sofa in the front room like a young Roman emperor and informed me he hadn't made up his mind which club to join.

Ray banned

There was a knock on the front door. *"For you, John"*, said father and the boy went to the door where a small group of boys stood bouncing a football. *"Coming down to the Rec to play football, John"*? they asked. *"Naw"* said John, *"I'm sick of football"*, and closed the door. He returned to his sofa. *"I'm watching telly this afternoon"*, he informed me. Enlightenment dawned. Of course, *Star Soccer* at 2.30, Stoke City v Manchester United. *"Naw"* said our hero, *"I'm not watching that — there's a Western on the other side"*.

To be Frank Barton

Three years later I switched on my car radio to hear a commentary on a vital relegation match featuring Stoke City. The commentator was Larry Canning. *"Stoke have a great youngster playing here tonight. The future of the game is assured as long as lads like this keep coming through"*. It was my hero of the sofa. *"Larry Canning doesn't know what I know"*, I told my radio. Four years and three clubs later John dropped into the obscurity of non-League soccer. Perhaps I had missed quite a few potential stars in my scouting career. But I don't think I was ever fooled by a charlatan.

Finally, the boy scout is a valued member of the community. The football scout is often seriously undervalued When I retired from my job as an education officer I decided it was time to retire from football scouting. My son, a dedicated Stoke City fan (though he is receiving treatment for it), told me that his beloved team were in dire straits. Could I not give them a helping hand? So I wrote to the club, told them of my thirty years in scouting, and offered to help in any way I could. I didn't want any payment and I wouldn't even claim expenses.

Some six weeks went by, then I received a reply. I was thanked for my interest but told that Stoke City didn't need any scouts. The signature on the letter puzzled me; it wasn't the manager's, nor the secretary's. Nor was it that of the chairman or one of the directors. My son knew the answer straight away. It was the groundsman's.

Eric Foster

Great Subbuteo Matches Of All Time
The Top Of The Pops Final, 1979

Who would win the last domestic honour of the season, The BSTOTP Cup? Tommy Doc's beaten FA Cup finalists, Manchester United, or Dave Sexton's high-flying QPR? Each team was allowed up to four guest players, whose only qualification was that they had to have appeared on Top of the Pops. In the semi finals, the Rangers had beaten Gornik Zabrze in a bad tempered game, the only goal being a sweetly taken penalty by Freddie Mercury. Manchester United, meanwhile, had thrashed Cowdenbeath 5-0, the goals coming from Stuart Pearson (2), Frankie Valli, Noddy Holder and David Essex.

The game was played in the brand new Bill's Grandad's Stadium (or Stade de Tomate, as we called it) and there was a capacity crowd of three well before kick-off. The pitch had a typical end of season feel to it; indeed emergency repairs, consisting of Bill's Crimbo pressie snooker table and double sided tape, had been effected only that very morning. QPR won the toss and elected to defend the Bedding Plant End. The first half was a drab affair, the one highlight coming when the referee (Jimmy Saville) was trodden on by a spectator, who was immediately ejected from the stadium.

After a fairly lengthy half time break, due to *Dr Who* being on telly, the match restarted in a tense atmosphere. Within seconds, a brilliant pass from Don Givens met the lethal boot of Rod Stewart. Alex Stepney had no chance with the shot. As the crowd began singing *"We are sailing…"* in praise of the scorer, Stepney was substituted for Demis Roussos, a telling tactical move by The Doc. From then on, the game swung from end to end. Greenhoff went close with a free kick, but Rangers' wall of Barry White and Isaac Hayes was impassable.

At the other end, Stan Bowles found the Greek warbler in a similar mood. The score remained 1-0 until, with ten minutes left, Barry White ruthlessly chopped down Elton John and Gary Glitter converted the penalty. The crowd was on his feet at this stage and extra time was looming large when, with a flash of pure magic, Coppell laid off a ball to Roger Daltrey who waltzed past the Sutherland Brothers and fired in a volley that Parkes never even saw. Seconds later Bill's Mum blew the whistle and the inaugural TOTP Cup, still full of dandelion and burdock, was on its way to Old Trafford.

In the euphoria that followed, pitch and players were forgotten about until two weeks later when it was time to play the Left-Handed European Championships. Unfortunately, the myopic Bill's Grandad had mistaken our greensward for a cleaning cloth. It's probably in that greenhouse even now; home no longer to the Bay City Rollers or the Red Devils, but possibly providing shelter for various species of insects hooked on Windowlene.

Nick Brown

Let's

"We'll never have a team worth watching in Bradford as long as we've got two clubs", my father used to say, simply because that's what his father told him. The theory was that there was just not enough people to share between Park Avenue and their older relations Bradford City.

"Damned nonsense", according to the late Dick Williamson, the sports writer who covered Avenue for more years than he cared to remember. *"Liverpool could not have supported two teams if they'd both been constantly on the floor the way that Bradford's have,"* he once told me.

It's a long way from the top of the First Division to the bottom of the Fourth, from the champagne celebration of the League champions to the humiliating re-election appeal of the 92nd club. Avenue's third successive re-election application was successful in May 1969 , but they were voted back with six fewer votes than they gained the previous year. It had been a difficult season. In fact, defeat was almost second nature, to players and followers alike. Perhaps the best example came from a supporters' club official who said to me, after a string of eleven defeats in twelve successive games, *"Do you think we'll win another match?"* I felt so helpless I didn't reply.

Final League chairman, Herbert Metcalfe

Matters got no better during that fateful final season of 1969-70. The club hit the headlines for all the wrong reasons for much of the campaign. At boardroom level the directors seemed to spend more time trying to unseat each other rather than building a winning team and the managerial trail reads like something from a *Carry On Managing* script. The outgoing transfer trail continued with the departure of stars-to-be like Kenny Hibbitt. Player after player was signed, many of whom came with latent ability which didn't show at their previous clubs and never did at Avenue. In my view, the club folded because at no time in these latter years did it have sufficient strength of character from the boardroom down to the newest apprentice.

Tender Moments From The Life Of Kevin Keegan…

Raunchy but approachable

Be Avenue

The last team

When Laurie Brown left, Avenue were sitting in 24th spot and Frank Tomlinson was appointed to complete the *Carry On* scenario. He came straight from behind the bar at a Lancashire club and tried to right a sinking soccer ship which was so holed below the waterline that it would have tested Matt Busby, Brian Clough and Bill Shankly put together!

A little bit of the city of Bradford died in the Cafe Royal, London, on Saturday May 30th, 1970 when Avenue were kicked out of the Football League after their fourth application for re-election was refused. Talking to people from all parts of the soccer globe I was left in no doubt at all why so many clubs had swung from Bradford and placed their faith in either Cambridge United or Newport County (based on the voting figures the previous years). Everyone mentioned the same point — the comedy of errors that had marked Avenue's downward path. They included managerial choppings and changings; coming and going of chairmen and directors; wholesale sackings and transfer listing of players. Throughout all this period there had been just one thread — almost total failure on the field.

At times supporters fared no better with lady luck and things occurred that could only happen to Park Avenue. The Bradford Supporters' Club coach to Swansea left the ground at 6.45 am with twenty or so cheering fans shortly before the end of the final League season. When the coach was some 30 miles from London somebody asked the driver: *"Where are you going?"* He replied: *"Isn't it to Wembley?"* — the League Cup final was on the same day. The Bradford supporters eventually arrived at the Vetch Field ten minutes after the start of the game.

Avenue limped along for three seasons as members of the Northern Premier League until they had to sell Park Avenue in order to survive. Bradford City's offer to share their Valley Parade ground was grasped as a lifeline. Unfortunately, their supporters departed in droves (as might have been expected with the club playing at the home of the enemy) and with only a few hundred

bothering to attend matches, the directors were faced with financial crisis. All the cash received from the sale of Park Avenue had gone to settle outstanding debts and, therefore, the coffers were empty.

Near the end of 1973-74 they decided enough was enough. Avenue went into voluntary liquidation in May 1974. The writer was one of some fifty shareholders present at that fateful meeting in the Midland Hotel, Bradford on May 3rd. Ironically Avenue had played some of their best football of the season during the last couple of months, going unbeaten in their final ten home games.

Nothing was done to develop or maintain Park Avenue after the club departed in 1973 and by the end of the decade the stadium was pulled down. The demolition men moved in during the Autumn of 1980 and this prompted a sudden wave of nostalgia in the city. Fans streamed to the ground to take just one more look. One old chap was carried to where he wanted to be on the weed-infested terrace and was left, leaning unsteadily on two walking sticks, staring silently at the unkempt grave of a football club and seeing God knows what.

He was only one of hundreds who came to pay their last respects. On the day that they began peeling off the roof tiles, demolition contractor Tony Fawthrop (a confessed Bradford City fan!) swore his gang drew a bigger crowd than Bradford Northern's rugby league game just up the road at Odsal. *"It's very sad, moving in a way,"* he said as a gale-lashed part of the end stand came down, *"but as they streamed in just to stand on their old favourite spot for the last time, I couldn't help thinking: if you buggers had been here when you were needed, I wouldn't be pulling the place down now."*

Bradford Park Avenue (1907) AFC was officially dead. However, a number of Avenue supporters were determined to keep the name alive. These fans formed a club — Bradford Park Avenue (1975) AFC — and started playing in a local Sunday amateur league. The aim was to get as far as possible

up the football ladder but, sadly, the club drifted along in Sunday football for many years making no apparent progress. The problem was that as the years went by the genuine Avenueites started dropping out, to be replaced by those who had little or no connection with the old club. The new members were quite happy to play Sunday football and it became increasingly clear that the club's original aims had been lost.

It was left to a former Bradford fan, Bob Robinson, to rekindle interest in Bradford Park Avenue in December 1987. Bob launched a campaign to set up a company aimed at reviving the football club and held several meetings in the city to test the views of old supporters. Everything went well and Bob received enough support to press forward. By March 1988 a new club had been formed and an application was made to join the West Riding County Amateur League, the premier Saturday league in the Bradford district. The club was accepted into the Third Division and obtained the use of Manningham Mills football ground in the Heaton district of the city.

The main stand, prior to demolition

After a shaky start, Avenue finished strongly to take the runners-up spot and gain promotion. It was felt that the club would have to step up into a higher grade of football if the support and interest was to be maintained. Unfortunately, after inspection, the Scotchman Road ground did not come up to the standard required by the various higher leagues which had been approached. No suitable ground could be found in the city so the net was spread wider to take in Keighley, Halifax and Leeds. An approach to Bramley Rugby League Football Club brought dividends as the directors of the West Leeds side were only too pleased to share their ground at McLaren Field. Avenue now had a stadium capable of staging GM Vauxhall Conference football and had little difficulty finding a league to accept them.

At the time of writing Avenue are alive and well, occupying a mid-table position in the progressive Central Midlands League. The old supporters, some not seen since 1974, are starting to drift back and who knows, in another ten years or so Bradford could have two football league clubs once again. And why not?

Tim Clapham

OK, *so the football equivalent of your old Max Bygraves favourite,* 'The Deck Of Cards' *has been done before. But there's never been a Middlesbrough version. So there…*

"When I see the Ace, I think of the 'Ace' goal scored by Billy Woof at Highfield Road, 1981; his last touch before being substituted.

When I see the two, I think of John Craggs' barrel-chest; it also reminds me of the number of left feet possessed by Billy Ashcroft.

When I see the three, I think of the Coopermen, Terry and Colin; it also reminds me of the seconds it took Alan Foggon to down a pint.

When I see the four, I think of the four goals scored by Man City in the League Cup Semi Final in 1976; a low point of my life.

When I see the five, I think of Dickie Rooks and his televised goal at Blackpool and the five strands of hair he had left on his head.

When I see the six, I'm reminded of the number of pints Alan Foggon used to sup after a match.

When I see the seven, I'm reminded of the number of pints Alan Foggon used to sup before a match.

When I see the eight, I think back to the eight we crashed past Sheff Wed in 1974; oh for such fire power now.

When I see the nine, I think of Big John.

When I see the ten, I try not to think of Alan Foggon but I can't help it because I remember when Man Utd bought him thinking he was Ken Foggo.

When I see the eleven, it reminds me I must go to the opticians.

When I see the Jack, I think of the Messiah of Boro sport in the 1970s. No, not Jack Charlton, Jack Hatfield (I got a free pair of shinpads off him once).

When I see the Queen, I think of the 6-1 drubbing by QPR, also on *Match Of The Day*.

When I see the King, I think of our great players of the past; George Camsell, Wilf Mannion, Brian Clough, John Hickton, Graeme Souness and Billy Woof.

When I count the number of cards in my pack, there are 51 (the dog ate the six of clubs) — the number of feet I had to walk before I could touch another supporter in the South Stand in 1984.

When I count the number of cards in a suit, there are 13; the number of yards Bobby Thompson missed a penalty by in 1982.

If I take the number suits away from the number of Jacks in my pack, I'm left with nothing — the number of times Boro have appeared at Wembley.

As you can see, a pack of cards help me relive memories, both good and bad. Now, where did I put that can of Fosters?"

Malcolm Riggs

Awesome Angel

The Positive Touch

On Teesside in the late Sixties Jack Hatfield's sports shop marketed a plastic football named after the supporters of the Holgate End. 'The Ayresome Angel' was white with red lettering and it outlasted the average orange Frido by up to a month. My friends and I used 'The Ayresome Angel' in the interminable games of football we played on the green of the village in which we lived, ten miles to the south of Middlesbrough.

Between tea and bedtime on most evenings a motley crew of budding stars would assemble under the lime tree that grew in the centre of our pitch. After a series of arguments over who would be captains, who should be picked first, and who should be left until last, two teams were arrived at. Then the real dispute began — which of us would be which player. There were three players whom all of us wished to imitate: George Best, Bobby Charlton and the Boro centre forward John Hickton.

Wearing the number 9 shirt at Ayresome Park during the reign of Stan Anderson was an onerous task. Aside from the mediocrity of the team, which seemed to finish every season in the top eight of the Second Division yet always avoided positions one and two, the Boro centre forward was further burdened with the weight of history. Whatever its other shortcomings the club had always been well provided with goal-scoring forwards: the Georges Elliot and Camsell, the Scot Andrew Wilson, in the Post-War years, Clough, Peacock and, Hickton's predecessor, the man whose goals had lifted Boro out of the third Division, John O'Rourke.

My first footballing memory is of sitting on my uncle's shoulders in one of the corner stands that flank the Holgate End. The Ayresome Angels sang *"Give us a goal. Give us a goal. John O'Rourke. John O'Rourke"*,

and he obliged with a couple. At the end of that season, perhaps in need of the money, or maybe, as my grandfather insisted, because they feared O'Rourke's goals might carry them into the expensive realms of the First Division and thus cause untold damage to the directors' wallets, the favourite of the Ayresome Angels was transferred to Ipswich.

John Hickton had already arrived at Ayresome Park by this stage and, within a couple of seasons, established himself as the hero of the Boro supporters, becoming the top scorer for six successive seasons. That he did so was as much a testament to his personality as to his ability. Hickton was tall and broad-shouldered with sandy-blond hair. He had the raw bravery needed to ride tackles and fling himself in where the boots were flying, and the cool, gunfighter's courage of the goalscorer.

On cold Winter afternoons beneath the floodlights, as the seconds ticked away with Boro a goal down, it was to Hickton that the half-chances fell and it was he who put the ball on the penalty spot when McMordie was dragged down, or Chadwick held back in the area. In a series of teams that had their share of hit-and-miss players — Crossan, Downing, Laidlaw — Hickton was the one that never let us down. When Boro were trailing 1-0 against Man United in the F.A. Cup Quarter Final it was Big John who charged onto a loose ball and hammered it into the net to earn us a replay. (*"That'll cheer the directors up"*, my grandfather cackled, *"A replay at Old Trafford. Charlie Amer'll get a new Rolls Royce."*).

In an Anglo-Italian Cup game, when Boro were bamboozled by Roma's catenaccio defence, it was Hickton who took direct

action — smacking a free-kick straight through the white-shirted wall and into the bottom corner to give Boro an improbable win.

Even my grandfather, who took me to most games and sat besides me in the 'Bob' End reminiscing about Wilf Mannion whilst calculating how much tax the club was avoiding by falsifying the attendance figure, was moved to conclude that John Hickton was *"not bad"*.

A family from the South-East moved into our village. A friend and I walked home from school with their son. He was a Spurs supporter. *"How can you like Middlesbrough"*, he said, *"They haven't got any good players"*. *"We've got John Hickton"*, my friend said. *"John Hickton"* the cockney boy sneered, *"He's never played for England"*. *"He could've"* my friend said, *"If he's wanted to"*.

John Hickton played for Middlesbrough during one of the club's many becalmed periods. There were a few high points — the FA Cup run that ended in defeat at Old Trafford, victory over United in the Third Round in 1971, and some low ones — a home defeat by bottom place Bury that cost Boro a First Division place. But mainly times were simply average. By the time Jack Charlton arrived to drag Boro kicking and screaming into the top flight, Big John's best days were behind him and my own love of the game had reached adolescence induced lull.

John Hickton was no Cruyff or Maradona. His name was never chanted on the terraces of Wembley or the Bernebau, but on evenings after school, on makeshift pitches all over Cleveland, after the teams were picked the hands would go up along with the cries of *"Baggy, baggy John Hickton"*. It was the biggest tribute that could have been paid to him. A player only needs talent to become a superstar; to be a local hero it takes much more.

Harry Pearson

Peter Bonetti obeys the whim of a disturbed photographer

What will be happening in football ten years from now? We commissioned a clairvoyant to give us some idea of what the football headlines will be in October 1999....

.....The Football League and the Football Association have finally reached an agreement on how this season will be named in abbreviated form. The official designation will be *"The ninety nine double-0 season"*, as opposed to the more defeatist *"Ninety nine oh oh season"*. Cynics still insist there are only nothings to look forward to....Newly appointed England manager Peter Shilton, commenting upon the World Cup qualifying group of Lithuania, The United German Republic and Liam Brady's Eire, said much could depend on trainer Bryan Robson's fitness. *"A sick man with the sponge is a definite disadvantage"*, Shilton explained, *"but there's no such thing as an easy game at this level"*....English Water PLC FA Cup holders, Oxford Maxwells have dismissed as *"scurrilous"*, press reports that they are about to move to a purpose built stadium on the Isle Of Dogs. Commercial manager, Suzanne Mitzi confirmed that they would continue playing in Reading for many years to come.....Luton Town have been docked six points by the Football League for having a sub-standard pitch for their recent game against Charlton Palace. An official said the bounce was far too even to allow for a fair game of footer.....Tottenham Hotspur, currently under investigation from the DTI for shareholding irregularities, say they will go ahead with their plan for an executive box only stadium. Although this will reduce capacity at the ground to 2,500, Irving Scholar says that comfort and money is all he's interested in....Sports Minister, Sebastian Coe has admitted that his proposal to ban the wearing of football scarves will be difficult to enforce but urged supporters to comply with the ban if they wished to see English teams compete in Europe....Manchester United brought their spending this season to £50,000,000 with the purchase of Liverpool Reserves....Hamilton Prophylactics, the Scottish Champions, are undeterred by adverse reaction to their new skin-coloured strip, donated by sponsors Durex. Reports that their away strip will be ribbed are unconfirmed....Politician and TV pundit Brian Clough is said to be shocked at the Green Party's takeover of his former club. A source close to the great man hinted that he particularly disliked the new club name; Notenough Rain Forest....Former England supremo Bobby Robson is writing his autobiography. Working titles so far include *It Wasn't My Bloody Fault; At Least I Didn't Go To Saudi; I Was Very Pleased With The Performance;* and the favourite with the bookmakers; *Spare Ribs For Robbo, PLEASE!....*

Potential. A small(ish), insignificant word, but one which long suffering West Country folk who admit to any allegiance to Plymouth Argyle FC are heartily sick of. Every couple of years or so a new manager heads for sunny Devon and arrives at Home Park with some all too familiar words for the media. You can guarantee that *"potential"* will feature in the first sentence. The usual cliches will all be there *"sleeping giant... lovely place to live and work... crowds will come back to support a winning team... if Norwich can do it then so can..."* and so on, ad nauseam.

Many managers have tried and failed to deliver the promise of First Division football to Home Park, and look where some of them are now. Malcolm Allison had two attempts (twice being tempted away to Maine Road) he deserves no better retirement home than Fisher Athletic, domain of various dodgy Dockland villains. Flash Mal goes down as the only man to lead Argyle to FA Cup defeat at the hands of a Non League club (a dreadful day at Worcester 1978) but is best remembered for some wonderfully eccentric tactical formations, which involved a bunch of decidedly average players indulging in bizarre impersonations of the Dutch 'total football' style. If you can imagine Kylie Minogue attempting the repertoire of Dame Kiri Te Kanawe you might just get the idea.

Sour faced Bobby Saxton's Plymouth Argyle team was a characterless outfit whose achievements have totally disappeared from my memory — and I suspect that I am not alone. Despite his subsequent, and faintly mysterious, continued employment in League football, he will perhaps be best remembered for his appearance as the typical Weather Beaten Old Pro in the *WSC* 'Just About Managing' slot. An honour surely to be savoured.

Suave stereotype Scot Bobby Moncur produced an attractive team but fell out with the directors. His 'escape route' from football involved yacht racing and running a

Bingo-calling at half-time

Argyle Style ——

Dave pleads for a drink

squash centre in Gateshead. Obviously though he hasn't been cured, as he has returned to the game as boss of Hartlepool. Mad, mad…

The team built by Moncur was, to everyone's surprise, taken to an FA Cup semi final by John Hore. As an Argyle player Hore was a country bumpkin version of Nobby Stiles, but as a manager his only credentials were a Western League title or two with Bideford. He belonged to the John Hollins School of Managers. (*"nice man but not quite up to it"*). He's now back amongst the bucolic locals of the Western League in charge of struggling Torrington (average gate: three farmers and a puzzled sheep…)

Bald Truth

Bald Eagle Mark Two, Dave Smith, actually achieved promotion with a rumbustious team whose style echoed the Wimbledon/ Sheffield Wednesday style of long ball simplicity. This side was rumbled by the classier Second Division outfits, however, and Smith departed for his home town to take charge of Dundee. His brief adventure in the Scottish Premier Division made Dave Bassett's career at Watford seem like a success story, and he's now back in Devon indulging in the usual unemployed football manager pursuits of itinerant scouting jobs and local radio chat shows.

Ken Brown (usual cliches: *"affable, avuncular, easy going"*) is now in the hot (well, warm) seat. His side plays plenty of pleasing football but the suspicion of lack of bottle persists and Brown has not convinced everyone that he regards the Plymouth job as anything other than a lucrative early retirement in a pleasant part of the country.

The trouble is that all hopeful new managers seem to think that possessing the hard to define quality of 'potential' is something to celebrate. Stuff potential. I never thought I'd say it but I'm jealous of

Wimbledon (to name but one other club). The only time potential is mentioned in the same breath as Wimbledon FC is when some property developer is speculating how many supermarkets he could build on Plough Lane. They've got a poxy ground and joke support — but at least they've made it to the First Division *and* they've won the sodding Cup.

But (apart from wishing them a swift return to the Beazer Homes League) that's enough of Wimbledon. Back at Argyle the fans only have the occasional Third Division promotion season and Cup Semi Final appearance to remember with any great joy. With so little success to celebrate Plymouth folk tend to see the funny side of football more than most. Incompetent players are tolerated, even glorified in only a slightly mocking way, far more than would be the case at, say, Leeds or Newcastle where success is impatiently demanded.

Good past players like David Phillips, Gary Megson, Barrie Jones, and Paul Mariner are remembered with pride and perhaps a little sadness that we at Plymouth didn't see the best of them. But they don't earn the amused affection that emerges when the true Argyle folk heroes are recalled. Just mention the name of (to choose four from many) Forbes Phillipson-Masters, John Uzzell, Gary McElhinney, and Home Park's ultimate hero, Gordon Nisbet, and you'll bring a smile to our faces…

Forbes Phillipson-Masters was an amiable lumbering carthorse of a centre half who smiled as he fouled; a man who comes second only to the immortal Wayne Wanklyn in the 'Footballers' Silly Names Contest'. On near deserted away terraces from Carlisle to Chester in the early Eighties we would embark on a ritual which occupied most of the first half. *"Give us an F… F! Give us an O… O!"* Not forgetting of course the obligatory *"Given us a hyphen…"*

John Uzzell, another unsubtle defensive hard man and destroyer of tricky wingers, stayed for over ten years and saw off at least three players bought to replace him, before departing this Summer for the familiar Argyle rejects rest home, Torquay United. He was well pissed off when an Argyle fanzine called him 'Bonehead', but the nickname stuck and even his team mates adopted it. His long balls from left back occasionally found the forwards, but more often caused severe structural damage to the floodlight pylons or the roof of the stand.

Gerry McElhinney was a daft Ulsterman who, bizarre though it seemed to those who watched his kamikaze centre half displays was once part of a Northern Ireland defence which kept a clean sheet twice in two years against West Germany. His dive-in head-first style brought him frequent injuries but he would always get up and soldier on, shirt stained with blood (not always his). He had been a junior star at Gaelic football back home, not surprisingly, but he would have been even better suited to Aussie Rules.

The unsubtle Uzzell

Gordon Nisbet was in a different class to the above three. Not just because he could actually play (and play bloody well too — how Phil Neal got so many caps when Nissie was around I'll never know); but because he could chop and trip with genuine style. Many left wingers suddenly became deep lying inside forwards after spotting Nissie in the no 2 shirt. After a booking for a superb ankle assault to halt Gillingham's Micky Adams in his tracks he was heard to say *"I could have got the ball, but I couldn't be bothered."* A true professional our Gordon, if he ever took up politics locally he'd beat Dr 'Death' Owen out of sight.

Argyle don't look as if they will ever get their act together and make it into the big League, but I doubt they'll ever sink down to the Fourth where football begins to get really funny. However the fans will have smiles on their faces as long as there are crazy characters at the club like Messrs Nisbet, McElhinney, Uzzell and Phillipson-Masters (don't forget the hyphen…)

Rupert Metcalf

Er

Desperate to see a Canadian soccer match? The report below is the next best thing. We may have saved you the cost of a plane fare to Toronto...

It had been brutally hot all day. Even as dusk begins to darken the sky the heat and humidity remain oppressive. Two hundred friendly people have crowded into the few square yards of shade provided by an elevated press box here at Esther Shiner Stadium in a barren suburb of North York. A tall muscular fellow hands out cream sodas to everyone from a huge cooler he has lugged onto the stadium. We are poised to applaud his generosity when the action on the field suddenly revs up. The Azzuri are on the attack. A woman with long dark hair leaps out of the shade yelling *"Guido! C'mon Guido"*. Guido has a clear run into the six yard box. Only the goalkeeper stands between Guido and glory. The crowd holds its breath. Guido kicks with all his might. The ball rolls gently by the near post and stops a few feet past the touchline. *"That's OK, Guido. Don't cry, baby"*. Guido is eight years old. His mother has rushed down to the sideline to console her weeping son.

Childs Play

The goal kick, meanwhile, barely reaches the edge of the penalty box. The swarming kids kick and chase the ball upfield. The referee turns away from the play, walks over to the distraught striker and pats him on the head. *"Are you all right, son"*? Guido nods as his mother wipes away the tears. He rejoins the fray.

In a corner at the other end of the field 14 men practice the debonair art of being a professional football team. They kick a ball around aimlessly, stretch a hamstring, toss bits of grass into the air to check the wind direction. However, men being men, most

of them are watching the young cheerleaders practice cartwheels. A stout man in a North York Rockets T-shirt, which barely covers his belly, huffs and puffs over to the distracted footballers. Tonight's match is a biggie! Mirko Basic, the Rockets', coach wants his troops to concentrate on the game, not on the thrill of a lifetime they might get after it.

Applause breaks out. Was it an especially nice cartwheel? No, the Moms and Dads, baby sisters and older brothers are cheering the 0-0 draw between North York Azzuri and the Willowdale Blues as the final whistle blows. *"There's more EXCITING!! soccer action in 3 minutes, folks, when the NORTH! YORK! ROCKETS!!! do battle with the Ottawa Intrepid, so DON'T go away"*!! The PA announcer's hysterical screams are largely unheeded as many rush for the air-conditioned comfort of their cars.

The spectacle of passionate football supporters stampeding towards the exits during the pre-game warm-up is a common sight at football matches in Canada. Professional soccer is simply not very important to Canadians. Hockey? Yes. Baseball? So-so. Thousands of parents encourage their kids to play soccer. Even Dad may drink a few cool ones with the boys after one of his recreational league games. But as a football concept, the North York Rockets v the Ottawa Intrepid does not excite very many people. You do not trade your allegiance to Napoli or Juventus for the North York Rockets when you emigrate to Canada. Benfica or Porto for the Toronto Blizzard? Hardly! Liverpool or Rangers for the Hamilton Steelers? You must be joking!

Other professional leagues survived for

several seasons before disappearing into a miasma of red ink. A few, like the Canadian Professional Soccer League in the early 1980s, collapsed after only a few matches. Besides, tonight's game is on the TV and no one is expecting a big crowd. However, there are no complaints about that. The Canadian Soccer League depends on European and South American immigrants for it understands and exploits the programming requirements and financial power of television. It may be the first football league in the world created and sustained by TV. We are three years ahead of Silvio Berlusconi's European Super League.

Is He Eck

The Intrepid make an appearance. This franchise has been bankrupt since the day it was formed. Three weeks ago the team was prepared to sell its two biggest assets, player-coach Paul James and the League's leading goalscorer, Ted Eck, to pay outstanding debts. The team is trying to survive on gates averaging around 1,000 when twice that number is the break-even point. The big sale never happened — divine benevolence, I guess — and both are here tonight. The Intrepid are only 4 points behind the 3rd place Rockets in the five team Eastern Division. Since only the top three teams qualify for the post-season championship play-offs Mirko Basic's anxiety is understandable.

A thin procession of spectators is coming in from the parking lot. It looks more like a Sunday picnic crowd than your usual

pty Canada

frothing football mob. Young couples holding hands, old codgers shuffling along, talking in whispers, dads with sons and daughters dressed in their soccer uniforms, small groups of middle-aged men laughing and gesticulating in a foreign language, Moms pushing prams while Dads tag along behind with the dog. The two policemen in the stadium are chatting with the cheerleaders. An intense young man wearing a Celtic jersey struts along, looking completely out of place among this crowd.

Everyone appears indifferent to the battle preparations on the field until that shrill voice on the loudspeaker demands that everyone stand for the national anthem. A scratchy record begins to play, skips, and an infant, being held by a man directly in front of me, begins to cry. Dad does a little rock-a-bye. The anthem ends. Everyone claps politely. There is a pause while the referee waits for the go-ahead from the television producer. The whistle blows and off they go.

Rockets and Intrepids are everywhere. The ball flies around like a runaway balloon. At this pace, and in this heat, all will collapse before half time. Here come the cheerleaders. Their faint voice tries to rouse the old Rocket spirit until the guy in the Celtic jersey stands up and shouts, *"We're tryin' ta watch the game"*! An old doll behind him is up immediately. *"That's not very nice"*, she says. The Bhoy flops down, rather contrite, and the rest of us turn back to the game. The cheerleaders continue, but in the same whispering voice. They finally give up and leave.

Not much is happening on the field, either. The best players, Ted Eck, and Vladan Tomic of the Rockets, could both sue for lack for support, so abysmal is the team play. There is a certain charm in watching the bumbling ineptitude of energetic children. Paying $8.00 to watch grown men do the same thing is embarrassing. How did Canada ever qualify for the World Cup?

In the 21st minute we get some drama. An Intrepid defender accidently handles in the box and a penalty is awarded. A harsh judgement, but that does not stop the big Rocket, captain Jens Kraemer, from gleefully blasting the ball through the net and over the clubhouse roof. The crowd claps politely.

A Tomic Explosion

Fifteen minutes later, the hilariously disorganised Ottawa defence gives Vladan Tomic a free run at goal. He barges into the six yard box and taps a soft shot past the diving keeper. It nudges the post and slips into the net. Tomic runs by the grandstand, a big smile on his face, and points to the crowd. One for Guido?

The CSL may not have any stunning football talent but it does have a lot of spunk. Down 2-0 away from home on a night better suited to twisting by the pool, and without any hope of seeing a decent paycheck until they quit the sport, the Intrepid fight back. Since they cannot defend they might as well attack. Everyone charges into the Rockets' half. Relentless swarming pressure forces the Rockets into a steady supply of giveaways. Fortunately for the home side, the Intrepid are not quick enough or fierce enough to score the goals they have earned. But, when the half-time whistle blows, it is the Rockets who leave the field with their heads down.

Half-time means the chance to win a basket of groceries, a pair of shoes and a free week at the Rockets Soccer School where Pietro Anastasi is the grey-haired superstar in residence. Someone has stuck a needle into that PA announcer's backside again. Boy, is he screaming. Something about Hamilton on Wednesday night. Can't wait for that one. Several hundred people, including me, are standing with our fingers in our ears. Time for a stiff drink, I decide. Try running to the bar with your fingers in your ears. It is not easy.

North York are still on the defensive as the second half begins. To witness so many squandered chances is surely one of the wonders of the world. The tension is not quite getting to the crowd, however. They are steadfastly polite to both teams. Many are chatting among themselves. Kids, grandparents in Italy, vacations in Greece. The action on the field is a sort of football muzak to these people. When Ted Eck finally scores for Ottawa in the 85th minute with a stylish bicycle kick, everyone claps politely. A second goal two minutes from time barely causes a ripple in the humid night air.

The game ends with applause for the 2-2 draw. The players, drenched in sweat and lying on the field, are too exhausted to crawl off. The announced crowd of 2,748 — a blatant lie, unless they are counting the kids playing baseball in the park behind the stadium — walk out in two straight lines, never glancing back at the reason why they came here on a brutally hot Sunday in July.

R A Patterson

Tender Moments From The Life Of Kevin Keegan...

Words fail us

Cor

Somebody probably once said that experience is the process of having your childhood illusions shattered. I have spent twenty something years nurturing two beliefs against all odds and still I battle.

The first is that I support The Greatest Club In The World. This was drummed into me from a very early age, as I voraciously read every word I could find about Manchester United. (Nor did I believe in ghosts. Never for a second did I doubt that George Best sat down quietly in his room at Mrs Fullerton's every Saturday evening to write his column for *Jimmy Hill's Football Weekly*).

Law Caught

At this time I truly believed that any team which did not win either the Football League Championship or the European Cup was simply not worth supporting. It was hardly my fault. At the age of eight or nine I'd known nothing else and England were World Champions. I thought that all football was played by teams including the likes of Best, Charlton, Crerand and Law.

Especially Law! He was the real hero of the playground where half the kids would run around holding their cuffs in their fists, shoulders hunched, raising one finger to salute a goal and spitting dramatically as things went wrong. I was just at the age when I had seen few players come and go; there were just current players and former players. Law had always been there, would always be there, and I would be a starry eyed Salford kid forever.

Ten Fancy Names For Football Shirt Colours

1. Amber (yellow)
2. Claret (dark red)
3. Flame (yellow)
4. Chocolate (brown)
5. Salmon-Pink (pink, for heaven's sake)
6. Aubergine (purple)
7. Silver (grey)
8. Primrose (yellow)
9. Maroon (dark red)
10. Tangerine (orange — despite what Blackpool fans say)

Five Reasons There Are So Many Football Books Containing Pointless Lists

1. They take up space
2. They don't need that much research
3. They seem to be in fashion
4. They take up more space
5. People read them (see?)

Football Un-Funnies

"He's the new target man"

Ten Football Writers Who We'd Buy A Coffee And A Sandwich For

1. Arthur Hopcraft
2. John (not Colin) Moynihan
3. Bill Murray
4. Geoffrey Green
5. 'Park Avenue'
6. Jack Rollin
7. Keir Radnedge
8. David Prole
9. Eric Weil
10. Patrick Barclay

Ten Other Sports That Gary Lineker Excels At...

1. Snooker
2. Orienteering
3. Indoor Skittles
4. Angling
5. Parascending
6. Shinty
7. Ice Dancing
8. Polo (as the horse)
9. Tobogganning
10. Oh, just everything, honestly

Menacing Denis

My second illusion was a faith in the reality of the aura of continental football, notably the tingle of trepidation generated by a European tie against a sinister sounding Eastern European team with strange looking foreign numbers on their shirts. European soccer remains magical for those who were introduced to football in those years.

Absolute winners

Without a comprehensive TV highlights service there was the added excitement of knowing your team were going behind the Iron Curtain, pausing only for a brief photograph wearing fur hats on the steps of the plane.

Then there was 'The Partisan Crowd'. How that expression conjures up images of gangs of brigands coming out of the hills, ammunition belts around their shoulders, unshaven, tough, gathering moodily in a pressure cooker stadium with the sole intention of terrifying your team out of the European Cup. To make matters worse, we all knew that our boys would be in bad shape; a six hour flight to a provincial airport, a seven hour drive on the bus to the hotel, checking in at midnight, town hall bells ringing on the hour every hour and the first of the Partisans already encamped outside the hotel, baying and hooting.

Abroad View

Then there was the opposing team. The air of mystery and fear was heightened by the fact that the newspapers always referred to very good Eastern European Teams as 'The Crack Czech Army Side' or the 'Tough Hungarian Police Outfit'. What chance did we have? And how come no Eastern European team had ever won anything?

Every season was a geography lesson, although history was apt to pass me by. Never mind Archduke Ferdinand or World War One, Sarajevo will always be a team that United beat along the way in 1967-8.

Within three years of seeing United crowned champions of Europe, my illusions were dented as the team faded and the club took to it s bed. It was to become a sleeping giant and wake as a monster. The *coup de grace* came on an eerie April Saturday in 1974, my innocence finally laid to rest as Law, spurned by Docherty, drew the final

curtain. Still my hero, it was his last kick in League football, and he was forgiven.

By then European football was, as now, a thing of the past. The clubs involvement in the Anglo Italian Cup, including a torrid encounter with the assassins of Lazio, underlined the depths to which we had sunk. At the age of fourteen I sounded like a seventy year old Huddersfield fan *"I remember when we had a team…"*

But suddenly we had a team again. Division Two was 'Taken By Storm' as the team led the table from week one, and just as importantly did it in the required manner. Anything less would have been unsatisfactory and the celebrations were tempered by the fact that none of this should have been necessary. The only sour note was the rise of the thug element which latched onto the club from the mid Seventies. Rarely would I stand shoulder to shoulder with a fan from another club from this period on.

The next job was to bring the League Championship and the European Cup back to their 'Rightful Place'. Maybe we were still 'The Greatest Club In The World'. Maybe I would again revel in the glory and the adventure of the European Cup.

Maybe. If. Too often since then United have been the nearly men. We have won the FA Cup, but so have several middle-of-the-table teams. We have played regularly in Europe, but others have actually won things; Everton, Spurs, Ipswich, Villa, Forest and Liverpool, Liverpool, Liverpool…. One special night which left Maradona, Schuster and Menotti shaking their heads in disbelief all the way back to Barcelona, evoked the dream, but it was only the Cup Winners Cup. Not *the* Cup, not the Champions Cup.

Around this time I saw for myself football played by some of those strange Eastern European teams on their own grounds: Bohemians of Prague, Ferencvaros,

Honved. I was left stunned by the mediocrity of it all; the lack of urgency in the play; a football ground in Prague which John Motson would describe as 'homely' if it were in the West Country and playing host to United in the FA Cup; a crowd of working men (few women) decrying a pathetic contest; apprentice hooligans on the Budapest Metro; and a player called Sloup who looked like John Cleese after a team talk from Juan Carlos Lorenzo (remember him?).

Then I read that the Hungarian games had probably been fixed anyway, and my myth about Eastern Bloc football was all but buried. When United were drawn against Dukla Prague in the Cup Winners Cup I wrote to Ron Atkinson assuring him that Czech footballers were not to be feared. This was actually just a ploy to gain an invitation to join United on the away leg. Strangely, Ron didn't ask me along for advice, and (given that Jimmy Greenhoff had earlier ignored my good wishes on his retirement) I decided to grow up and stop writing letters to footballers. Since then I have stuck to giving them my money, because that is basically all that they are interested in.

Jackie's brother

United supporters' belief in the divine right to success has irritated every other fan for years. Aren't United successful enough? How many will ever see their teams play in the First Division? Or even the Football League? But success is the extent to which achievement exceeds anticipation, and on that basis we have been on a 22 year lean patch which may not be over yet. Please fellow supporters, be gentle with us. We are like unhappy millionaires, taking for granted those things which others will never have.

There again I wonder if our still great rivals of the sixties — Real Madrid, Benfica, Milan — would have settled for as little? Do they remember us? Do they know that I support The Greatest Club In The World?

Tony Smith

The Debu

It's hardly an exclusive club. Of the 1,015 players selected by England, no fewer than 313 have won only one cap. Brian Marwood, with his ten minutes against Saudi Arabia, must feel he's already the latest member. Overlooked for all World Cup matches, pushing 30, competing with the likes of Barnes, Waddle and Rocastle, his international career may well have ended when it began. He should take heart. He's in very good company.

Albert Allen, Jack Yates, Walter Gilliat, John Veitch, Frank Bradshaw. Not names he'll immediately recognise. Nevertheless distinguished fellow members: they scored a hat-trick in their only England appearance. Whatever the performance on the field, that second cap has never been a formality.

Perhaps in the game's early days this state of affairs was understandable. International football was a kind of public school social whirl, with invitations handed out through the Old Boy network - so that England's first seven teams (1872-78, all against Scotland) included a remarkable 39 single-cap men; and a genuinely exceptional player like Robert Sealy Vidal, the first 'Prince Of The Dribblers', won no more caps than moderate journeymen like administrator Sir Charles Clegg, the Olympian CB Fry, great Test batsman and world long-jump record holder but distinctly ordinary full-back, and such luminaries as Elphinstone Jackson and Cecil Vernon (later Brigadier) Wingfield-Stratford CMG.

Some weren't especially good players but such thoroughly decent chaps that they captained England in their only internationals, from Charles Adcock in 1875 (as FA Secretary he helped select himself!) to a spate of amateurs in the whimsical Twenties including Wimbeldon doubles champion, Max Woosnam. Proof that the selectors have always had their favourites - and a fair bit to answer for. Except in such cases as David Pegg, who died in the Munich air-crash, or Tony Kay, banned for life after the Sixties bribery scandal, there seems to be no good reason for giving any player just the one game. Either he's international standard or he's not. Either a run of matches or none at all. In fact, a number of players were lucky to have been capped even the once, eg 19 year old Nick Pickering on an ersatz trip to Australia and George Robb, the Spurs winger pushed forward by the London press, out of his depth against the great Hungarians of 1953.

Sometimes there was at least some kind of thinking behind the dropping of a player after his debut. A bad result, for instance. Ron Henry, elegant full-back in the Spurs Double team, didn't survive Alf Ramsey's first match as a manager, the 5-2 European Nations Cup defeat by France in 1963 in which the French wingers each scored twice; Conrad Warner kept goal in a 7-2 disaster against the Scots in darkest 1878; clever little Ernie Taylor, consumed like the rest by the 1953 Magyars; Jessie Pye, prolific Wolves centre-forward, didn't score as Eire won at Goodison in 1949.

Others were simply stop-gaps, and probably knew it: Bill Nicholson in place of the endless Billy Wright, Alex Stepney for Gordon Banks. One, William Carr of Owlerton was punished for apparently arriving late at the match against Scotland in 1875, leaving England to play the first twenty minutes with ten men.

One Hit Wonders

Several, on the other hand, were treated with something like cruelty; injured in their first game and then discarded: Fred Fox kept goal against France in 1925, but had to go off after being shoulder-charged into the net. Inside-forward Billy Walker replaced him, England went down to nine men, contrived a 3-0 lead, and held out to win 3-2. Perhaps the selectors decided that since poor Fred wasn't needed during the match, they could do without him for good! Even shorter was the international career of Jimmy Barrett, who lasted just the first 8 minutes of the Ireland game of 1928.

Treated badly in a different way were those who scored in their only appearance: 33 of them, including the five hat-trick men and several who scored twice (Harold Halse; Jack Haines; Joe Payne of ten-goal fame; Capt William Slaney, scorer of England's first ever) as well as Paul Goddard, Tony Kay, journalist Norman Creek, Danny Wallace - and Bill Nicholson, who scored after less than a minute against Portugal in 1951.

Just as disenchanted must have been the goalkeepers who didn't concede a goal yet were never picked again: the likes of Phil Parkes, Nigel Spink, famous 20-stone Willie Foulke - and John Rawlinson, who had the easiest game of any England player: he stood back and watched as his team-mates won 13-0 against the Irish innocents of 1882.

Perhaps some of the one-cap players learned from their treatment by the powers-

England players celebrate being selected

that-be, and became better managers as a result: Arthur Rowe and Nicholson, Ken Shellito, Ken Brown, Brian Miller, Major Frank Buckley of Wolves. The majority, however, must have been simply bemused and dejected, especially those who everyone agrees deserved better: Charlie George, Colin Harvey, Clem Stephenson, John Hollins, Jimmy Hagan…maybe Steve Perryman - who all won fewer caps than John Fashanu.

Some at least had the hefty consolation of caps in other sports: rugby union (Reginald Birkett and Charles P Wilson) or cricket (five including Charles Burgess Fry and the Hon Alfred Lyttleton).

The list goes on. George Eastham's father George senior; Derek Temple; brothers Rex and Bertie Corbett; Bernard Joy, journalist and last amateur to win a full cap; the first stopper centre-half, policeman Herbie Roberts; the sumptuously-named Segar Richard Bastard (who later took to refereeing, where his name became a byword) - and now Michael Thomas and Clough junior, who'll be hoping their membership of the club is only temporary.

And yet, compared with some, these are 313 favoured sons. They can put England after their names. They stood, once, on the summit. Others were chosen for England squads (Alan Oakes, Howard Kendall, Jim Montgomery, Duncan McKenzie, Maurice Setters, Peter Dobing, Remi Moses and the rest) or even an England game (Peter Kippax, Vic Mobley, Billy Bonds) but never capped at all. A club with fewer but even more reluctant members. Tony Dorigo must wonder if he'll ever be allowed to leave.

Unpaid Bill

Cris Freddi

ant's Ball

...am

Funny, isn't it, the sort of bloke who gets an England cap? It's no surprise to discover the likes of Roy Coyle and Bertie Lutton knocking up dozens of caps for Northern Ireland, but did Brian Greenhoff really play 18 times for England? Steve Whitworth 7? Tony Towers 3? Possibly most startling of all, we find that Ian Gillard, last heard of helping Aldershot towards the Conference, actually won 3 caps! A fact surely more astonishing than Len Ashurst finding paid employment.

If lists were to be made of the most useless lists of all time, England's one cap wonders since football began in 1966 would be up there with Great Cookers Of The World. Here are a few then.

Jeff Blockley (1973, Yugoslavia)
Jeff's most notable features were his spectacular sideburns which bamboozled opposition forwards. Once the most expensive player in English football, Jeff was Arsenal's replacement for Ian Ure, and very possibly Ian's love child. Jeff was a shocking player.
Reason picked: Sir Alf attempting to demonstrate a sense of humour.

Phil Boyer (1976, Wales)
Phil was a journeyman forward blessed with cunning, skill and a nose for goal. He'd score with hands, feet, bum, back and inner thigh. Followed Ted 'Fuck off, kid, I don't sign autographs' MacDougal from club to club. Ted scored more goals but Phil was the better player. One cap seemed about right, somehow.
Reason picked: Injuries to squad.

Peter Davenport (1985, Ireland, substitute)
Peter was the kind of player for whom Manchester United would pay a lot of money and everyone else just knew it was wrong. He had the tactical awareness of General Galtieri and the scoring rate of Gary Sprake. The normally reliable Bruce Rioch bought Peter who instantly transformed Middlesbrough from mid-table First Division types into looking up how to get to Port Vale.
Reason picked: A general conspiracy against Manchester United.

Charlie George (1977, Ireland)
Poor old Charlie, forever on his back after securing Arsenal the double. Who can forget the sad sight of the man ending his England career after an hour and walking around the Wembley touchline, head bowed, pretending to hobble? Charlie should have had a cabinet full of caps, but he was an awkward bugger and he was crap against Ireland, *and* he was past his best by 1977. Charlie is now helping to run a garage.
Reason picked: Appeasement.

John Gidman (1977, Luxembourg)
With a General Noriega complexion and a free transfer from Liverpool to his credit, John was an unlikely England player. There hasn't been a decent England right back since Ernest Blenkinsop. John was another attempt to fill the vacuum. He was injury prone, occasionally classy and never too far away from the professional foul.
Reason picked: Why does anyone pick a right back against Luxembourg?

Colin Harvey (1971, Malta)
How strange that the engine room of Everton's 1970 Championship midfield, 'Wiggy' Kendall and Colin Harvey, should only receive one cap between them. Colin's silky skills were not suited to a hard Valetta pitch and although the Maltese were crushed 1-0, he was never given the chance to parade at Wembley in a figure-hugging white shirt.
Reason picked: So he'd be injured on the concrete and never trouble Sir Alf again.

John and only

Phil Parkes (1974, Portugal)
Sir Alf's last game saw the old buzzard pick a remarkable seven new caps, though Phil was the only one never to reappear. He even kept a clean sheet in this silly friendly. Phil resembled a dopey cartoon dog and was often injured in later life.
Reason picked: Because there were only two capped goalkeepers at the time.

Nick Pickering (1983, Australia)
Nick's inclusion in the spectacularly successful Australian tour (a win, two draws) must have been a mystery even to Mrs Pickering, who must have been hoping for a holiday in Benidorm. Perhaps Bobby Robson meant to pick Mick Pickering, though, then again, probably not. To confuse matters further, midfielder Nick played at full back as England secured a creditable 1-1 draw.
Reason picked: Possibly unspoken family connection with Bert Millichip.

John Richards (1973, Northern Ireland)
Around this time, foreign teams were too scared to visit Belfast and although John would have played a Druze/Christian select in East Beirut to secure that elusive cap, it was at Goodison Park that he mumbled his way through the national anthem. Unfortunately, he had a stinker and that was that. He looked a bit like David Cassidy.
Reason picked: General consensus.

Tommy Smith (1971, Wales)
Tommy was the toughest man in the world in 1971. Wales hadn't beaten England since 1955 and these things mattered to a struggling Sir Alf. With Tommy in the team, any Welshman who entered the penalty area would be kicked to death by this worryingly Bronson-esque figure. Tommy ended up barely able to walk but more than able to write ghosted articles for *The Sun*. A moral to us all.
Reason picked: Terror.

Alan Sunderland (1980, Australia)
The 1980s saw two tours to Australia. In 1980, England flew out for one game and then flew back again. Still, Alan didn't mind, though he was substituted as Australia were stuffed 2-1. Alan didn't score, but in truth, he didn't score much anyway. He always looked like he'd make a tacky disco record at some point. We still wait.
Reason picked: They couldn't get enough people to go.

Trevor Whymark (1978, Luxembourg, substitute)
Trevor was one of those First Division war horses best suited to outpacing Gary Collier in the 85th minute to score a consolation goal against Coventry. Sadly, such qualities do not an international footballer make. He was last seen at Southend outpacing Mel Pejic in the 85th minute to score a consolation goal against Hereford.
Reason picked: To test the theory that any old donkey can score against Luxembourg.

John Aizlewood

Albert Stubbins

I went to my first football match in Liverpool on a Winter's night towards the end of 1963. My older brother took me to see the Blues play Man U. We sat at the Gwladys Street end of the Bullens Road stand, unheard of luxury for terrace folk. It ended 3-3 in an atmosphere that could singe your face, but stopped short of the hateful bile so often generated by Scousers versus Manx.

Denis Law was the first player I saw who made me almost afraid with anticipation. He also came back from Italy with boots cut so low that the white foot of his all red socks shone off his feet. This was serious style. I had a soft spot for Law (a real bad ass) for years, and took much stick for it in classrooms where the *only* forward talk was of St John and the anaemic Alex Young.

Family Ties

Apart from this aberration, we were a typical Liverpool family, mad about football. My Dad, a red hot Liverpudlian, Kop and Anfield Road, before firstly the scallies and then the Men With Seats made the latter alien territory for the old terrace guard. My older brother, as first borns are liable to do, wilfully chose Everton, which

left me ripe for pre teen football flirtations. My brother's Blues fixation cut no ice with my Mum, who told us starchly never to trust Catholics, but was little help in identifying them. Liverpool FC, a supposed Protestant stronghold, was the only just cause. And yet these sectarian ties, like the city itself, were already in steep decline.

My first authentic football heroes were Liverpool forwards I never saw. Albert Stubbins and Billy Liddell were supermen from an age so distant from the modernity of the Sixties, they made Law and his Italian friends seem like Vulcans. From my dad's awed description I still have a complete picture of Stubbins' horizontal header from a bullet cross shot by Liddell which knocked Birmingham City out of the Cup in 1947 (it was 'the' Cup then). Twenty years later we saw Tony Hateley do the same thing for the Reds against Chelsea, but my Dad and his mates assured me and the other young 'uns that Stubbins and Dixie (Dean, of course) used to power in headers from as far away as Huyton. We believed them.

Liddell's mazy runs down the left were a constant source of comparison with the work of the mysterious and fragile Alan A'Court, who followed him into the side and later, in the same spot, the mercurial Peter Thompson. We are talking a different age

here. In front of the Kop, Liddell once presented a female marathon walker who had ended her trek at Anfield with — a handbag! A few years later there were honorary awards of the same kind from Kopites for Gordon West, a Blues keeper prone to nervous error and therefore clearly 'a Mary'.

Science Lesson

The early Sixties on Merseyside was all Everton 'School Of Science', with the Reds catching up — winning the title in 1963-64 — and the city spewing out pop stars as quickly as the contracts could be drawn up. The BBC even signed the Kop, but reneged on the payments. Incongruously, we had a rocker in the side, Alf Arrowsmith, complete with quiff and sideburns, a centre forward out of his time who came, and scored and then quietly drifted on. Across the (Stanley) Park, Tony Kay was found out on 'a nice little earner' and Alec Young, the 'Golden Vision', had a television play written about him and his raw followers. (We really *did* think that Merseyside was the centre of everything then).

When Young was replaced at Blackpool in 1966 by a 16 year old tower, Joe Royle, some

Knew My Father

of the Vision's worshippers laid boot to Harry Catterick, a manic depressive who ran the side between bouts of analysis.

Horror stories? I remember my brother coming home from Blues against Leeds in '64, the match in which the sides were taken off for ten minutes while the ground staff recovered the severed limbs that were strewn around the field after the opening exchanges. He went silently upstairs and just lay, motionless, on his bed. I did the same ten years later following a misjudged visit to *The Exorcist*. No-one actually *saw* Bremner give with the green bile, but a few of us had our suspicions.

Final Reminder

I didn't go to Wembley in '65. Today's Reds fans don't even blink at a trip down the Jubilee, but then it was down to season tickets, and fellahs who knew fellahs — out of our class. We had the newspaper photos up in our window, of course, and the curtain closed, lest the sun should fade our boys' new all red 'Cup' strip. Stuffing Leeds, and the opportunity to see Willie Stevenson parade himself on TV, was some consolation

for being kicked out of the European Cup by Inter and the hired men in black.

Those European games at home — Inter, Ajax, Cologne and the rest — were like exotic time outs, before 'the boys' discovered that the continent was *much* more fun (though Celtic fans brought some of 'their' boys, bottled up, to us, in '66). Europe brought us loads of stuff; Roger Hunt was the first English player I saw throwing imaginary javelins after scoring; Tommy Smith a man with a face like a chemistry experiment, the first No 10 playing central defence; Tommy Lawrence, the first Sumo wrestler to keep goal in the European Cup. The list is endless.

In the summer of '66, Pele, the greatest player in the world, came to play on Merseyside. He was not treated to bananas but got a fearful kicking from the Portugese. I saw Hungary, inspired by Florian Albert — the second great Albert to play in the city, according to my Dad and local quizmasters — destroy the forlorn Brazilians, and looked forward to seeing England at Goodison in the Semis.

The 'national' side preferred to stay at Wembley, however, and the dispossessed North West saw, instead, a young West German curl a wicked shot past a Russian goalkeeper dressed all in black and sporting

hands like jellyfish. Strange smelling Russian sailors in the crowd near us jabbered in disbelief that the great Yashin could be beaten from that range by an inexperienced midfielder called...Beckenbauer. (*I* knew Yashin was great, because I had read it in Kenneth Wolstenholme's *Book Of World Soccer*.)

Machine Age

The Liverpool side of the late Sixties never quite recalled the sweet pleasures of a few years before. The game was changing too; a running machine, converted from full back to midfield had arrived at Anfield to herald the do-it-yourself, close them down early 70's. Emlyn Hughes — and later Kevin Keegan — symbolised the end of the age of A'Court, Young, Kevin Lewis, Stevenson and the rest. I never saw another handbag on the pitch either — until this year. The Hillsborough demonstrations of respect allowed a woman to lay one on the pitch, along with flowers, in remembrance of the dead. Different times.

John Williams

Ever wondered if you might just be a loony? Compare your behaviour patterns with those outlined below and keep it to yourself if the answer's yes.

Nuts

Thanks largely to the popular press, the nouns 'fan' and particularly 'supporter' have come to represent something rather lukewarm and insipid, something that supports its local side but otherwise has neither emotions nor opinions — just an allegiance. What follows below is a six-point definition of what I would wish to term a 'nutter', the embodiment of the slave to a passion, the genuine article. Before the advent of the fanzines, I thought I belonged to a small and exclusive band of such weirdos, but now I am not so sure.

I remain faithful to the idea that there is a distinction between 'supporters' and 'nutters', but leave it to the reader to decide into which category he or she best fits. Incidentally, psychiatric counselling is not difficult to obtain, but can be expensive.

I write of the person who stands glumly on the echoing terraces of some 4th Division outfit on a bland sunless April afternoon watching his favourites struggle with tired ineptitude to a 0-1 defeat. He slouches home, shoulders hunched in philosophical gait to hear of the latest successes of the glamour clubs and to see on the last moments of 'Grandstand' that his team has slipped yet further into the ignominy zone of the division. He gives the sports paper a perfunctory glance. His whole week is affected. But even on that Saturday evening, he was thinking of one thing only; the next home game in a fortnight's time. Time is an inconvenient irrelevance between football matches. Behold the nutter.

1. THE REACTION TO A GOAL SCORED BY THE OPPOSITION

The nutter will have little trouble in recognising himself here. The first thing of which he becomes aware is the flailing arms of the opposing players. The next, on his home patch, is the stony silence as the awful truth begins to sink in. As he stares at the small bouncing mass of away fans in a trance of jealous disbelief, the brain quickly scans around for mitigating circumstances to protect its host. If the goal was a good one, the nutter may turn to his silent neighbour and say, *"Good goal"*, nodding slowly and wisely. This prompts the comforting delusion that the goal was somehow unavoidable.

Before this, he will have located the referee with owl-like precision, hoping beyond hope that the goal has been disallowed. Maybe the linesman is flagging, erect in his conviction that everything is going to be all-right after all for the nutter. These forlorn hopes are seldom rewarded. When it's 0-4, he kids himself that he doesn't care, that football is an absurd pursuit and that he may not come again. Of course, he always does.

2. THE DREAMS OF THE NUTTER

Dreams commonly express fear, desire, or a combination of the two. Some subliminal expressions of these twin facets are often too surreal and complex to interpret satisfactorily. Football dreams, however, seem fairly simple to understand.

The most common 'nasty' for the nutter is the one which finds him some way from the ground with only minutes to go before the kick-off. No matter how he tries, his legs seem burdened with invisible weights, friends hail him in the street and insist on chatting, he suddenly finds he has no clothes on, etc. Sometimes the crowd contrives to let him know, to his utmost agony, that his team is scoring goals at an uncharacteristic rate of knots. The worst version is where the nutter finally reaches the ground after an almighty struggle only to find that the ground no longer exists, having been moved to some unknown part of the town.

Every nutter has pulled on the club shirt and scored before the adoring eyes of surprised friends and locals. It may be at Wembley, but this clearly depends on the status of the particular club and the egotism of the nutter involved.

3. THE SUPERSTITIONS OF THE NUTTER

As is common among those who feel that they have little control over events in general, the nutter does all manner of bizarre things at a game. He notices, for example, that each time he has put his hand in his left jacket pocket for any sustained length of time, his team has played ineptly. On the other hand, when he was sucking a fruit gum his team scored, etc, etc. If subsequent events disprove the theorem, he tries new ones, like balancing on his left leg, or putting his right hand into his pocket.

Some items of clothing may become taboo, simply because the wearing of them seems to have coincided with some particularly traumatic defeat. Certain sections at the ground are similarly 'unlucky', and he will never sit or stand in them. So strong are these superstitions that

the nutter will adhere to them for a lifetime, against all the better appeals of logic.

Every nutter debates with himself about his team's prospects in the privacy of the bog or the bath on a Friday night. He always believes firmly that his team will lose. If they do, he merely feels a sense of circumstantial endorsement, a sort of psychological shoulder-shrug which says *"I told you so"*. If they win or achieve a creditable draw, he feels the pleasure of surprise.

4 READING THE PAPERS

The nutter always reads the local sports paper on the Saturday evening, the Sunday papers and then the Monday reports. This constitutes three days of intense reading and study.

The hour between the result and the arrival of the evening sports edition of the local paper is a painful time, especially if his side has won. A full hour must be reserved for a well-nigh technical perusal. He pores over the kick-by-kick convention of such reporting, awaiting the bold type of the scorers rather in the manner that people prolong the tasting of the best part of a meal that they are eating.

If his team has climbed in the table, he stares for long periods at this wonderful sight in a hypnotic trance, only snapping out of the reveries to work out where they might progress (or regress) to the following week.

The results are of general interest to him only when his own side has won, for in the event of defeat, the goals and successes of others on a day of personal gloom can be most depressing. However, the Sunday ritual can be most pleasant in the aftermath of victory. The nutter potters downstairs

And Reasons

and casually prepares the ground for the morning's study. Coffee must be made first, for all the comforts of relaxation must accompany the reading. The nutter of the little club scours the print for a mention. He is acutely perceptive to the sight of the name of his club and can spot it amongst the morass of print like a mother seagull spies her nest upon the crowded cliffs.

Having sated himself, he may nip down to the newsagent and flip sheepishly through the back pages of the rest of the press to see whether his team is featured.

On other midweek occasions, the nutter tends to switch off the TV and wait to read the result in the morning paper. The rationale behind this foible is reasonable, since to know of defeat too early is to suffer a putrid evening and depressing awakening. The prolongation of suspense preserves at least the possibility that a result has been attained, and the next morning leaves something left to live for, viz: the opening of the morning paper.

The suspense as he approaches the publication is like that of the child creeping downstairs on a dark Christmas morning. As he slides his hand across the home team, he begins to wail as an ominously thick wad of scorers appears. Never mind. There's always Saturday.

5. THE WAY IN WHICH THE NUTTER CONVERTS HIS GIRLFRIEND TO THE CAUSE

No sexism implied here, but it is surely the case that it is usually the male who does the converting, simply as a matter of statistical history. Apologies to female nutters.

During the natural processes of a developing relationship it is noticeable how each partner takes a keen interest in the hobbies and obsessions of the other. It is equally noticeable how these initially separate interests can become the bones of contention when the partners have become a bit less sympathetic to each other's quirky habits.

The nutter has surely experienced the first 'shopping' Saturday, maybe taking the new girlfriend to another town for the day. In the gathering evening gloom he carefully urges his companion towards a shop that displays televisions. You shiver in the dark with the little crowd, hoping that she won't think you too eccentric. Division 4. We've won! You jump up in the dervish fashion, wave your fist and shout conspiratorially *"You bastards"*! as though you know them. Condescending little sideways glances from the First Division folk.

She smiles, for it's still early days. When you calm down, the realisation seeps through of what a jerk you must have looked. It's then that you explain this achilles heel, this dotty yet endearing trait that you have. Yes of course she'll come to the match next week. It's love — you knew it from the first tender moment.

6. THE FEELINGS OF THE NUTTER AT AWAY GAMES

"How shall we sing the Lord's song in a strange land?"

The nutter experiences feelings of ambivalence at away matches and never fully enjoys himself in what is an alien environment. Other grounds may seem grander but they lack the associations and comforts of familiarity present at the home venue. Rather like moving to a new house after a long period in one place, the overriding sensation is one of discomfort, of insecurity. He cannot believe in the basic ordinariness of their grounds — that these clubs have traditions, stories, atmospheres

and nutters just like himself. Yet it nags him in the back of his mind that these people may well think the same about his team and ground.

It is akin to culture shock, especially the first time. People speak differently not only in terms of accent but also in content. They speak of their own players animatedly, yet to the eavesdropping alien the anonymity of these players makes it mind-boggling that they should be thus discussed.

Nevertheless, the nutter cannot help feeling that when the sides come out, the opponents look stronger and more like a real football team. He often parks himself among the away supporters, for he wishes to learn what they think of his players, to listen for some grudging praise. The experienced away nutter will take his time, but may well admit his affiliation to someone whom he has selected as non-violent and a possible fellow-nutter. This can be most rewarding — rather like the Germans and the British exchanging cigarettes and banter in No-Man's Land on Xmas Days during World War One.

In conclusion, one could add several categories to this list, but space is at a premium. Categories such as the way the nutter watches his favourites on the telly (why does his team always look potty?), his behaviour during the purgatory of the close season, his pre-match routine (set meal times on Saturdays), his attitude to footballers in civvies (he's always embarrassed to speak to them, so much is he in awe), his belief in the face of near mathematical certainty that his team will still make the play-offs, etc, etc.

Above all, the nutter is both sensitive and knowledgeable, has never raised a boot in anger, and treats with scorn those who think that Arbroath 36 Bon Accord 0 is the answer to a difficult question.

Phil Ball

Welling is a suburb in the South East London/ Kent borders and home to a GM Vauxhall Conference team. Their average attendance last season was around 1,000. Are there 10 great things about Welling United? Well I think so, but then I'm biased.

1. Paul Barron

Paul came to Welling as a sixteen-year old forward in 1970. At the time the club had loads of forwards and no keepers. Barron later donned the gloves and had a long Football League career before returning to Welling's Conference team for the 1988-89 season. His desire to be a centre forward had not died, however, as he ended the season with a number of forays into the opposition penalty area. A forgetful linesman turned up without his shorts for an FA Trophy replay last season, and had to borrow Barron's spare pair. During the match, the following exchange occurred between the two:-
    Barron: *"Hey, Line-oh, get the flag up; that's f*!?ing offside!"*
    Linesman: *"Cut the verbals, or the ref'll send you off."*
    Barron: *"If I go then my shorts go with me!"*
    The linesman, realising that his modesty was at stake, let the matter pass.

2. Being confused with Bexley United

Until 1977 Bexley United, (a Southern League outfit) occupied Park View Road. They were singularly unsuccessful and went bust. Ten months later Welling moved in. It was very difficult for a teenage turnstile operator (okay, *the* turnstile operator) to explain to the Old Codgers that they weren't the same team — it didn't help that both played in red. The difference became more obvious as the years rolled by because Welling were heaps more successful than Bexley ever managed to be.

3. Andy Townsend

The Republic of Ireland World Cup star started his senior career at Welling's home, Park View Road.
    Andy worked for the local council as a computer operator and was more than a handy snooker player. He also sported long, straight black hair (unlike today) which earned him the nickname 'Gypo'. If you had mentioned 'Eire' to Andy in 1982 he would probably said it was something swimmers came up for.

4. The Untypical Non-League Story

Through good soccer, shrewd manoeuvring and no little luck, Welling have navigated from the local Under-14s League to the Conference in eighteen years. Welling reached the Spartan League Premier Division in 1978. They were fortunate to move into a Southern League ground (see **2**) and gained entry to the Athenian League.
    After two seasons an application to join the Southern League was rejected due to lack of ground facilities. Twelve months (and a few ground improvements) later, the Southern needed a team in a hurry to replace Bognor who had defected to the Isthmian. Welling were in and after six seasons won the Premier Division with 93 points (from 38 games).

Keeping the Rovers at bay

Entry into the Conference has halted the progress — but Welling don't have the ground to enter the Football League anyway.

5. Tony Sitford

Sitford was the typical Les Bence-type Non League manager; an ex-pro who was rumoured to have broken his toe in the act of taking a penalty kick for Brighton (I hope it's true, it deserves to be). After a successful spell at Gravesend, Sitford was brought in to add some 'professionalism' to the set-up. He made a number of signings, some good, some awful and also claimed credit for Welling's entry into the Southern League. Sitford was also supposed to be a handyman and spent some of the quieter hours renovating the dressing rooms and other facilities at Park View Road.
    Unfortunately his flair for DIY matched his management skills and soon after his departure everything he had put up started to fall down — literally! A piece of Sitford logic just about sums everything up. Welling had just been 'giant-killed' by lowly Three Bridges in the FA Vase — an awful performance. After the game Sitford fined eight of the team for *"lack of effort"*, but retained them all for the midweek league fixture. He did, however, manage to drop one of the three players who escaped a fine, and had been praised by the manager in the press that week. Thanks, Tony, don't call us....
    Sitford moved on to manage Southern League Corinthians (and is still there, I think). The rest of the soccer is thus free of his managerial skills and, more importantly, his prowess with a hammer and a nail.

6. Paul The Groundsman

Groundsman and referees have one thing in common — they both believe that players ruin their lives. Welling's 'curator' came via a YTS spell at Millwall (if it's good enough for players why not groundstaff?). As well as tending the pitch Paul can be found fetching errant match balls from the Park End; serving behind the club bar; throwing out potential trouble makers; throwing in potential supporters; answering the telephones; painting the stand and even appearing as substitute in a Capital League fixture. Since Paul arrived at Park View Road the playing surface has improved from a quagmire to being half-decent, though like all groundsmen he is never satisfied. Known as the 'market gardener' (due to his lack of formal training) Paul should not really warrant a mention except that he is a good mate of mine.

7. Park View Road

Home of Welling United. Through continual enhancements it's now a good Conference venue. Not outstanding like Boston or Alty, but, then again, not crappy like Fisher or Runcorn. There is now an away entrance for big matches via the local park (just like Aldershot) and parking facilities are about nil (just like QPR). A good atmosphere can be generated if the crowd reaches 1,000, although if it's raining that is about as many as can get under cover. The ground would be excellent if it had a covered end and some parking facilities.

8. Les The Tannoy Man

Les is the most outrageous tannoy man in Non-League soccer. The impression is of 'The Bloke Behind Me' whisked away and stuck behind the microphone. Famed for his rebukes to young ruffians: (*"Will the idiots behind the goal please pack it in and act their age?"*) and for his questioning of the ref's timekeeping after late opposition goals: (*"In the forty-seventh minute of the second half..."*).

9. The Hobbins Family

Although they are now in the background, this family is largely

ere

responsible for the formation and continued existence of Welling United. Syd Hobbins (Sam Bartram's understudy at Charlton Athletic) started the club for his two sons, Barrie and Graham, and their mates back in 1963. Syd remained as Chairman until his death, Barrie quit when the soccer got serious and became club secretary (and still is today). Graham took charge of the team at about the same time and 'moved up' to general manager in 1988. On match days you can find various other family members behind the scenes, in the tea bars and directors' room; and Graham's brother-in-law has taken over from Syd as Chairman.

Many may criticise these close connections but you cannot question the family's commitment to the club or deny that without them there would have been no Welling United.

10. The Nickname

Most clubs have a stupid nickname and Welling are no exception. Take the 'ell' out of 'Welling' and you are left with 'Wing'; hence the name 'Wings'. The name was selected after a competition in the club programme — so the fans must take the credit....

Nigel Ransom, just prior to dropping the Kent Senior Cup

The story of Welling United, its eccentricities, it's terrific players and the cock ups along the way, is a story of hope.

No-one seriously believes that you can start a park side and take them to the very brink of the Football League but it happened — and I saw most of it. The difference between dreams and reality is usually a combination of hard work and belief, the story of Welling United is a testimony to that.

I don't see as many Welling matches now as I used to, but the memories recounted here will not fade, whatever the future holds...

Andy Legg

Eye-Spy

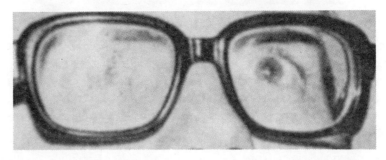

Remember all those intriguing little 'I-Spy' books that your Granny bought you when you were too young to know better? Yes, you know the ones; where you had to spot hundreds of dogs, cats, trains, boats, Nazi war criminals....and then pretend you'd seen them all down the end of the garden? Well, plenty of strange things reappear time after time at our football grounds during Yuletide. This Xmas, you can expect to see...

1. Peculiar and gaudy orange footballs.

2. Chocolate snowmen being thrown at tiny brats in the family enclosure.

3. *The Saint and Greavsie Christmas Special ("Well Saint, s'ppose you're used to all this snow in chilly Jockoland, hur, hur.")*

4. Red-faced policemen laughing and swapping jokes with the crowd (only because they're on double time).

5. Buses, trains or taxis on Boxing Day morning when you want to travel 300 miles to an away game in an obscure mining village no-one's heard of.

6. Liverpool versus anyone worth a good hammering, live and exclusive on ITV, only twenty minutes after forty League games have just finished and thousands of supporters are trying, hopelessly, to get home.

7. Visiting fans singing obscene versions of 'Jingle Bells' when their team scores.

8. Experts declaring openly for the umpteenth time that Christmas is the turning point in the season.

9. Players with hangovers (or should that be players *without* hangovers?).

10. The goalmouth at the other end, when the blizzard sets in.

11. Overseas players wearing (snigger) fluffy mittens.

12. Frozen cups of brown liquid (reputedly tea, they say...)

13. Those loyal fans who turn up because they didn't want to watch the Disney film, shouting and gesticulating at the team because they've paid their money and demand to see a storming win.

14. Teams *still* wearing short-sleeved shirts.

15. Bobble-hats knitted by Auntie twenty years ago.

When you have spotted all fifteen anomalies, put where and when you saw them on the back of a postcard and shove it down the side of the cooker. There, that wasn't too much trouble, was it?

Nicholas Brown

More Questions

We'd like to think that the difficult (nigh impossible) WSC Quiz has an important place in the hearts of our readers. It isn't true, but we pretend sometimes, to boost office morale. Anyhow, in a spirit of Xmas goodwill, we've printed the answers. But we're not going to tell you where they are. Ha ha, no, come back, they're at the bottom of page 95.

1. *"Sorry — It's all London!"* Identify the Labour MP who declined to buy a copy of *WSC* for the perplexing reason quoted above?

2. Which was the last club to win the League championship wearing striped shirts?

3. Which current Football League striker is also one of the biggest whippet breeders on Humberside?

4. What is the lowest recorded attendance for a Sherpa Van/Freight Rover Trophy match?

5. Which Cypriot team boast the sponsor's slogan 'Pourquoi Pas?' on their shirts?

6. **Professional Ambition**: *To win a European Cup with Burnley.* Identify the player quoted above in a 1970 issue of *Shoot!*?

7. Which England cricketer played in goal for Corinthian Casuals in their F.A. Cup tie against Watford in 1965?

8. Why are Stockport County called that? Derby County and Notts County makes some sort of sense, but Stockport has never been a county. What do you reckon?

9. Which TV newcaster quit his job in support of the firemen's strike in November 1977 *on the same day as the England v Italy World Cup match?*

10. *The Soccer Tribe* by Desmond Morris is quite possibly the worst football book that has ever been published, but it does contain some nice pictures. True or False?

11. Which company supplied England's catering requirements for the 1970 World Cup and how many cases of tomato sauce did this entail?

12. Name the member of the Plymouth Argyle FA Cup Semi Final side who left football to become a probation officer?

13. Which FA Cup-winning team consisted entirely of army officers?

14. Which two players who appeared and scored in English League football in the 1967-68 season are still playing professionally?

15. Who did an MA degree which included a thesis on the life of a professional footballer?

16. Fred Davies was the 'man in a coracle' who used to fish balls out of the River Severn for Shrewsbury Town. How much was he paid per ball?

17. Which British football ground hosted the World Stock Car Championships in 1985?

18. Which one of the these never happened to Brentford keeper Chic Brodie? a) Career ended by a tackle from a runaway dog on the pitch? b) Hand grenade thrown into his net? c) Knocked unconscious by part of a floodlight pylon falling on his head?

19. Which Italian club sacked their coach after he made the following statement — *"They may not have won the championship since I took over, but they haven't been champions since the War and only won in 1942 because their coach was Benito Mussolini"*?

20. Who, or what, is Zyber Konci?

21. Which former Manchester United defender is landlord of the Rising Sun pub in Spon Street, Coventry?

22. Which team had the most blocked shots in the Major Indoor Soccer League in 1987-88 season (some sort of quiz, this, eh?)?

23. What was the name of the Bogota jewellers' shop from which Bobby Moore was accused of stealing a bracelet in 1970?

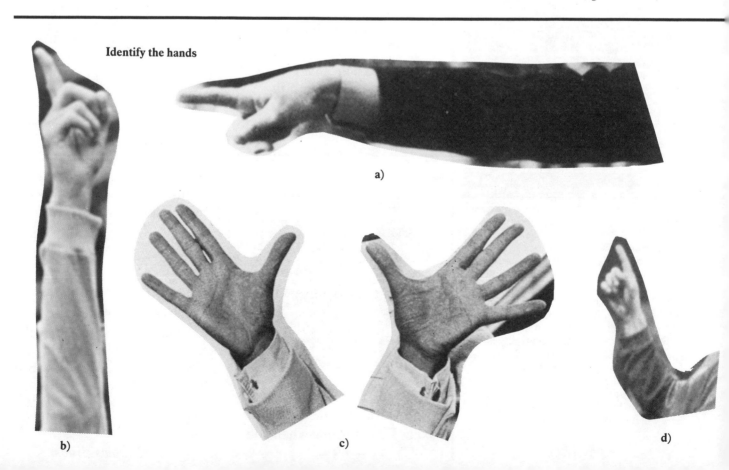

Identify the hands

a)

b)

c)

d)

24. Which one of the four Celtic players sent off against Racing Club in the 1967 World Club Championship play-off refused to leave the field?

25. (On a similar theme) Which Swansea City player was sent off for assaulting a ball boy at Home Park, Plymouth in April 1985?

26. (One more for luck) Which Copa Libertadores match ended with nineteen players being sent off?

27. Who are the only First Division club in Europe (in 1989-90) wearing an all-black strip?

28. What is Jim McLean's middle name?

29. In August 1969, the *News Of The World* rather prematurely ran a feature called *The Soccer Story Of the Seventies*. Which star of that era boasted *"I'm no pin-up boy - I'm a big mouth"*?

30. Which member of Brazil's 1970 World Cup squad came close to signing for Fulham in the late Seventies?

31. Which of these statements is true? a) Port Vale gained their name because Stoke was on the coast in the 19th Century b) Port Vale were once known as Bedlam Port Vale c) Port Vale once played an away League match against Loughborough in a vicarage garden d) Port Vale's ground was originally designed to hold crowds of 120,000

32. Name the current Football League chairman who had his ankle broken in the first minute of a pre-season friendly against Wimbledon?

33. Which League ground is highest above sea level?

34. Andre Duclos is *World Soccer*'s French correspondent, but who is he *really*?

35. Why are Wagon Wheels on sale at every League ground?

36. Which Icelandic club play on the slopes of a dormant volcano?

37. Which Football League club is furthest away from a main-line railway station?

38. How many times does the phrase 'The rest, as they say, is history.' appear in this book?

39. What is Paul Mariner's hobby supposed to be? (It's an unlikely one)

40. Which former England centre-forward of the 1950s advertised Andrews Liver Salts?

Who are the doggie owners?

a)

b)

c)

d)

When a football team dies there is always a great deal of sentiment aroused, even in people who were never supporters and had never seen the team play. Why should this be so when the many firms which go broke each week produce merely a resigned shrug from all but those whom such events directly affect?

The reason is that even now, as the cynical Eighties give way to the nonchalant Nineties, the local football club is the focal point of many towns. It becomes a meeting place, a major catalyst in the community's progression. A football team puts the town on the map. This has happened recently to the town of Newport, Gwent. Unfortunately, only for the saddest reasons.

Although no longer a League team, following their relegation to the GM Vauxhall Conference, their demise in early March 1989 had made them the most noteworthy club to fold in mid-season since Accrington in 1962. This was due to debts of nearly £150,000, run up after years of flirting with extinction thanks to inept management in all departments.

Their passing had not left me unmoved. Although not counting myself among their supporters, Newport County were my father-in-law's 'other' team, and I'd always promised Jack I'd accompany him on any visit to Somerton Park.

We achieved this last year when Tranmere Rovers became the penultimate league visitors to what had become a very sad enclosure indeed. The ground was sprinkled with a mere 1,100 diehards, and the original main stand, the entirely wooden 'Social side', was long closed, following the Bradford-inspired re-designation of the Safety of Sports Grounds Act. Amber paint was peeling everywhere, and the corrugated iron which seemed to dominate our side of the pitch quietly rusted in sympathy. However, the people that we met were extremely affable, and, not surprisingly, in

possession of a fine sense of humour.

Our next trip to Somerton Park was appropriately on the morning of Saturday April 1st 1989, inspired by the fortnightly auction of bankrupt stock to be held in the Newport Docks. Not usually a large date in our diaries, but this week the attraction was the 'Auction Sale of the assets of Newport County Association Football Club Ltd in compulsory liquidation.'

On the way from the M4 we visited Somerton, now looking extremely dilapidated, its low floodlight pylons nearly lost among the proliferation of signals and gantries from the neighbouring railway lines. The 'Welcome' sign on the back of the stand now bowed to the inevitable, hanging at 45 degrees. Large holes had appeared in the stand roof, and the grass on the pitch was long.

We took some nostalgic photos, a vanload of amused railway workers our audience, then moved on. A patch of grass adjacent to the ground was adorned with the sign for 'Somerton Road'. Alongside it was a smaller one bearing the legend 'No Ball Games'.

We entered Abbey Auctions Maltings headquarters and registered to bid. All the remnants of Newport County were laid out. The liquidators had taken everything from Somerton; several full kits, balls, boots, tracksuits, all the ephemera of a football club, as well as the trophies of which there were few, needless to say. There were also the things that were particular only to Newport County, such as the pennant presented by Carl Zeiss Jena's captain Konrad Weise had presented to Newport skipper Keith Oakes on 4th March 1981 in East Germany, prior to the First Leg of *that* Cup Winners' Cup Quarter Final. Another gift from Jena, presented on their arrival in South Wales for the Second Leg, was less

impressive, looking like some errant meteorite.

The telegrams of congratulation from Real Madrid and Barcelona, the beautiful replica viking ship from the Norwegians of Haugar, and the commemorative pennant from the First Round tie with Belfast Crusaders were all there, and would all subsequently attract healthy prices when their lots were called.

But alongside the glamour there was the truly pathetic. An ice making machine (Lot 595), and also from the club bar, an eight track tape machine with approx. 55 tapes (working order) (Lot 424). The latter was proved by the strains of Bob Marley's *Exodus* accompanying our viewing. There were also 'Two large teapots', 'A Tombola drum (black and yellow)', 'Large Meat Plate', and a 'Bingo machine with balls' -- the last item equipped it seems with a quality sadly lacking in management circles at Somerton Park until it was too late.

Bidding For Victory

The auctioneer announced the sale to loud boos and jeers from the collected throng. *"Everything must go,"* he informed them. Jena's meteorite went for £360 after a spell of frantic financial table tennis between two principal bidders in front of us. Apparently, one of County's most fervent fans was the eventual buyer. Fitting, I thought. Obviously I was surrounded by people of a similar viewpoint, as a large cheer went up as the gavel fell, and simmering resentments broke the surface as a voice behind me cried, *"Send the bloodsuckers home!"* For a moment or two I certainly felt like an intruder, but my acquisition, Lot 193, 'A Non League Yearbook 1989', was hardly the stuff of Welsh football folklore.

I learned the following Monday that the auction raised £12,000, a mere drop in Newport's £350,000 ocean of debt. The last amber and black football shirt went for £300, and as we drove past Somerton Park for one last look on our journey home, one was struck by the ironies that piled up around this ex-football club.

That same week, Charlton had received the green light to return to their Valley home, as Newport, with the last throw of a gambler, had offered to play home matches at Cardiff's Ninian Park. Charlton's move from their temporary 'home' at Selhurst Park was assured, as was Somerton Park's future as a housing estate.

Furthermore, Newport's best ever side was rumoured to be not necessarily the Tynan/Aldridge ensemble who faced Jena, but was regarded by many to be Billy McCandless's Division Three (South) Champions of 1939, who defeated Southampton and drew with Spurs in two of their three fixtures completed before the outbreak of the Second World War curtailed the 1939-40 season.

Decimated by the conflicted, County retook their place in Division Two seven years later, only to lose 24 of their league matches, conceding 133 goals in the process, including a 0-13 hammering at Newcastle, to which Len Shackleton commented, *"And they were lucky to get nil!"* Adolf Hitler, his part in Newport's downfall?

County Down

One further irony was on the night in September 1987 when I first saw County in the flesh (a 1-4 reverse at Leyton Orient), Merthyr, the Ironside's Non-League conquerors in the previous season's Welsh Cup Final were doing battle in the Cup Winners' Cup with Italy's Atalanta Bergamo. What might have been.

Instead, there was elimination from that season's Welsh Cup by the might of Havordwest County at home in front of 581 spectators, and inevitable demotion to the Conference. Their league hosts on that season's opening day, Stafford Rangers, only knew the fixture was going ahead at 11am on the day before the match. Indeed, County only signed their goalkeeper, Tony Bird from Cwmbran Town, at 10pm that eventful night.

So now, less than ten years after playing Third Division football, County are no more, their league record having been completely wiped from the Conference table.

It's a crying shame that just when Newport were in dire need of the steadiest of guiding hands, they were directed by 'A large quantity of mugs' (Lot 475).

David Rawlings

Christ, more crap about Newport County and how ill-served their fans were by feckless managers, ne'er do well directors and players who literally couldn't get a job anywhere else. Well, yes, but amid the dross one name stands out as spanning the bad old days and the revival of the early Eighties, a player who came on a free, survived serious injury, always gave 100%, quit as manager after seeing relegation averted and now finds himself entrusted with the revival of the town's footballing fortunes. Every lower division cliche you can think of, in fact. I make that 10 so far.

John Relish's first appearance at Somerton could hardly have been less auspicious — an own goal which gave County a Boxing Day win in 1973. No doubt some drunk tottering on a rotting railway sleeper yelled *"Sign him up"*. The management, ever mindful of supporter opinion, did just that when Chester dispensed with his services the following summer.

Unlike so many of the County's 1970s intake — remember Stavros look-alike Willie Brown, the puny Willie Screen, the horseless jockey look of Tony Byrne — John bore more than a passing physical resemblance to a professional footballer, nor was he an ex-inmate of the Sloper Road home for knackered footballers. He immediately got stuck into a career at left back, but broke a leg after a couple of dozen appearances. (In 20 years of watching the 'Port I don't recall any other player making a successful comeback from serious injury, which says much for the physical and mental state most of them must have been in when they arrived).

By 1976-77 the club was in desperate straits, out of credit at the bank and with the AGM licking its lips. Absurd sky-blue kit clashed with day-glo orange ground fittings and the first half of the season saw fewer goals than post-war managers.

John came back from his injury into midfield and the tide gradually turned. Only once have I ever heard the legendary swish of the net as the ball went in (you've had needed a ground tracking station to

eavesdrop from the Cromwell End), which was for John's 30 yarder at a near-deserted Vetch Field away end on Grand National Day, my first ever away match. By the end of the season, we needed five wins from five games to stay in and the bare statistics show Eddie Woods and Brian Preece as largely to be thanked, but from where I was standing Relish got the credit.

Never again, we were told, and, sure enough, things picked up with sensible signings and eventually the heady days of promotion, the Welsh Cup, and Europe. John Aldridge became the second best Liverpudlian to wear the amber shirt. Eventually the pinnacle — the top of the Third as we ground down Cardiff on a never to be forgotten Easter morning in 1983. Even my Dad leapt up and down as the one goal went in from short range as the boots flew in. The most crucial goal for years. The last man up from the ruck? Stand up John Relish. And a week later he was happily crediting it to John Aldridge, who apparently got another touch.

A Moment To Relish

Relish, who had been eight years at the club before he first faced First Division opposition and who was always to the fore in community-linked activities like seeing a party off to Lourdes (disabled supporters, not players) took a well-earned testimonial. On the field and in the boardroom things went downhill fast. When Bobby Smith quit in the middle of yet another financial and points crisis, we looked doomed to relegation and quite possibly to Leighton James as player-manager. The board saved us from that by appointing John over the player-coach's head, and somehow the team was motivated for one last struggle. A desperate 0-0 at Blackpool kept us up.

John must have sneaked a look at the books as he quit immediately to take up a post with the PFA, advising youngsters on YTS traineeships, though he did come out of retirement once or twice to add to his 300-plus appearances as the County plummeted from sight. I imagine it fell to him to tell the trainees that they had been stuffed when the club was kicked out of Somerton Park for the first time in 1988-89 The lamentable Steve Sherlock filled the left back slot in the last season, but even in his mid-thirties I'm sure Relish could still have done a better job. I didn't attend the funeral auction, but I should think a 1983 vintage shirt with a number 3 on it would have attracted more bids than most.

Like all good cliched profiles, this has an optimistic ending. In the teeth of council opposition and the absurd posturing of the FAW, who oppose affiliated clubs joining the pyramid, a new Newport AFC has been formed. (For a while it appeared that two little phoenix chicks would rise from the speedway track ashes, but Jerry Sherman's bullshitters have been shown the door by the Vauxhall League). The new club starts from scratch in the Hellenic League, affiliated to the Gloucestershire FA and ground sharing at Moreton-in-March. This all sounds deeply unpromising, until one reads that the new club's first player manager is... one John Relish. We have our fingers crossed.

Phil Tanner

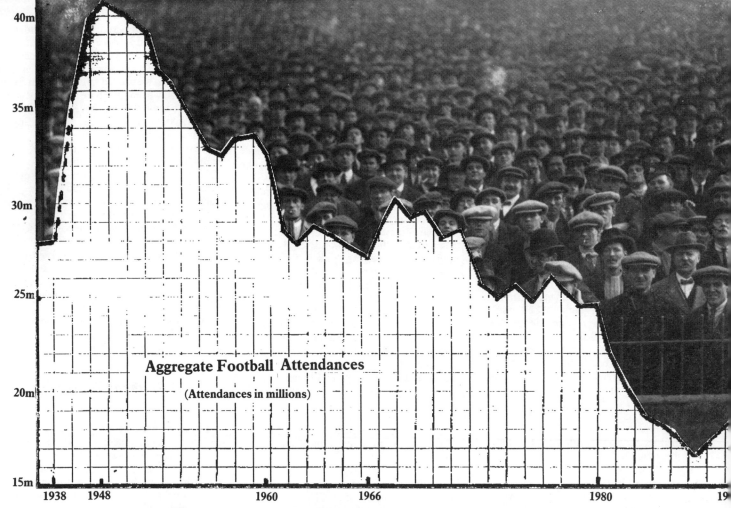

The graph shows:

Aggregate Football Attendances

(Attendances in millions)

Y-axis: 40m, 35m, 30m, 25m, 20m, 15m

X-axis: 1938, 1948, 1960, 1966, 1980, 19

No Requiem

No sport is as fascinated by its own crowd figures as football. They've always been the lifeblood of the game and the very fact that they're always published alongside the match results demonstrates their influence. And, like some great matches and players, myths have arisen about them too.

From the 1960s onwards the fc__all press have been wailing about the decline in post-war attendances from a 1948-49 all-time peak of 41.2 million. Where, oh where, have the missing millions gone?

Myth Number One: *"The Good Old Days"*.

The large aggregate attendances of 1947-52, from which football's decline is always measured, were themselves a fluke, an aberration caused by the unique social and economic circumstances of the time. (*"I've just won the bloody war so you're not stopping me from seeing every Doncaster match. And Barnsley too."*)

It is only because the Football League began collecting official attendance figures in 1946-47 that the statistical picture customarily starts at this point. But on the Saturday before the war broke out the average League gate was lower than it is today! And, as far as anyone has yet made out from newspaper reports, gates in the 1920s and '30s were broadly similar to the 1960s and '70s. So not only was there a well-chronicled post-war decline, but also a pretty significant and unprecedented rise too, which isn't generally mentioned by the gloom merchants.

Myth Number Two: *"Gate figures have fallen steadily and fallen everywhere"*.

Look back 25 years and you'll find 16 League clubs with lower gates than during last season - among them Bradford City, Barnsley, Aston Villa, Ipswich and QPR, all of whom did nothing much in 1988-89. Moreover, gates don't fall steadily; they lurch down a step, seemingly at the beginning of every decade, then, usually, hold steady for a while. What was the biggest season-on-season drop? Post-Heysel? No, in fact it was the season of the Spurs double, 1960-61. Gates were brought down by a record 12%! It may have been caused by higher admission charges, greater TV viewing of *Grandstand/World Of Sport*, or just a boring, one-horse First Division.

1980-83 saw a sudden 24% drop in attendances. At the same time, beer consumption fell, for the first time in years, by 12%. There was a big recession that hit the once-industrialised regions particularly hard. Whilst not significantly changing their League positions, Liverpool's gates fell by 11,000, Sunderland by 10,000; Aston Villa by 4,000 and Cardiff by 3,000. Since hitting the all-time low average of 8,131 in 1985-86, there have been three successive, well-publicised increases, to 9,069. The more important trend, however, has gone largely unremarked.

Myth Number Three: *"The gate figure is the one that counts"*

Increasingly, this is not true. There are two ways of measuring a business - the number of people who 'buy' (gate figures) and, more importantly, how much they spend (gate receipts). When terraces took up most of the available space in a ground and the League set standard admission charges, there was a strong correlation between the two. Not now. For instance, Rochdale's record crowd is 24, 231 for a 1949 FA Cup tie. But their record receipts came from a crowd of only 5,779 at a league match last season.

Over the last decade, and in the South in particular, football has become much more expensive. Ten years ago, the minimum adult charge was £1. Now there are only half-a-dozen clubs who will let you in for £3. Even when you take inflation into account, the long-term price rises are still very steep. To take one very exact comparison - in 1960, Port Vale charged a record crowd of 50,000 an average of 16.8p each for a 5th Round Cup tie. In 1988, again in the Fifth Round, against Watford, they gained record receipts by charging an average of £3.90 per head. If their Watford tickets had ben index-linked to inflation, they would have only cost about £1.40!

With every First Division seat nearly a tenner, more seats going in all the time, plenty of TV money, the Government subsidising the youth policy through the YTS and a third of the club's income

— 74 —

or the Masses

coming from sponsors, lotteries, Clubcall and so on, maybe it's not such a ricketty business, after all. Have a look to see how recently your club's record receipts were taken. You might find the odd million.

Myth Number Four: *"If we just had more attractive football/better facilities/less hooliganism then gates would soar"*

Broadly speaking, all these theories are bollocks. Or, to be more precise, post-rationalisations and excuses used by people who don't go any more in order to justify themselves, and feel superior, to those who do. You could play the nicest football since Holland in 1974, but if you went 2-3 down at home to Portsmouth you wouldn't see the doubters for dust. Winning (in the nicest possible way, of course) is what builds up gates.

There have never been better facilities in the Football League, so long as you have the right bits of membership plastic to use them, but the long-term gates trend is still down and many of those seats remain unused. If hooliganism is such a barrier, why do you still see so many pensioners, the most frightened portion of society, at grounds today? Or why do so many people skip ordinary League games but travel hundreds of miles to Cup Semi Finals and Finals where the odds of a chance encounter with a mob of the other kind are so much greater.

All these factors give football a negative image, to be sure, but they don't stop big crowds from turning out to see their team. But nowadays they only want to see *some* of the matches and, herein, lies the crux of the problem.

Football's origins were in a mass, male-oriented, habitual society where there wasn't anywhere near as much recreational stimulation on offer. Going to football used to be a big something to do. Now it has to compete with DIY, driving the children around, moonlighting, shopping, playing squash. The question is no longer 'What can I do?' but 'Can I fit it in?' Like church-going or cinema-going (both of which have declined far more than football in the last 50 years) more people go only when it's special. Even so, in this day and age there's not a lot else that will get 6,000 people out of their homes in Burnley on a cold January night. Frankly, it was even more remarkable, if not miraculous, that, in their heyday, every other man in the town seemed to go to Turf Moor on a Saturday.

What Of The Future?

Crowds will probably get lower in the next few years, though the effect will be modified by increased receipts. The 18-24 population, who make up a large portion of the football audience, will decline by a fifth in numbers. The Government and, therefore, the media, will continue to put

the boot in, the hooligans won't give up yet either and the game's leadership looks as greedy, short-sighted and imbecilic as ever.

Marketing at club level seems to take the tack of trying to persuade youngsters that football is the next best experience to the NFL, like what they have on telly and in America. Dispiriting stuff, but probably correct; if you don't get them between 10 and 15 you never will. The overall outlook, despite recent increases, looks bleak.

It is essential that the Football League put pressure on the TV companies to cover as many teams as possible - even regional highlights will do. The younger generation may then recognise their local 'heroes' and believe in something other than Liverpool.

For the rest of us over-21 year olds, there are three small glimmers of hope. Firstly, the 1990s *might* see a return to local pride and traditions rather than regional markets - Blackburn Pride rather than a train to Manchester Piccadilly. Secondly (it sounds like heresy, but hold on) the ID scheme *might* work if it doesn't cost the fan, is properly marketed and distributed by Barclays and Littlewoods and if it doesn't break the clubs (and the careers of a few marginal Tory MPs). Thirdly, football is ripe for a Campaign For Real Ale-style venture, where the baddies respond to the punter for a change. It's all down to the 'fanzine generation.'

Roger Titford (who is currently researching and writing the seminal text on Football League attendances)

FOCUS ON

Professional Ambition: To captain a League Select on a Commonwealth tour

Greatest Influence On Career: My old Battery Sergeant, who sadly left us at Ypres

Countries: Egypt (away fixture v Rommel), Germany (great cup tie atmosphere)

Miscellaneous Likes: Watching 'television'.

Dislikes: Powdered eggs and Communism

Car: Ford Popular

Music: Edmundo Ros And His Orchestra; Max Bygraves

Favourite Reading: *Movie Goer; Picture Post*

Biggest Disappointment: The end of the Second World War (wonderful comradeship)

Pre Match Meal: Spam, bangers and mash, and sometimes a sticky pudding

If Not A Footballer : Car assembly worker

Person Most Like To Meet: The Shah Of Persia

Favourite Phrase: *Alright, me old cock?*

...the 1970s

Professional Ambition: To be in the England side that wins the 1974 World Cup

Greatest Influence On Career: Games teachers who encouraged me to develop my talents, and probation officers who didn't.

Miscellaneous Likes: Running, walking, standing still, sitting down somewhere posh

Best Countries Visited: Benidorm and Africa

Miscellaneous Dislikes: I like to think I have many

Car: E-Type Jag

Music: Lovelace Watkins, Tony Monopoly

Favourite Reading: Leslie Thomas, Sven Hassel

Biggest Disappointment: Missing the jackpot (for charity) on the Golden Shot

Pre Match Meal: T-bone steak, scampi, prawn cocktail, anything sophisticated, really

If Not A Footballer : An electrician or an art designer of some sort

Person Most Like To Meet: Muhammad Ali; Sylvie Kristel; and the Pope, when he presents the World Cup winners' medals.

Favourite Phrase: *"Ooh, you are awful..."*

Jobson's Choice

The Positive Touch

Who was your boyhood idol? An infrequently asked, and often underrated, question. A childhood hero often influences ideas, mannerisms or even the way people dress. Perhaps you worshipped prolific goalscorers like Kenny Dalglish or Trevor Francis? What about Eddie Gray, with his mercurial dribbling? Or maybe it was Charlie George, all flowing mane, glamourous image and glorious volleys? Not me, though. I devoted my early teenage life to the adoration of John Jobson and the football grounds he trod on.

No, this isn't a pseudonym for some *Roy of the Rovers*-type comic book star, but Meadowbank Thistle's devastating, and record shattering, goalscorer of 1979-82. He was the man who dragged Thistle from the middle of non-achievement to the verge of promotion and previously undreamt-of success.

John Jobson arrived at Meadowbank in the close season of 1979-80, just another hand-me-down from Berwick Rangers Reserves, a virtual unknown, except for two facts: the previous season he had scored an eight minute hat-trick for Berwick and won himself a cradle of bubbly as a reward and, more startlingly, his brother Richard, famed poet and broadcaster, was lead singer with popular band The Skids. This caused a ripple of excitement amongst the more discerning of Thistle's 100 supporters, especially when he attended the occasional home match.

John's impact on the field was immediate. His explosive shooting, cavalier-charges at defences and an unnatural ability to rise like a souffle when going for crosses, yielded ten goals in as many games, elevating Thistle (albeit briefly) to eighth in Division Two.

With his craggy features, athletic physique and quivering quiff, he had the structure of a star. Sharp and fast, lean and dynamic, why did he never endorse Stylo Matchmaker boots in *Shoot!* or open charity fetes, I ask myself?

With the passing of time his collection of truly great goals increased. He smashed Thistle's individual League scoring record with seventeen crafted strikes, during a first season sadly terminated by injury in February.

The following season Jobson again lead the line sublimely, specialising also in a novel approach to goal-accumulating: the 45 yard thunderbolt. Delicately using the customary eastward hurricane at the Commonwealth Stadium, Jobbo would unleash ferocious shots which the best Division Two goalkeepers were helpless against. I remember during one particularly torpid midweek match with Montrose — you know, the type that seems to be lasting until Thursday afternoon — he received a short free kick on the halfway line and promptly dispatched a shot past the bewildered Ray Charles (and please, no jokes about pianos and white sticks).

Jobson continued to set new standards, attaining a status of demi-god and writing his name forever in the wafer-thin volume of Meadowbank folklore. There was the first hat-trick by a Thistle player — which sank League leaders Clyde and had the eight Thistle fans four deep in the enclosure acclaiming the master above the cacophony of the Rutherglen boo-boys. And what about his cup replay winning goal at home to Stranraer? Gathering the ball on the touchline 50 yards out, Jobbo threaded his way through five clumsy tackles, rounded the 'keeper and nonchalantly flicked the ball past two diving, despairing defenders. Off he set, arm aloft, blowing kisses at the vast banks of deserted stand seats. The 180

spectators went wild, stamping their feet on the concrete -- eleven of us singing his name in unison.

This man had character. Such acts of demonstrative behaviour made him deeply unpopular with opposition referees and fans it has to be admitted. Nicknamed 'Jobby' by some away supporters, his 'conversations' with match officials were extremely animated and on many occasions led to Our Hero being allocated first use of the Radox. Thistle supporters frequently felt the force of his verbal blasts too. At Stenhousemuir during the obligatory 3-1 defeat, one fan ventured to suggest Jobbo should be trying just a little harder, perhaps. He was told, by a purple-faced Jobson, that he would *"fucking sort you out later, you bas!"*

As with all legends, rumours of sightings in bars and in the busy streets of Central Scotland persisted even after his retirement. One friend swears that, one dull evening at an East Stirlingshire versus Cowdenbeath game, Jobson spotted him amongst the small crowd nestling behind the goal, and rose, ghoul-like, from his perch in the stand in order to shake his hand, saying *"You're that Thistle fan, eh?"* Unlike the majority of ex-Meadowbank centre forwards, Jobson didn't find solace in the demon drink after he breezed out of Edinburgh. Instead he became youth team coach at Dunfermline, no doubt bringing a level of sanity to a club overshadowed by extrovert, clown and occasional manager, Jim Leishman.

But I don't care about all that. At the age of fourteen I was prepared to convince my Premier Division supporting pals that John Jobson was immortal, and were he not 22, would surely rate a mention in the Scotland under-21 team.

All that is gone now, and I'll never have another boyhood idol. What remains for me are memories and a full set of autographed Skids' singles.

Colin McPherson

Blame it on John Atyeo, really. Dalymount Park was the venue, 19 May, 1957 the date, a play off for the World Cup Finals in Sweden the prize. Ireland were leading England 1-0, only seconds away from their greatest victory ever. Then Atyeo, a striker with Bristol City, equalized. The disappointment was shattering, the day still part of Irish soccer legend; grown men broke down and cried, the silence could be heard as far as O'Connell Street etc etc.

For three decades John Atyeo was a shadowy, half remembered bogeyman haunting the Irish game, until Ray Houghton buried the ghost in Stuttgart. Now Atyeo can finally be forgotten; the Republic of Ireland are set for their first World Cup Finals.

For the younger people brought up on the Atyeo legend the prospect is delightful enough. For those who remember the horrid day itself, and endured close on 30 years of frustration, heartbreak and near misses, the wilderness has been left behind, the land of milk and honey reached. Jack Charlton is indeed the Messiah.

Deutschland 1988 was great, a brave new world for the boys in green. The team was wonderful, the supporters did themselves proud. Now Italia 1990 beckons; vino and lasgne, the Trevi and Tuscany, burning sun and azure skies. We won't win the thing of course. But let's have no crap about *"just being glad to be there."* We're big boys now, and last year's European Championship is going to be the yardstick for now on, no Brady, no Lawrenson and still only eight minutes and an offside goal from the Semis. With a little luck and (even more unlikely) a half decent draw, there's no reason why Jack's lads can't make the Quarter Finals.

Most of all though, the Republic's chances in Italy rest in their own hands, and hang on the extent to which they modify the hit 'em hard and hit 'em early style. Charlton was surprisingly prompt in agreeing to the need for this refinement in the wake of the Dutch defeat. But he welshed on that promise (so far, anyway) and the team haven't come within an asses' roar of repeating their marvellous display against the Soviet Union in Hanover.

Jack with invisible friend

Ireland's World Cup qualifiers at Lansdowne Road have been more mini Somme than soccer; the troops screaming frantically across a ploughed field to breach the opposition citadel, shrieked on by 50,000 frenzied fans.

Unfair? Put it this way, Ireland haven't been in the thoughtful football business in their home games. Get the ball in the air and into the box quickly and you're bound to scare shitless the likes of Malta and Hungary. They were much better in Belfast, where bad finishing cost them a point, and should have taken a demoralised home team in Budapest, except that Charlton was happy to settle for a draw. And happy to settle for a 2-0 defeat in Spain, with the promise that *"we'll get you in Dublin"*.

Admittedly the team was decimated by injury in Seville that night, but did O'Leary and McCarthy really have to hoof the ball upfield at every opportunity and the team generally not worry too much about trying to create a goal? It says much for Charlton's standing that the media gave him the softest of rides over that gutlessly unconstructive performance, admittedly a one off for Ireland under his reign.

It says much for Charlton's achievement s too that fans can afford to bitch about 2-0 away defeats. John Giles and Eoin Hand may well grit their teeth and think of what might have been had they got even one of the breaks Jack has enjoyed.

Profit And Loss

The song had remained the same during the Sixties and early Seventies, too many good players ending up getting hockeyed too often. They had a chance in 1965; a play-off with Spain to decide who would go to England the following year. The players aparently still believe that the game, fixed for Wembley was moved to Paris because the FAI took up the Spanish offer — *"You can keep the gate money if you agree to play it in Paris."*. They did. 50,000 noisy Spaniards turned up and Ireland lost 4-1.

Things changed with Giles. He was professional, competent, knew the ropes. Brady, Daly, Stapleton et al were beginning to bloom. A new era was dawning. Ireland as contenders rather than cannon fodder. But Giles was cursed in the three team qualifying group for Argentina. Goal disallowed in Paris (it ended up 2-0) and a typically disgusting hometown decision in Sofia to give the Bulgars a 2-1 win.

The following Nation's Cup campaign was disappointing, with three points dropped to 'Norn Iron' and the nadir coming when Kevin Keegan chipped Ron Healey (anyone remember him?) at Wembley to give England an embarrassingly comfortable 2-0 victory. The pressure on Giles and his team's rigid style of play mounted. He decided that he could do without the hassle and headed back across the water. In came Eoin Hand, then player manager at Limerick.

Coming U

John Atyeo's fateful goal

If Giles had been unlucky, Eoin Hand's misfortune was simply beyond belief. No matter that Stapleton was at his peak, Brady had just moved to the Giovanni Agnelli works team, Lawrenson was fast becoming Britain's classiest defender and the 'my Granny came from Cork' bandwagon was thundering along. No tragic flaws here; the problems all came from outside. Shakespeare could never have written a great play about Eoin Hand.

The group for Spain was incredibly difficult. Holland, finalists in the previous two World Cups; France, destined to be European Champions in 1984; Belgium, subsequent conquerors of Argentina; and Cyprus. But that wasn't enough for the heavenly forces who had it in for the boys in green. They got the referees on their side too.

Robbed! (Number One). Paris October 1980. Played off the Parc des Princes for half an hour with Tigana having a blinder on Brady, the real republic came back in the second half. The TV pictures went, and potbelly Mike Robinson (he whose professional ambition in a *Shoot!* Focus On a year earlier had been *"To play for England."*) equalised. Pandemonium in the school theatre. When everyone stopped jumping around five minutes later they discovered that the goal had been disallowed for a non existent hand ball by Moran when knocking it down. France made it 2-0 eight minutes from time.

Robbed! (Number Two). Brussels, the following March. Thunder and lightning and the rain hammering down. Stapleton scored in the first half. The referee, a Signor Nazarre from Portugal, disallowed it. To this day nobody knows why (possibly he was browbeaten, a photograph taken from

For Eire

Hand's second World Cup campaign was a disaster with early defeats in Oslo and Copenhagen. Eamon Dunphy in the *Sunday Tribune* began putting the boot in. Not just on Hand, but also on Brady and Stapleton (*"non-triers"*), the FAI, the 'decent skins' and everyone else he saw as conspiring to further their own interests to the detriment of the national team. Irish soccer, cosy in the 'I scratch my back you scratch mine' relationship between officials and the press has never seen anything like it before. With Ireland managing a measly six points from eight games, Dunphy clearly wasn't talking rubbish.

A 4-1 home defeat to Denmark in the final qualifier (Mick McCarthy couldn't play because he had injured himself beforehand in a race with a hack who claimed that he could run faster), meant au revoir to Eoin. In fairness to hand it should be remembered that he was part time, and that he'd beaten Paddy Mulligan to the job by nine votes to seven because — wait for it — one member of the FAI Council thought Mulligan was *"the person who'd thrown a bun at him on one of the trips a while back"*. Charming innit? **The Eoin Hand Story** is essential reading for anyone who wants an insight into the Republic pre Charlton.

Ireland Race

Billy McNeill was the choice to replace him. Peter Swales thought differently, however. Ergo the infamous ballot which saw Jack Charlton get the job ahead of Bob Paisley and John Giles after machinations that made General Noriega and Ferdinand Marcos look like infant vote riggers. Fleet Street/Wapping had a ball. The fisherman was in and the rest is history.

Has Charlton been as outrageously lucky as people like to make out? Not really. Sure, he's had some breaks; Pfaff's last minute rush of blood to bring Stapleton down in Brussels; Lineker's misses in Stuttgart; most of all Gary Mackay's winner in Sofia. But then there was the ref in Sofia when Ireland played brilliantly and still got done; an obvious penalty in Hanover when Dassaev hauled Galvin down; and Aldridge blazing wide a cross he merely had to walk into the net to make it 2-0. And Kieft's offside goal robbing the Rep of a semi final spot. Things do even themselves out.

Interesting guy this Jack Charlton. A classic, no bullshit, red meat, black and white type, yet still capable of amazing sophistry. Lineker threatened in Stuttgart not because McCarthy was burned for pace but because Bonner wasn't coming off his line quick enough! David O'Leary was not interested in playing for his country! Brady and Sheedy would want to watch themselves (ie I'm wary of skilful players)! So would Aldridge and Cascarino (although they never get a decent chance created for them)! Chris Morris is not a bad crosser of the ball!

Is it any surprise that Ireland played two lousy games in Germany and still came home heroes and moral champs?

The other changes that he has brought about have been equally remarkable. European coaches are scratching their heads wondering whether it is possible to be consistently successful using Charlton's tactics of playing your game in the opposition's half and pressurising them into making mistakes. The FAI, so long an objectionable, self serving closed circle who ran delightful away trips for their human Bass advert members (ie we're only here for the beer!) is now a professionally run business; £851,000 netted from West Germany, massive receipts from the current qualifiers, and £2-4 million as the potential Italian pay-off. Bonanza for an ex beggar.

Liam the greatest?

The once piercing parrot cries of *"those English lads have no pride in the green jersey"* have thankfully been silenced. That tiresome David O'Leary saga appears to have reached a happy ending. And most satisfying of all, the London media have been brought down crashing from their high horses of superiority. Initially Jack's lads, like so many Irish things, were worthy of mere affection/contempt. Now that they're successful, like McGuigan, Roche and Kelly before them, and Alison Doody more recently, they just have to be 'our boys'.

Somebody once said that Vincent O'Brien's monumental training feats in the Fifties provided a much needed confidence booster and role model of the Irishman as winner in an era whose freezeframe was the young emigrant taking the Dun Laoghaire mailboat. In a similar decade Jack Charlton and his boys are providing an enormous focus for national pride among a nation of wild geese flung from Queens to Kilburn, Brisbane to Ballyhedob. That Charlton is an Englishman and most of his team aren't purely Irish makes it perhaps all the better.

But the bottom line really is that Jack Charlton has taken the nearly out of the nearly men; has brought out their full potential. Never mind that the bubble may burst, or that some Hoddle type will expose the team's vulnerability to the early ball played over the top. Our day came at last, and that's all that can be asked for.

Enda McEvoy

---

behind the goal shows Stapleton wheeling away in joy and five Belgians with their arms raised in best Tony Adams style). Three minutes from time Gerets took a dive on the right, the free kick came off the bar and Ceulemans nodded in.

There was a lot of nonsense talked afterwards — there would be a replay, Nazarre would never ref another game again, and so on. In the event a 2-2 draw in Amsterdam and a thrilling 3-2 win over the French at Lansdowne Road was not enough and the table ended up thus

	P	W	D	L	F	A	Pts
Belgium	8	5	1	2	12	9	11
France	8	5	0	3	20	8	10
Eire	8	4	2	2	17	11	10
Netherlands	8	4	1	3	11	7	9
Cyprus	8	0	0	8	4	29	0

Sicko stuff eh? That England and Northern Ireland fluked their way through with nine points each from far easier groups (the North scored just six goals) and went on to do well in Spain only twisted the knife deeper.

To take their minds off the disappointment the Republic went on a South American tour, brilliantly timed to coincide with the height of the Falklands War. A friendly with Argentina was mercifully cancelled but they still lost 7-0 to Brazil and 2-1 to Trinidad and Tobago. The following European qualifiers meant more let downs, culminating in a 3-2 defeat by Holland after being 2-0 up at the break. Probably just as well. Spain 12 Malta 1 and all that.

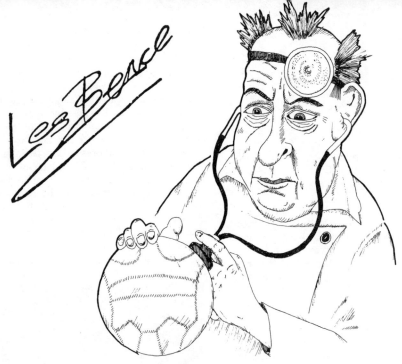

Les Bence

Soccer Surgery

Les Bence answers some common football queries.

Dear Leslie

Let me make it clear straight away. I am not the kind of person who tells tales but I make an exception when it comes to the wellbeing of The Stiffs

After watching our shambolic training session last Thursday evening, when no less than six players failed to turn up, I called in for a shandy at the Duck and Forceps. Imagine my horror when I spotted Dave Doyle and Terry Wade, both absent from training, drinking at the bar with someone else who did not make the workout — you, Leslie Bence!

I demand, as do my fellow supporters, an explanation of this disgraceful behaviour.

A Loyal Supporter (Miss)

Dear Miss Loyal

Your letter perfumed the air for me with a whiff of nostalgia. Reading it I was transported back to my schooldays by thoughts of creeps and little sneaks.

"Please miss, look what Leslie is doing under the desk" "Please miss, Leslie Bence is trying to show me something nasty." Let me state categorically that during the season I NEVER enter a public house more than three or four times a week and then only to drink.

It should be remembered that a 'tanked up' Athletico are a far better proposition than an Athletico that knows what it's doing.

Les Bence

Dear Les

What's going on eh? You have had the big job now for three seasons, but we are still piddling about in Division Three. Perhaps you've forgotten Les, but the day you were appointed a few of us went back to your place and you told us that with you in charge we could look forward to promotion, new exciting players, Football League status by the year 2000 and free school milk for all. You're a bloody liar Bence!

It is the same rubbish year after year and no amount of excuses can hide the fact. What we want to know Les is when are you going to deliver?

Vic

Dear Vic

What a pain in the backside your letter was. There is nothing more pathetic than a whingeing supporter who seeks to blame everyone else for his team's failure. That's right, Vic, I blame you! You and all the other Bog End bores who inhabit the Tip on a Saturday afternoon. If you had any love for this great club then you would be only too willing to pay five quid at the turnstiles. One hundred and eighty odd fivers comes to…quite a lot of money and would mean I could entice some very average players to the Tip, allowing me to ditch the dross. Instead of that you expect top quality entertainment at MFI prices, so, like their furniture Vic, you haven't got a good leg to stand on.

By the way I do not recall promising you those things when you came round, but I DO remember lending you my Peggy Lee album. I am still waiting for it back scumbag.!

Yours in sport
Les Bence

Dear Mr Bence

I am eighteen years old and have just completed my exams at Technical College, gaining good grades in Needlework, Biology, Religious Instruction and Sociology.

I would like to pursue a career in football management and thought that I would write to you in the hope that you may be able to offer some advice. Are there any leaflets? Courses? Do you know anyone in football? Naturally as it will be my full time employment I will need to manage a proper club and not, as my Dad calls Athletico *"a bunch of degenerate Swede bashers"*.

Yours Jeremy P.

Dear Jeremy

So you want to be a Football League manager do you? Well the first thing to remember is that you will be up against some pretty tough opposition, namely L M Bence.

Unlike most careers, the job of football manager does not require any experience. In fact experience can prove a handicap as my good friend Michael Channon would testify.

Having said that, there is no substitute for working your way up from the bottom. I have been fortunate in this respect in having been given the chance to manage Athletico Whaddon. Remember a trainee jockey begins by mucking out the horses, a raw recruit slops out the toilets and a virgin football manager runs a club in the Mothercare Swan Vesta League Division Three.

My advice to you is to find a chairman with a bottom that's worth licking, be a big fish in a crap club and pray. As John Motson once said *"God will need to be in Lineker's right boot this afternoon."*

Les

Dear Les

I have just read in the *Whaddon and Mitchley Argus* that you intend to introduce ID cards at the Tip from next season. As you are well aware there is no requirement for Non League clubs to implement this scheme, so what are you up to? If you go ahead it could be the death knell for the semi pro game.

Yours Sincerely

Mr Ashdown

Dear Thickhead

If I had a pound for every time the local gutter press misquote me then I could afford to buy the likes of Brian Robson or Boris Becker to strengthen our squad!

No, I have no intention whatsoever of introducing Identity Cards here at The Tip. What I am setting up is a scheme of my own that will require supporters to apply for IQ Cards. In future only supporters who have no opinions of their own, and intelligence below that of a duck, will be admitted to the ground.

Yours

Les Bence
(Branch Chairman SOLDASS) *

(* Social and Liberal Democrats Against Spectator Sports)

A Vision Of Hill

It was the 1983-84 season and one man stood out from all the others as I surveyed the Highbury pitch from my vantage point in the depths of the North Bank. He had style. He had panache. He had… rickets. Well, that was one explanation for the way that Colin Hill played football. Another was that he was an out of work Thunderbird puppet, rejected for being too wooden. Many a tedious match was livened up by a quick game of 'Spot the Strings'. If only Colin could have added basic football skills to his list of assets he might have been a great player.

Colin Hill was a regular in the Arsenal defence for only one season, somehow notching up 46 appearances in his Highbury career. A couple of appearances in 1982-83 did not bode well, but the arrival of Charlie Nicholas in the summer of 1983 brought a new confidence and air of expectation to our corner of North London. Colin's awful early performances were thus lost in the glare of publicity surrounding Charlie. All eyes were on the Bonnie Prince, and if the youngster at full back looked a bit dodgy, well, he had time to improve.

In mid October a crushing 4-1 win over Forest brought Hill his first and only goal for Arsenal, as he notched up our second just before half time. It couldn't last, though, and gradually Arsenal fans began to wake up to reality. A truly dismal performance at home to West Brom (0-1) shattered any illusions that I had. I was now convinced that Hill was that rare breed, a truly awful Arsenal defender.

Tied In Notts

He saved what was probably his worst performance for an early January match against Notts County. We struggled to hold a very bad side to a draw after their delighted realisation that all they had to do was attack our right back. Colin responded by constantly falling over and, eventually, rushing off to hide behind the centre backs. By now I had worked out the four vital ingredients of 'How to play football the Colin Hill way'.

The impact of the method can still be seen in the Arsenal defence today. Colin was the originator of the Tony Adams 'Hands Up For Offside' technique, although in Hill's case it was more of a last resort as yet another winger sailed past him. Technique no 2, the 'Fall Over The Ball At Vital Moments' tactic was passed on to the ever popular Gus Caesar. Colin's third and most famous trick, though, was the 'Desperate Lunge'. Our Gus (obviously a dedicated Hill-ite) got sent off while practising this in Miami. The prototype Hill version, however, never landed Colin in trouble, usually because he was so slow that the winger had long gone (although he occasionally clipped the full back who had come up in support).

My lasting memory of Hill will be of the bemused look that appeared as he ambled around the pitch seemingly on the point of asking the other players what to do. Like many comedians, his true genius only shone in a partnership. On rare occasions the long suffering Highbury faithful were allowed glimpses of the John Kay And Colin Hill Show, a pairing to rival Laurel And Hardy, Morecambe And Wise, and, even, Hankin and Hawley (another pair of Arsenal jokers who had recently done the rounds).

Sleeping Partners

Hill would frequently go AWOL from the defence and amble back. He would then give Kay a look that would seem to say *"Another fine mess you've gotten me into"*, blithely ignoring the fact that it was his own fault and that Kay's incompetence was merely incidental.

To Arsenal fans brought up on traditions of defensive impregnability, the culture shock of having a defender of West Ham proportions was too much to bear. Hill rarely appeared after that season, and after a successful loan spell at Brighton (successful for Brighton anyway, because he never appeared for the first team), he was set to leave Highbury. Viv Anderson was now entertaining us with his quiet, modest approach to football, and Colin took the long and winding road to Colchester.

Like a recurring nightmare, the vision of Hill reappeared last season when I saw his current team playing at Grimsby. There he was, falling over the ball, lunging and panicking in the same old way, although he had now persuaded the rest of the defence to join in.

Grimsby fans looking at their programmes assumed there had been a typing error. Surely he couldn't really have ever played for Arsenal? Shamefaced, I had to admit that he had, although Howe I'll never know. On that cold January day I knew that Hill had finally found his level. Bottom of the Fourth Division.

Mike Baker

Paul Goddard never scored that many goals anyway, Gazza wanted to be away, and Neil McDonald had an acne problem so severe that the linesmen always ran down the left hand side rather than risk bumping into him. So easily were the 1988 Summer departures from Newcastle dismissed.

What of the replacements? A goalie, a real goalie, even *the* goalie of the moment, Dave Beasant. The first decent goalie since before I started watching the lads.

Andy Thorn, a £900,000 centre-half from Wimbledon. Who? He had played for the England U-21s and was 'highly thought of'. Two forwards arrived. John Hendrie, from Bradford, a long time target of McFaul's. He was Bradford's best player, more creative than Stuart McCall, a bargain at only £500,000. John Robertson, from Hearts. A regular goalscorer in Scotland, another good buy at only £750,000. The only slight concern was the lack of replacement for Gazza in midfield, but Michael O'Neill and/or Ian Bogie were naturals.

Goals To Newcastle

How would our season go? Well, O'Neill had scored 14 goals in his first 20 league games so you could count on 20 for a full season. Mirandinha would start the season refreshed and more than a handful for any defence — 20 goals, at least. Robertson and Hendrie must get 25 between them. Already we had 65 goals and that wasn't counting any that big Dave would score direct from goal kicks.

Pre-season friendlies included a surprising 7-0 win at Peterborough. Their keeper lived in Yorkshire and, to his horror, had to share the only northbound train out of the town that night with Newcastle fans. The poor lad had the piss taken out of him all the way back *"How's your back, mate?"* *"Can I get you a can of 7-Up?"* etc. Joe Neenan went out for a celebration pint or ten when we were relegated. Newcastle's

management consisted of McFaul as manager and John Pickering as coach. They had two ideas for the season. The first was the small, nippy forward line — Hendrie, Robertson, Mira — all fast, all small. What a fool Tony Adams would look with these three buzzing around. The second idea was to play three centre halves and no full backs, with the midfield covering back on the flanks.

I clearly remember thinking how pleasing it was to have a manager who was setting out a game plan and buying players to fit it. I said to a friend that for the first time since we were promoted I knew I wouldn't have to worry about relegation. Even as I finished the sentence I could sense the foreboding.

What went wrong? The first sign of problems was the 4-0 stuffing at Everton on the opening day of the season. Regardless of the scoreline it was the performance that really caused embarrassment. Beasant is not a Shilton nor a Southall. Shots do not stick, and we conceded a stack of goals from rebounds off him. Andy Thorn was like a trainee Tony Adams.

The new tactics were an instant flop. John Robertson never settled in and the Robertson/Mira/Hendrie forward line never played a full 90 minutes together. The whole idea of small forwards was to play the ball to their feet. What is Beasant famous for? That's right, kicking the ball higher and harder than any other goalie around. If he didn't do this then we were stuck. We had no midfield. The previous years' dependence on Gazza suddenly became crystal clear. The honest hard-working runners who had been carried by Gazza's brilliance were now shown up to be what

they really were. The lack of responsibility taken by David McCreery, for example, was a major disappointment.

The three centre halves trick didn't work out at all. The worst performance was at home to Coventry, who played two wingers and Speedie in a deeper role behind Regis. The centre halves had one player to mark while Coventry's wingers had no full backs to beat. 3-0 by half time.

During his all too-short career with Newcastle (only 7 appearances), John hadn't even had a decent shooting chance. The inept midfield had bombarded him with balls that King Kong wouldn't have got his head to.

In the midst of it all this we won at Liverpool (and stopped them winning the League?). I had money on Liverpool to win 9-0 (I'd dreamt it), so I was as surprised as anyone. How did we manage this famous victory? The defence was bolstered by the perceptive introduction of full backs, and the aforementioned midfield grafters were in their element. In our hearts we knew it was a fluke.

The blame for Newcastle's shortcomings is always put upon the shoulders of the anonymous board of directors. *"Sack the board"* is now the number one chant at St. James' Park. Managers come and go but the same families remain in control. Various individuals have tried to get a seat on the board over the years. They all failed. The present generation on the board has produced Gordon McKeag as its leader.

The departure of Gazza, after the previous partings of Beardsley and Waddle,

Wisdom

was the breaking point. A group of nouveau riche local businessmen joined together and called themselves the Magpie Group. They were led by John Hall, self made millionaire, professional Geordie, visionary and a bit of a bastard by all accounts. Their (his) stated intention was to buy out the present board/shareholders, have a share issue and give the club back to its fans.

I have not spoken to one Newcastle fan who does not support the Magpie Group's aim. The board have a very weak case, with no domestic success for 33 years (apart from the Texaco Cup a couple of times in the '70s). McKeag revealed his attitude to the club when he said that he looked on it as part of the family silver, and would fight to retain control to the bitter end.

Making Hay

As the results worsened, McKeag sacked McFaul with no replacement lined up. Arthur Cox and Howard Kendall were both offered the job, the latter on whatever terms he would like. Howard's not that daft. Those rumoured to have turned it down included Joe Royle, John McGrath, Mel Machin, Bob Paisley (!), Jim Smith, Steve Coppell, Lou Macari and Keith Burkinshaw. Finally it was announced that David Hay had accepted the post. He revealed in an interview in the *Daily Record* that it was only until the end of the season, and that he wanted to have Lou Macari as his assistant. Newcastle withdrew their offer.

A year earlier, Colin Suggett had asked to move from first team to youth team coach as he couldn't take the pressure. McKeag made him manager, with Mick Martin, now a local bookie, as assistant. They were both appointed on the understanding that if McKeag found a real manager they'd be out. Suggett's teams did not score in the six games he was in control.

Enter 'The Bald Eagle', Jim Smith (or as he is now known, 'The Toothless Sparrow'). Just about everyone was surprised that a manager with as good a track record as Smith should decide to be the board's new Yes-man. Surely a man with his reputation wouldn't kow-tow to their wishes. Smith's management over the rest of the season was a disaster. He sold most of the existing players to raise money for seven new players, of these Kevin Brock from QPR, impressed, the rest did not. He never played the same team in two consecutive games, and never gave Mirandinha or O'Neill a full game, always using one as a substitute for the other thereby encouraging a loss of confidence in both players.

Held To Ransom

Fans became increasingly disenchanted with Smith, who continually made bewildering team changes. After signing right back Ray Ranson and Kenny Sansom, whom he described as *"the best left back in the country"*, he proceeded to play Ranson on the left and Sansom as sweeper against Middlesbrough. Supporters thought that the cold North-East wind had penetrated his baldy head and blown his brain down to his arse, especially as he always found a way to blame Mirandinha for every defeat. He even blamed the fans after one game, claiming to have picked the *"Supporters' team"* and not his own choice.

Generally, Smith followed the Don Revie school of thought; *"If you don't concede goals you don't lose games"* and employed five defenders and two defensive midfield players to make sure the team never got a pasting. He succeeded in that respect - only Wimbledon really hammered us.

The worst feature of this defensive ploy was that it continued in home games against fellow strugglers. The likes of Villa, Charlton, QPR, West Ham and Sheffield Wednesday all eventually sussed what was going on and gained an unexpectedly easy three points.

Newcastle were relegated because: a) They had inadequate players (most of the good ones had been sold for a large profit); b) They had three inadequate managers; c) They have the most unambitious board of directors in the country. It has even been rumoured that McKeag is so mean, he has his house double-glazed so his grandchildren can't hear the ice-cream van.

Surely the fans deserve better. A home average of 22,839 watched Newcastle play very little football last season. Not a bad figure for a team whose highest position in the League all season was 17th out of 20. And that was secured only once, on September 3rd!

Smith admitted he may have made mistakes but explained that the club was in a terrible state when he took over. Always a good one, that. The 1989-90 season started with Newcastle having two players in the team that had played in the first home game of the preceding season. Smith cannot say that the team is not his own now.

The boardroom battle reached an impasse. Or so it seemed to the fans who desperately wanted to see a change. In reality the board strengthened their hold over the club while creating a huge bank overdraft. If promotion is forthcoming it will not be due to their financial backing.

Newcastle's supporters are, by nature, optimists. Whether it is next week, next month or next season, their team will one day deserve them. In the meanwhile, season 1988-89 has been stored away as a bad dream.

Ian Ferguson, with additional contributions from Gary Burke

The Arch Duncan

The Positive Touch

To those of you not able to remember, the 1970s were an aesthetic nightmare. At the start of the decade we had Weimar Republic-style inflation and some of the most boring bands you could imagine. *Stairway to Heaven* was the alma mater of every discerning trenchcoat and loon pant-wearing youth. It took a while, but the advent of Bowie, Roxy Music, T Rex, The Sweet, Sparks and Mr G Glitter Esq. at least made everybody stop dressing up like Rory Gallagher's roadie. What was more startling, however, was the transferring of the feathered hairstyle onto the football pitch. Why anyone wanted to look like Keith Chegwin, was a mystery every bit as perplexing as the Bermuda Triangle, or, indeed, why Everton continued to draw crowds at the time.

Skill On Sight

During these days I often used to look up heavenwards and think *"This is a practical joke, right?"* The drivel factor would have driven me away entirely if it hadn't been for a single player, who whilst on the ball, would for a split second invoke images of matches involving Brazil. I give you…Duncan McKenzie.

All I knew about the man when his arrival was announced was something about jumping over Minis. Billy Bingham signed him to bring a bit of flair (and not just on his kecks). *"The last two that signed him have been sacked, heh heh heh!"*, said the laconic but unwittingly precognisant Bingham, unaware of the huge '3' over his head, visible only to the little people (no, not Bremner and Giles)

'Flash' became an instant favourite with the Goodison cognoscenti, brought up on this type of player. His flicks, shimmies, backheels, swerves and dummies caused 30,000 to purr and made 'good' players like Dobson, King, Rioch and Thomas, look like Berwick Rangers reserves (Darracott and Pearson, of course, wouldn't even have

made their bench). He couldn't save Bingham's bacon, however, and the door was shown to the affable ex-boss after he had led the team to a Wembley final.

On the pitch, 'Flash' had been turning in his usual performances. He dominated the return leg of the League Cup Semi at Bolton. Like all brilliant ball artists he was absolute shite at taking penalties; he missed one that night and tossed his head skywards. A gold chain spilled onto his shirt and glistened in the Burnden lights. Such adornments were unusual at the time and Duncan must have been unaware of the 'Big Ron' proverb: 'Those who wear gold, never pick up silver'. We went on to lose the Final to Villa.

Meanwhile, after failing to get a place at Hammer Films, Gordon Lee did the next best thing and joined the Blues, determined to turn the club into a metronomic unit of efficiency.

On the field the FA Cup Semi Final came, against our handsome near neighbours from Anfield. 'Flash' had a great game, torturing crusty old psychopath Tommy Smith and even giving him a taste of his own medicine in the form of a hefty kick. The Anfield Iron got up from the floor. *"Who the f*** did that?"*, he spluttered. *"I did. So what?"* replied 'Flash', by this time thirty yards away and increasing. He later struck one away in a 2-2 draw that will forever be remembered by Evertonians as the game in which Clive Thomas decided to disallow a perfectly good last minute winner by Bryan Hamilton. The erstwhile official turned first to his linesman, who signalled a goal, and then towards Mick Lyons, deciding that the Blues shouldn't be allowed to beat the Reds while they had ideologically unsound types like him playing for them. A free-kick was given against Hamilton for possession of an Irish accent.

The McKenzie/ Lee relationship was doomed from the start. 'Asimov' Lee's penchant for *"robust team men"* (read robots), alienated 'Flash' and mutual hatred was nurtured. Lee's judgement must be brought into question if only because of his disturbing habit of walking into inanimate

objects while wrestling with his muse (an Everton team with ten Mick Lyons).

Things came to a head when Media United came to Goodison one Boxing Day and gubbed us 6-2. Lee stormed into the dressing room after the game, nearly slammed the door off its hinges (it must have closed easier than his coffin lid) and asked his team to explain one by one how they thought they played, from David Lawson, through Darracott, Lyons, Rioch Darracott etc. All seemed to think they tried their best and some, like 'Flash' even went so far as to say they felt they played well. When he got to David Jones he said *"Well it must have been all my fault boss, I've let a team of f***ing world beaters down."* Later on Lee unearthed (sic) his famous quote *"Even when you're dead, you shouldn't lie down and let yourself be buried."*

Rover's Return

McKenzie escaped Lee's clutches and joined Chelsea. I can remember his return and especially him waltzing contemptuously around the series of garden gnomes that constituted our defence and clipping in a beauty. 30,000 eyes turned towards the home bench, dispatching stares of the paint-stripping variety to the person who *they* felt should have left.

A self confessed nomad, Duncan decided to move back to Merseyside when his playing days were over. He responded well to his adoring public and settled amongst them. He is now responsible for Youth Development: Football in the Community, no doubt giving coaches like Arthur Cox and Dave Bassett coronaries with his methods, and he still plays to the galleries in the odd exhibition game. Much to the chagrin of Evertonians, the drivel factor has shown distinct signs of returning to Goodison recently. Pat Nevin, come on down! It's your turn next.

Frank McConville

Embarrassing Moments Part Four

Billy Wilson gets it off his chest…

1. I covered all my schoolbooks in pictures of players cut out of *Shoot!*

2. Wrote letters to Kevin Keegan (cringe) before he became a German. Not alone in this, though, because after KK had scored for Southampton v Liverpool in 1982, I heard an anguished Scouser shout, *"I used to write letters to you, you c**t!"*

3. Waited behind for autographs after a Corby Town match.

4. Not only bought the *Kop Choir* LP but also *Ally's Tartan Army* in 1978.

5. Had the handles of my 'carry-out' bag snap under the weight of the cans of lager inside and saw the cans roll in a hundred (well, twelve) different directions under the feet of thirsty Scotsmen on route to Scotland v England, 1977.

6. Could only manage four of the above mentioned cans.

7. Started a small capitalistic venture at school, selling 1977 Wembley grass to football fanatics. Grass taken after 2-1 Scotland win (those were the days).

Football Un-Funnies

"He's the new surrealist"

Tender Moments From The Lives Of The Stars…

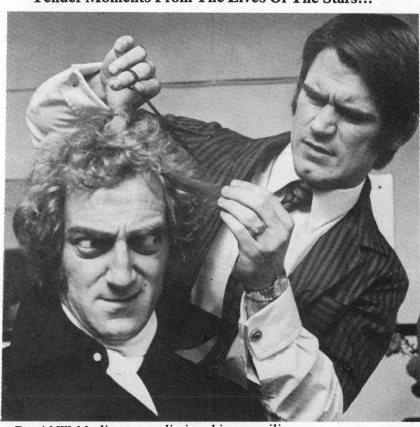

David Webb discovers a limit to his versatility

Port In A Storm

Jim Fryatt, always in the mood

Admitting to being a Southport fan was, and still is, guaranteed to produce loud laughter and questions about my sanity. Driving through sleet and snow to Hartlepool on a Monday night, I wondered myself whether I had all my marbles. But, from the day my father took me to Haig Avenue as a birthday treat (an early example of parental cruelty!) I was hooked. Names like Blain, Blore and Fielding became as important as the likes of St John, Young and Law were to youngsters with less taste than me.

Memories of the early Sixties have faded, but some things still stand out; Eric Jones, a flying winger who dislocated his shoulder more times than Bryan Robson, but played better with his arm in a sling; Workington arriving in the unaccustomed role of Division leaders and the always inconsistent Southport going 4-0 up after 12 minutes, and finally winning 6-3; local lad John Coates making his goalkeeping debut in a 4-4 thriller against Lincoln and being credited with two own goals...

Everything changed dramatically in 1965 with the arrival of Billy Bingham as manager. Results improved and I had my first experience of Cup fever when we reached the Fifth Round after victories over Second Division Cardiff and Ipswich. The defeat at Hull was watched by nearly 40,000. This was what supporting a small club was all about; national press and TV coverage, and, for a short while, envious schoolmates wishing there was life below Liverpool, Everton and Manchester United.

1966-67 saw two memorable events. Southport gained promotion for the first time, but more importantly, *GOD* arrived, in the shape of Eric Redrobe, 6ft 1in and usually weighing in at around 14 stone. 'Big Red' is still my all-time hero, unusual in that he *tried* in every game. His 'direct and robust' style certainly upset opposing defences and supporters. The final away trip of the season was made memorable by Eric

scoring the decisive goal in a 2-1 win at Tranmere in front of 15,000 fans.

In 1968 we even appeared on *Match Of The Day* in a 3-3 thriller at Swindon, the highlight of which was a thirty-yard screamer from Eric. Two years later, however, we were back in Division Four and by 1972, Eric had moved to Hereford. My final memory of him comes from a Cup tie against West Ham when he was prepared to take on all comers after one of his little challenges upset Billy Bonds & Co.

This period saw the boys on a run which will probably never be equalled. From 1969 until the end of our League career we never got past the First Round and three Non League teams sorted us out. Runcorn and Boston were bad enough, but the most shameful result was at Northern League Spennymoor United, when, despite scoring first, we were lucky to get away with a 4-1 thrashing.

Amidst these Cup disasters, there were still some bright spots. Tony Field scored some great goals before a sudden burst of hat-tricks attracted the attention of Blackburn Rovers. He later joined the exodus to the States, playing with some distinction alongside Pele at New York Cosmos.

Season 1972-73 was the final highlight in what had been a fairly undistinguished League existence. We actually went up as champions, managed by Jimmy Meadows with the headline-grabbers being twin strikers Andy Provan and Jim Fryatt. Both ended their playing careers in the States and the ever-cool Fryatt was last heard of as a croupier in a Las Vegas casino.

A Way Out

After that highspot, everything fell apart and relegation the following season was just the start of a long downward spiral to present-day near-oblivion. Away trips were rarely rewarded with a win, and sometimes just getting there was an achievement, notably when a two-car convoy travelling to York in 1977 was involved in a near miss with wandering cattle.

The club never had a happy relationship with the townsfolk, and until Wimbledon some time later, we had the lowest-ever average for a Championship team. Mind you, the club never went out of its way to encourage support. In the final season, a couple of fans made the horrendous midweek journey to Swansea, but weren't allowed to return on the team coach and had to spend the night on a bench at Cardiff BR station, waiting for the mail train to set off. Even fund raising attempts went sadly wrong. A pop concert was cancelled at the last minute - the Commercial Manager and any cash already taken haven't been seen since. When a raffle for a car was organised, the winning ticket belonged to a director's wife...

Billy Whizz

Now we are in the HFS Loans League and those days don't seem so bad at all. Over the years, the standard in this league has got steadily worse and any one of us faithful 250-300 would readily sell our souls to be travelling to York or Doncaster instead of Shepshed Charterhouse.

I have often thought of running a competition to find the worst ever decision made by a board of directors and would like to nominate the one made by those of Southport at the end of our first season in Non-League football. The top eight teams in the Premier League were invited to join the newly formed Alliance, forerunner of the Conference, but we declined on the grounds that it wouldn't even last one season, and none of the Southport players were interested because of the extra travel involved!

Three months later, the team had fallen apart, and despite occasional FA Trophy and FA Cup runs, each season has got steadily worse. The hardcore fans put up with mediocre playing standards and a fairly regular turnover of managers. These last two seasons must have set some sort of record with over 80 players having made at least one appearance! There have been occasional highlights — a brilliant FA Trophy win at Telford by 4-2, one of the goals scored in spectacular fashion by a young striker called Andy Mutch — some Midlands readers may know of his whereabouts now. The FA Cup run of last season brought more publicity and the TV cameras appeared at Haig Avenue. Oh, the memories: queues outside the ground, pubs full before kick-off, police horses chasing fans down the road.....

Over the years, this club has caused us heartache and inconvenience and ruined our social life, but we still turn up each week. Roll on the FA Cup First Qualifying Round!

John Massam

Time: 4.33 pm
Date: 24th April 1982
Place: Millmoor

A vital top of Division Two clash reaches its climax; the score is third-placed Rotherham United 2, fourth-placed Luton Town 2. Constant pressure by the Millers has been matched by some fine counter-attacking play by David Pleat's young team. Yet again, the genius that is Tony Towner torments the left side of the Luton defence only to be chopped down by a typically subtle Peter Nicholas challenge. Penalty! With only minutes to go, up steps 'Crowd Favourite' Gerry Gow. The ground falls silent. The whistle blows. The ball hurtles skywards...

Most people think of Rotherham as being a dirty little Yorkshire steel town. Actually, er, they're right. Although the traditional coal and steel industries were amongst the hardest-hit in the '70s and early '80s, the local council fought hard for new jobs with some success. But as well as being one of the staunchest strongholds of the People's Republic of South Yorkshire, the town is also the home of the 'Merry Millers'.

Rotherham United have never been in the First Division, though in season 1960/1 we were pipped on goal difference by only 1/100th. In 1960 we made it to the first ever final of the League Cup, narowly losing over two legs to Aston Villa. Apart from that, our main claim to fame is the Tommy Docherty one liner; ("*I promised Rotherham I'd take them out of the Third Division...*") There was also, of course, our heroic victory in the BBC Kop Choir competition in the late Sixties. Ah, I can still hear the strains of our winning rendition of *"We all live in a red submarine"*. What an age of innocence.

Great players of those days included Trevor Phillips, Neil Hague, David Gwyther and the inimitable Trevor Womble (whose name prompted predictable chants concerning a possible anatomical deficiency). With the two nearby Sheffield clubs, and Leeds United competing for the affections of younger supporters, crowds were modest by the standards of the day. Even so, throughout the dark Division Four days to follow, the club could always depend on a hardcore of two or three thousand souls.

The caption-defying Nigel Johnson

During the years 1965-1979 Rotherham Utd Ltd were controlled by the Pursehouse family, a local butchery dynasty. In 1979 after years of careful (and boring) stewardship, they decided to sell out. After a few days of speculation a bid of £70,000 was accepted, a surprisingly low sum for a tidy little club with book assets amounting to a quarter of a million pounds. The buyer turned out to be an Essex 'businessman', Anton Johnson. On finding that Johnson wanted to pay by monthly instalments, the Pursehouses tried to pull out of the deal. The threat of legal action forced them to reluctantly go through with it, though they were fearful for the future of the club in the hands of a man like Johnson. Still, Anton with his big cigars and his helicopter landing in the centre circle, promised exciting times to come.

An untried manager, Ian Porterfield, was appointed and money was spent on new players like Seasman, Towner and Ronnie Moore. Millmoor got a much needed lick of paint. Things were on the up and up. Nobody complained.

And the exciting times *did* come. 1980-81 saw a heroic Third Division championship made more sweet by beating the old enemy Barnsley to the finishing line. The combination of Towner bouncing the ball into the net off Ronnie Moore's head, together with a rock solid defence founded on Jimmy Mullen, Paul Stancliffe, and the great Ray Mountford in goal. The team were undefeated at Millmoor, equalling the divisional record for the fewest goals conceded.

Blades Runner

Next season Porterfield dropped a division to take over the Blades (Sheffield United). His replacement was another untried ex-player, Emlyn Hughes, whose first action was the inspired purchase of Gerry Gow from Manchester City. On his home debut Gow was booked before the ball left the centre circle at the kick off. A minute later he was sent off for a tackle which left a Derby player writhing in agony. Obviously a man on a one way ticket to the hall of fame. Stiffened by Gow's 'committment', the team came within a whisker of their first trip to the top flight.

A string of vital penalty misses robbed the Millers of glory that season; against Newcastle to end that fabulous run of nine straight wins (eight of them in February); against Derby, another promotion contender; and a vital miss against Luton which helped them and not us to the First Division. Even two sound thrashings of Chelsea (6-0 at home and 4-1 away) couldn't quite make up for the disappointment of missing out on a first time trip to the top.

Perhaps unsurprisingly Rotherham have never made it to the big time in terms of sponsors but the team shirts for the 1982-83

The caption-defying Martin Scott

campaign were classics. You may remember a brief period in the early Eighties when it was popular to have players names emblazoned across the back of their tracksuits. On the first day of the season I was somewhat puzzled to see every member of the Millers team turn out with 'PATRICK' written in huge letters across the front of their shirts. After a few minutes' speculation about a wholesale close season swoop on the Irish Leagues, I was told of a last-minute sponsorship deal with a French sports company of that name. My Rotherham shirt of this vintage is an ideal conversation starter at parties.

The 1982-3 season saw the Millers start well, being ninth in the table by January. However a serious injury to mountainous centre half Paul Stancliffe, forced a defensive reshuffle leading to an alarming leakage of goals. A string of disastrous results followed, with manager Emlyn Hughes living up to his Crazy Horse nickname by selecting himself to play each week. Inexplicable behind the scenes deals further eroded morale and the team slipped into the relegation zone. The premature, though predictable, sacking came after a 4-0 thrashing on the newly-lain plastic of Loftus Road.

False Leeds?

With games running out new manager George Kerr dipped into that famous pool of talent, Grimsby Town Reserves, and promptly turn a slump into a landslide. Even so, three points from the final fixture at Leeds would see the team avoid

The Mill Town

Johnson was among the first of a new breed of business sharks to become involved in football. Sadly he wasn't the last.

In the 1984/5 season, with decent local businessman Syd Wood taking over as Chairman and trying to sort out the mess, Rotherham struggled for self respect in the Third Division. Grimsby rejects like erratic striker Kevin Kilmore (never was a striker so obviously but wrongly nicknamed 'Killer') and the excruciating Bobby Mitchell made it a losing struggle. As they had been together at a number of clubs George Kerr referred to Mitchell as 'my John McGovern'. Supporters viewed the Clough/McGovern allusion, as being rather less apt than, say, Harry Corbett/ Sooty. Indeed Mitchell, christened 'Jogger' by the crowd, showed all the power and athleticism of a glove puppet.

Burns Unit

The precocious talent of brilliant Bobby Mimms (how do you make a chant out of Mimms?) was the only shaft of light in the gloom. Poor Bobby. The light that shines the brightest burns but briefly.

The dog days of George Kerr faded into the equally forgettable era of Norman Hunter flailing machines, with a dash of the awful Dave Cusack thrown in along the way. Chairman Syd Wood passed on the torch to scrap metal supremo C F Booth, whose yards surround the ground on three sides. Cynics made all the predictable jokes. They seemed justified when the team finally slid into the Fourth Division in 1988, albeit thanks to an extremely dubious Plummet Airlines performance by Fulham at Chesterfield.

New manager Billy McEwan was a member of the Third Division

Bobby dazzler (caption!)

championship team. He's a wiry Scot with a faintly disturbing touch of fanaticism about him. His obvious determination to lead from the side has led to him having more trouble with referees than anyone actually playing in the team.

With some shrewd buying and the sensible use of younger players he produced a team that always looked like last season's Fourth Division champions, despite an alarming inconsistency. They played lovely football, despite a brief experiment with the long ball game after the purchase of the lanky Stewart Evans (ex Wimbledon). In one match we played four wingers which must have confused the opposition no end.

The caption-defying Tony Grealish

Current darling of the terraces is top scorer Bobby Williamson, a bargain buy from West Brom. With his close cropped hair and a tendency to shout the odds to all and sundry, he has the air of being a reformed hardcase; perhaps Sergeant Major McEwan has brought the best out of him.

Another key ingredient is the midfield blend of Tony 'Mr Sunshine' Grealish with talented youngster Shawn Goodwin. In defence, international Kelham O'Hanlon keeps goal behind centre half Nigel Johnson and right back Martin Scott. Johnson is back at the club after a big money transfer to Manchester City went wrong when injury wrecked a promising career. Scott is a young defender with enormous talent and a hell of a left foot (ask Coventry or Everton).

With the club now on a firmer footing financially and a new mood of optimism prevailing, further progress up the League seems a definite possibility. The dangers and the disasters of the Anton Johnson era, the subsequent brushes with bankruptcy and the agonies of watching hopeless teams are in the past. A single season's brush with glory, followed by seven years in the wilderness. Was it worth it? If only that penalty had gone in…

Graham Slack

relegation. At the interval the Millers were 2-1 up only for Leeds to equalise midway through the second half. Despite being in mid table the home team spent the next twenty minutes on one of their famous specialities; time wasting. By niggling fouls, petulant argument and booting the ball out of the ground, they managed to hang on for a draw. The die was cast; back to the Third Division after two heady seasons of optimism and with worse to come.

During decline and relegation a number of inexplicable decisions by Chairman Johnson baffled the fans. In the spring of 1983, with relegation threatening, the club's best player Tony Towner, was 'loaned' to arch rivals Sheffield United. Insane proposals to merge the two club were rumoured with the merged club to play at Bramall Lane and Millmoor to be sold off.

Unaccounted For

In addition the Chairman was becoming involved with other football clubs, much to the disquiet of the Football League. In particular an allegedly dodgy unsecured loan to Derby was widely questioned. Somehow the Millers were supposed to be hugely in debt. In April 1984, Johnson sold out, leaving a big red mark in the account books and a lot of questions about 'consultancy' payments to his mates. In little more than four seasons the books show the balance going from a healthy surplus of £250,000 to a deficit of nearly £400,000.

Many of the financial dealings of the Anton Johnson era remain a mystery.

Michael Alway's *search for the true essence of English football leads him into a consideration of the matchday programme...*

Art

The late Sixties — Justin De Villeneuve, The Herd, Cecil Beaton's hat, *The Frost Report*, the Italian bistro and... the Matchday Magazine. In the vanguard, Coventry City's *Sky Blue*, West Bromwich's art catalogue *Albion News*, Queens Park Rangers distinctive chessboard design - owing more than a little to the Brigit Riley school of Op Art - Burnley's *Claret & Blue*, *Molinews*, a flight of fancy from Southend (of all people) and the issues of the (then go-ahead) Birmingham clubs.

By 1974, most clubs had experimented in radically restructuring the format of their official programmes in line with the whimsical ventures of design and layout undertaken by the above.

Unlike today's formularised efforts, early incursions into juxtaposing the ever more entwined worlds of pop and football were entirely fascinating journeys into the unknown. Graphic Design was the new religion. Outrageously camp and exotic letraset fought for visual attention with mystically blurred action photographs. The most down to earth and prosaic of managers and players were elevated to celebrity status by this imaginative approach to publishing.

Sky Blue was the paragon of disposability, perfectly encapsulating the period's neo-psychedelic lust for invention. In artistic terms, it remains an item of some beauty. The aesthetic guidelines for programme production had to be completely re-drawn. As most clubs were still contracting the work to local printers, somehow the imagined character of each team and its regional flavour remained intact. The importance of this last point

should not be underestimated; to a small boy, *Albion News* **was** West Bromwich, a fabulously glamourous place. Later, the grim reality was discovered and an innocent dream exploded.

Without doubt, the best of these productions should have a unique place in the inner sanctum of any self-proclaimed 'style guru'. The dividing line between Ronnie Rees and Rembrandt had never been more fine. Pretention was everywhere, although some clubs went too far, when, following the lead of Derby County's *The Ram*, they completely lost their marbles with the introduction of newspaper issues. These were hated by programme collectors for being outsize and tatty before their time.

Murphy's Law

Like pop music, however, the last fifteen years have seen a gradual erosion of character in club productions, a dour trend toward uniformity, accelerated by the syndication of printing and, especially, writing. With the noble exception of Colin Murphy, the editors of the past, the madmen and adventurers who hoisted the proud flags of their clubs, have disappeared from the scene in the name of commerce. Despite obvious technical advances, dismal standards prevail today.

Gone are the romantic images of twenty years ago to be replaced by grey photographs that somehow fail to capture the atmosphere and sexuality of the moment. There are exceptions, but generally, local colour, a sense of place, has been lost. The marvellous potential of the English language is rarely exercised, indeed, most columns today would not engage an infantile mind.

The chain broken by the current television fiasco has not helped as there always seemed to be a complimentary relationship between the two mediums. Our heroes would leap from animated pose in the matchday magazine into exactly that same gesture on *Match Of The Day* and *The Big Match*. A transformation so surrealistic as to leave one gasping.

Apart from a handful of brave clubs, (notably Wrexham, Clydebank and Stirling Albion) and the estimable Mr Murphy, where might one find experimentation and reason for the stylist to think twice before consigning those tank tops, loon pants, platform shoes and flowerpower ties to the dustbin or museum forever?

A small survey of Non League productions has convinced me that although these clubs cannot possibly reproduce the visual opulence of the matchday magazine in its heyday, the programmes of our smaller (sometimes amoebic) friends are the places to find humour, detail and bizarre visual panoramas. In relation to attendances, the achievements of these Non League journals' editors are quite astounding and are something of which the nation should be

Official Match-Day Magazine   Volume 3 Number 3

Molineux, Saturday, 5th September, 1970   Kick-off 3p.m.

WOLVES v STOKE CITY

Of The Matter

proud - indeed, fight to maintain.

Loquacious former Leatherhead giant-killer, Chris Kelly is the manager of **Kingstonian** and, in his very first notes of the new season, starts as he means to go on by proclaiming, quite unabashed, that new striker Mark Smith had been found in 'Options' nightclub. The programme cover displays a (surely deliberate) out of focus photo of their new Kingsmeadow stadium to further enhance the feeling of deja vu.

Great Yarmouth evoke the Sixties by depicting a line drawing of their pavilion grandstand; a piece of architecture so curious as to recall the work of Clough Williams-Ellis of Portmerion (*Prisoner*) fame.

Selsey is now home to at least two great English eccentrics in cricketing stargazer Patrick Moore and former Middlesbrough and Carlisle goalpoacher Joe Laidlaw, who manages the locals. Joe, hardly the most florid footballer of his day, expresses his annoyance, in no uncertain terms, at having been forced to introduce himself against Pagham, *"to instill some decorum into an undisciplined midfield."* Along the coast at **Lancing**, the editor wittily describes the disappointing goalscoring return of one Richard Styles (11 goals in 111 games) as *"nicely symmetrical."*

The neat issue of **Metropolitan Police** sows the seeds of internal schism by complaining that Mario Russo's inability to regain fitness after injury was down to *"being aggravated by chasing villains at work."* In a player profile at **Ringmer**, Paul Thompson declares an ambition to be a

ballet dancer and has to answer other questions like *"How many training sessions have you missed through bullshit?"* and *"Do you think things can get any worse?"*

In Essex, at **Southend Manor**, Bobby Hodges proves himself to be something of a connoisseur of the good life and confounds his lager-quaffing counterparts by admitting to being partial to *"Lobster Thermidor and cointreau."* A weighty **Exmouth Town** programme sees match sponsor and local builder Terry Davey contribute a tale of *"being caught short up Snowdon with a Bangor supporter"* and, later, failing to make the latrine in time *"because it was occupied by an Oriental gentlemen."* Meanwhile, **Racing Club Warwick**'s boss is pissed off that he must field a team *"depleted by invitations to Bobby Hancock's wedding."*

Wadd Of Notes

Such is the tradition at **Falmouth Town** that following an unthinkable two successive defeats, manager, Dave Wadd insists *"It'll never happen again."* **Chester-Le-Street** describe referee Mr Docherty as a *"failed family planning consultant"* and on a sartorial note, a guest writer for **East Ham United** describes manager Ruben Gane as *"bearing a resemblance to a County Sligo potato farmer."* **Waltham Abbey**, uniquely, run a medical column and we learn that *"in treating a dead leg, on no account should the area be massaged or heat applied."*

The bizarre continues at **Biggleswade Town**, who have their priorities right by emblazoning the words *"Coming Soon - Jacket Potatoes And Soup"* and at **Didcot Town** we see that the photographer has run out of film and instead submits a Cocteauesque 'artistic impression' of Dave Shorter's goal at Maidenhead.

The trivia goes on and on, **Franklands Village** are not ashamed to remember their 'worst ever sides' detailing the circumstances of surrender at Crawley Reserves, 13-0, and Ardingly, 11-2. What can only be described as dandyism can be found in the works of fanatics at: **St Albans City, Harrogate Railway, Three Bridges, Wivenhoe, Newtown, Penhill** (*"Welcome back, Vinny Zarola"*), **St Osyth, Evesham, Bury Town, Clacton** (80 pages!) and **Chelmsford City** , who whimsically staple down the short side. **Wealdstone** exercise the supreme irony by allowing a column to the exotic and persuasive Sudhir Rawal while banning his own independent *Elmslie Ender* from Lower Mead.

In my view, the programme editors of the Football League would do well to take on board the esoterica of these characters and use their greater resources to produce the necessary pop artefact whilst assimilating the influences of such timeless figures as Warhol, Jackson Pollock, Mickie Most, Luis Bunuel, Peter Wyngarde, Powell & Pressburger and the Pre-Raphaelites.

Michael Alway

Frankie Speaking

The Positive Touch

When your local team boasts one of the finest pairs of strikers outside the First Division and only an erratic defence can be held responsible for the failure to mount a serious promotion bid, it might seem downright perverse to swear allegiance to the right back. However, although I, on my youthful early visits to Boothferry Park, gloried along with everyone else on the goalscoring brilliance of Chris Chilton and Ken Wagstaff, my heart pounded most fiercely when defender Frankie Banks was on the ball.

This, in fact, did not amount to spells of extended heart pounding, as Frankie did not spend very much time on the ball. If he did receive the ball in space, his preference was to hoof it forward without further ado. For ten years from 1966 to 1976 as he compiled a record of just short of 300 Second Division games for the Tigers, he was the essence of the dependable full back, finally meriting the standard pen picture description of *"tenacious and sturdy"*.

This was an era when full backs were not born but hewn out of rock. Frank took over the coveted Hull City right back spot from a man comprised almost entirely of granite, Andy 'Jock' Davidson, a one club and three broken leg man, who still holds the Boothferry Park record for League appearances.

Elsewhere in the League those vital number two and three shirts were filled by graduates of the 'Take No Prisoners School Of Defending', such as Millwall's awesome Harry Cripps and Swindon's John Trollope, who trained by ploughing fields with his bare hands and teeth. Also regularly to be seen on Saturday afternoons exhibiting little regard for the provisions of the Geneva Convention when it came to dealing with flying wingers, were the likes of Gary Pendrey at Birmingham, Bolton's Sid Farrimond and Len Badger of Sheffield United.

Frankie, to his immense credit, rarely took the violent option. His tackling skills were of good quality and he was usually able to time challenges with sufficient precision to take the ball first and the man only incidentally. He was an unglamourous, glorious contributor.

Frank's early life links two of the East Coast's more fashionable leisure resorts, Hull and Southend. He was born in East Yorkshire but brought up in Essex. His career began with Southend United but in 1966 he joined Hull City and stayed for ten years. That decade span was a turbulent one for football chic and Frank was surpassed by few stars in his fashion consciousness. The Banks sideburns circa 1973 were a match for anything in the League and had he played for a geographically less peripheral club surely they would have earned him an England call up. After all, coiffeur rather than football ability, can constitute the only

explanation for the award of caps at full back around this period to such as Frank Lampard, Mike Pejic and Ian Gillard.

It is easy to allow the reckless modern day attacking posturing of Gary Stevens, Mitchell Thomas and Kenny Sansom to obscure the fact that twenty years ago a full back departing his own half of the pitch would travel equipped with a map, a compass and a slab of Kendal mint cake. Frankie was very much of this tradition but he did occasionally sneak forward, and scenes of unrestrained joy greeted his seven goals for City.

These were largely scored from 25 yards out, when a loose ball would run free from the penalty area melee to Frank, who, having absent mindedly wandered into the last third of the pitch, would realise that he was horribly out of position. Panic stricken, he would promptly tonk the ball into the net rather than face the awful prospect of a vain chase back to his defensive duties in the wake of a pacy winger exhibiting a clean pair of heels.

You knew you'd made it as a footballing stalwart in this era when you were the subject of an article in the *Football League Review*. Frankie's moment of glory came when the *Review* highlighted his remarkable

proficiency as a cartoonist, including a couple of examples from the Banks portfolio. As far as I can tell Frankie remains undiscovered by the art world at large; perhaps, as is so tragically often the case, it will only be after his death that he will be recognised as a truly original talent.

In 1976, Frankie left Hull for Southend United, taking up coaching duties shortly afterwards. The Shrimpers' meanderings of recent seasons have taken their toll on Frank, who has risen and fallen in their set up, but a glance of page 337 of the 1988-89 *Rothmans* (come on, admit you've got it handy) will reveal Frank Banks listed as Assistant Manager. He is in the photograph too, greying at the temples, surely indignant as a matter of professional pride at having to stand next to Chris Ramsey, possibly the feeblest full back ever to play in a Cup Final, and a man who has never even tried to grow sideburns.

Southend's 1989 relegation clearly proves that Frank was not promoted to a sufficiently high level in the club's structure. In any event, I hold nothing but fond memories of the integrity of Frankie Banks and I hope that his glory days in football are not over.

Steve Weatherill

I T WAS CHRISTMAS DAY IN THE TRENCHES .... IN THE SPIRIT OF GOOD WILL SOLDIERS FROM THE OPPOSING ARMIES ENGAGED IN A FRIENDLY GAME OF FOOTBALL.

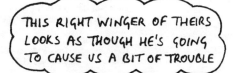

(Not A) Great Own Goal Of Our Time *Claimed by David Bamber, Barnsley v Portsmouth, 9th Feb, 1985*

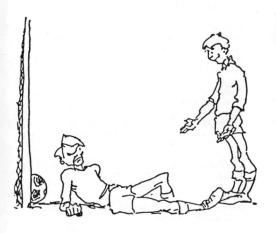

It was one of those days, when Winter had the land in its icy grip. Every club from Inverness Caledonian to Plymouth Argyle is likely to end of the day with a big 'P' beside it. The gentlemen of the Pools Panel are cossetted in their Savoy suite and the BBC set up a snowman on a pitch, dressed in a scarf and electronic headset and film it with a voiceover from Archie McPherson. You assume everything is off and so don't even bother to turn up at Euston. Then that nice Mr Lynam smiles and tells you, at 12.30pm, that your team's match at Barnsley, of all places, is one of the five that will be played that day.

Highlights were to be shown on *Match Of The Day*, which was just as well because

otherwise I would never have seen one of the finest 'Not The Great Own Goals' that I have ever spotted.

Then as now, Portsmouth were struggling for goals, which was not surprising when I reveal that our strike force was Scott McGarvey and Dave Bamber. McGarvey had already tested the goalkeeping abilities of the Barnsley fans behind the goal when Paul Hardyman produced the fifth *"Oooh!"* of the afternoon from Barry Davies as his tackle on Billy Ronson sent the ball sailing towards the goal requiring a fingertip save from Baker.

From the resulting corner, the ball sailed in towards the near post from where Paul Futcher headed it powerfully away, but only onto the back of Ian Law's unsuspecting head. In a crazy split second it flew past Futcher and Baker and was nestling in the back of the Barnsley net.

About four yards away, on the six yard line, Dave Bamber had jumped, if that isn't too extravagant a term, an inch or two in the air and, much to the amazement of all, was accepting the congratulations of his team mates. Barry 'Oooh' Davies confirmed in the second half that Bamber had claimed the goal. This tenuous statistic proved to be the only 'goal' of his brief career at Fratton Park, even though videoed evidence clearly showed he got nowhere near the ball.

Alan Kerby

Publications

All prices and addresses were correct at the time of going to press. Don't forget to enclose a large SAE when sending away for any of the magazines listed below.

General Magazines:

The Absolute Game (Scotland): 50p from P O Box 303, Southern D O, Edinburgh EH9 1NE
Blow Football: 50p from 91 Dawlish Road, Selly Oak, Birmingham B29 7AF
Crazy Horse: 50p from Top Floor Studio, 27-29 Union St, London SE1
Don't Just Stand There (East Midlands/General): 30p from 12 Gresham Road, Derby DE2 8AW
Each Game As It Comes: 20p from 22 Stanley Street, Norton, Stockton-on-Tees, Cleveland TS20 1HG
Elfmeter (West Germany): 50p from 32 East Ave, Porthmadog, Gwynedd, N.Wales LL49 9EN
European Football: 35p from c/o Chris Littleford, 11 Cottan House, Thames Street, London SE10 9DG
Five To Three: 40p from P O Box 10, Pwllheli, Gwynedd LL53 5BE
Football Utopia (South East London): 30p from Spring Place, St Aubyns Close, Orpington, Kent BR6 0SN
Head the Ball (Ireland): 50p from P O Box 2466, Dublin 8, Rep Of Ireland
Hit The Bar (North-West): 60p from 10 Grafton Street, Blackpool, Lancs
The Ivor Thirst Good Pub Guide To The Football League — Vol no 1 The Midlands: £2.00 (inc post) from 61 Stratford Road, West Bridgford, Nottingham
The Lad Done Brilliant (Humour): 50p from 11 Khama Road, Tooting, London SW17 0EN
Les Bence — Manager's Notes (Humour) 50p from 5 Clark's Place, Trowbridge, Wilts, BA14 7HA
More Than A Game: 40p from 56 Springdale Road, Broadstone, Poole, Dorset
Non League Football Fanfare (South East England): 40p from 26 Orchard Road, Kingston upon Thames, Surrey KT1 2QW
Offside Trap: 50p from 66 Westlands Road, Hull HU5 5ND
On The One Road (Ireland): 50p from 10 Mendip Way, Highfield, Hemel Hempstead, Herts HP2 5QY
Rodney, Rodney: 40p from P O Box 19(SEPDO), Manchester M19 5RZ
The Scottish Non League Review Of 1988-89: £1 from Stewart Davidson, 12 Windsor Road, Renfrew, Scotland PA4 0SS
Storming With Menace (South West England): 40p from 11 Chatsworth Way, Carylon Bay, St. Austell, Cornwall PL25 3SL
Tayside Football Review (Scottish): 60p from 45 Sutherland Crescent, Dundee DD2 2HP
What's The Score? (Merseyside/General): 50p from PO Box 221, Liverpool L69 7DD

Club Magazines:

Aberdeen:
The Northern Light: 50p from P.O. Box 269, Aberdeen AB9 8EN

Airdrie:
Only The Lonely: 50p from 6 Ossian Road, Glasgow, G43 2JJ

Albion Rovers:
Over The Wall: 50p from c/o 15 North Drive, Tooting, London SW16

Aldershot:
Shots In The Dark: 50p from P O Box 238, Guildford, Surrey GU2 6FY

Arsenal:
An Imperfect Match: 50p from 80 Stapleton Hall Road, London N4 4QA
The Arsenal Echo Echo: 40p from 30 Dene Road, Guildford, Surrey GU1 4DD
The Gooner: £1.00 (Championship Special) from BCMM Box 7499, London WC1N 3XX

Aston Villa:
Witton Wisdom: 50p from 60 High Road, Byfleet, Surrey KT14 7QL
Heroes And Villians (Aston Villa): 50p from 48 Tewkesbury Rd, Perry Barr, Birmingham B20 3DU

Ayr United:
4-1: 50p from 8 Maple Place, Kilmarnock

Ballyclare Comrades:
Calling All Comrades: 50p from 50 Rashee Road, Ballyclare, Co Antrim BT39 9HP

Barnet:
Buzztalk: 50p from 4 Seymour Road, London N3 2NH

Birmingham City:
Tired and Weary 40p from 133 Longmore Road, Shirley, Solihull, West Midlands B90 3EF

Bishops Stortford:
Cross Rhodes: 30p from 36 Wetherfield, Stansted, Essex CM24 8JB

Blackburn Rovers:
4,000 Holes: 50p from 'The Garth', Commons Lane, Balderstone, Blackburn BB2 7LL

Bolton Wanderers:
The Normid Nomad: 50p from P O Box 2, Worsley S O, Manchester M28 6XY
Wanderers Worldwide: 40p from 62 Queensgate, Bolton, Lancs

Boston United: **From Behind Your Fences**: 60p (Big Summer Special) from 82 Osprey Road, Biggleswade, Bedfordshire SG18 8HE

Bournemouth:
Not TheEightthousandfivehundredandtwo: 25p from 56 Springdale Road, Broadstone, Dorset
Out Of Court: 40p from Flat 3, High Point, 50 Midanbury Lane, Bitterne Park, Southampton SO2 4HE

Bradford City:
City Gent: £1.00 (massive issue) from 46 Ainsty Road, Wetherby, LS22 4QS
Bernard Of The Bantams (Football Comic): 50p from 83 North Road, Wibsey, Bradford BD6 1TR

Bradford Park Avenue:
Avenue Fightback!: £1 from 46 Ainsty Road, Wetherby, LS22 4QS

Brentford:
Voice Of The Beehive: 30p from Flat 2, 84 Milton Grove, Stoke Newington, London N16

Brighton:
And Smith Must Score!: 50p from 88 Friar Oaks Road, Hassocks, West Sussex BN6 8PY.
Gulls Eye: 20p from Flat 5, 4 Oxford Road, Worthing, West Sussex

Bristol City:
The Bountyhunter: 50p from P. O Box 576, Bristol, BS99 1QJ

Bristol Rovers:
The Gashead: 50p from 39 Co-operation Road, Greenbank, Bristol
9 1/2 Months: 50p from The Laurels, Park Road, Paulton, Avon BS18 5QQ

Bromley:
Down The Lane: 50p from 2 Toynbec Close, Chislehurst, Kent BR7 6TH

Cambridge United:
The Abbey Rabbit: 30p from 220 Abbotswold, Harlow, Essex, CM18 6TP
RahRahRah!: 50p from 283 Campkin Road, Cambridge CB4 2LD

Cardiff City:
Bobbing Along: 40p from 2 Moy Road, Roath, Cardiff CF2 4SG
Intifada: 40p from 13 Brym Terrace, Careau, Mid Glam CF3 4OUR
O Bluebird Of Happiness: 50p from 90 Llandaff Road, Canton, Cardiff CF1 9NN
Watch The Bluebirds: 20p from 49 Nant-y-Fedw, Ynysboeth, Abercynon, Mid Glam

Celtic:
Not the View: 50p from P.O. Box 306, Glasgow G21 2EA

Charlton Athletic:
Addickted: 5p from 4 Dacre Place, London SE13
Voice of the Valley: 50p from P.O. Box 387, London SE9 6EH
The Valiants Viewpoint: 50p from 47 Bradbourne Cr, Bexleyheath, Kent DA7 5QJ

Chelsea:
The Chelsea Independent: 30p from P.O.Box 459, London E7 8LU
The Red Card: 50p from 42 Hillside Close, Banstead, Surrey SM7 1ET

Cheltenham Town:
Murphy's Frog: 30p from 46 Long Mynd Avenue, Up Hatherly, Cheltenham, GL51 5QN

Chesterfield:
The Crooked Spireite: 40p from Flat 3, 119 Newbold Road, Chesterfield S41 7PS

Chorley:
The North Stand Blues: 50p from 60 Ashfield Park Drive, Standish, Wigan, Lancs WN6 0EG

Cliftonville:
The Wee Red: 50p from Flat 4, 1 Myrtlefield Park, Belfast BT9 6NE

The Casbah: 60p from the Red Shop, Solitude, Cliftonville Street, Belfast 14

Colchester Utd:
Floodlight: 30p from 8 Maple Drive, Kirby Cross, Frinton-on-Sea, Essex

Coventry City:
The Westender: 40p from P O Box 128, Coventry, CV1 5TQ

Crewe Alexandra:
He's Not Danny Grady: 20p from 63 Egerton Road, Fallowfield, Manchester, M14 6UZ

Crystal Palace:
Eagle Eye: 50p from 30 Manor Court, York Way, Whetstone, London N20 0DR

Darlington:
Mission Impossible: 40p from 8 Bramley Parade, Bowesfield Lane, Stockton-on-Tees, Cleveland TS18 3JG

Dartford:
Light At The End Of The Tunnel: 50p from 19 The Terraces, Dartford, Kent DA2 6BX

Derby County:
Bloomer Shoots — Shilton Saves: 50p from 10 Quorn Rise, Sunnyhill, Derby

Dulwich Hamlet:
Champion Hill Street Blues: 40p from 106 Wolverton, Alvey Street, Walworth, London SE17 2AF

Dundee:
It's Half Past Four And We're 2-0 Down: 70p from HPF, Eassie House, Glamis, Forfar, Angus DD8 1SG

Dundee United:
The Final Hurdle: 30p from P.O. Box 91, Dundee DD1 9DW
Freakscene: 35p from 14 Banchory Ave, Eastwood, Glasgow G43 1EZ
One Team In Dundee: 20p from Box 1909, 11a Forth Street, Edinburgh EH1 3LE

Dundee United/West Ham:
UTD United: 50p from 3 Douglas Terrace, Dundee, Scotland, DD3 6HN

Dunfermline:
Walking Down The Halbeath Road: 50p from Box 6168, 11a Forth Street, Edinburgh EH1 3LE

Emfa Kilkenny:
Every Man A Football Artist: 50p from 75 John Street, Kilkenny, Rep of Ireland

Enfield:
Talk Of The Town End: 30p from 20 Calder Close, Enfield, Middlesex EN1 3TS
In Defence: 40p from 43 Anglesey Road, Ponders End, Enfield, EN3 4HZ

Everton:
Blue Wail 50p from 62 Liverpool Road, Crosby, Liverpool L23 5SJ
When Skies Are Grey: 50p from 32 East Ave, Porthmadog, Gwynedd, N Wales LL49 9EN

Exeter City:
The Exe-Directory: 50p from P O Box 106, Exeter, Devon

Falkirk:
Falkirk Unofficial Fanzine: 50p from 2 Rose Terrace, Stenhousemuir FK5 4DW

Fulham:
There's Only One F In Fulham: 50p from 37 Ember Lane, Esher, Surrey KT10 8EA

Gillingham:
Brian Moore's Head: 50p from 11 Watts Avenue, Rochester, Kent ME1 1RX
The Donkey's Tale: 50p from 43 Fox Street, Gillingham, Kent ME7 1HH

Gloucester City:
Tiger Roar: 20p from 70 Sussex Gardens, Hucclecote, Gloucester, GL3 3SU

Grimsby Town:
Sing When We're Fishing: 30p from 4 Nicholson Street, Cleethorpes, S.Humberside, DN35 8RW

Hearts:
The Good, The Bad And The Ugly: 40p from 37 Swanston Drive, Edinburgh EH10 7BP
The Gorgie Wave: 50p from 5 Oxgangs Road, Edinburgh EH10 7BG

Hibernian:
The Proclaimer: 40p from Mr and Mrs Shinyheid, 2 Northumberland Place, Edinburgh EH3 6LQ.
Hibees Glasgow Gossip: 30p from 2, Guthrie Street, Edinburgh EH1 1JG
Hibs Monthly: 50p from 59 Comely Bank Road, Edinburgh, EH4 1EJ

Hull City:
Hull, Hell And Happiness: 60p from Spring House, Seaside Road, Easington, Hull, East Yorkshire, HU12 0TY

Ipswich Town:
Dribble : 50p from 117 Maldon Road, Colchester, Essex
A Load Of Cobbolds: 50p from 62 Raynham Road, Bury St Edmunds, Suffolk IP32 6ED

Kidderminster Harriers:
The Soup: 50p from 29 Gilgal, Stourport, Nr Kidderminster, Worcestershire

Kilmarnock:
Killie Ken: 30p from 34 Boyd Orr Crescent, Kilmaurs, Scotland
Paper Roses: 50p from c/o 12 MacCallum Place, Kilmarnock

Kingstonian:
NHS — No Home Stadium: 40p from 34 Hunters Road, Chessington, Surrey KT9 1RU

Leeds United:
Crossbar : 40p from 12 Belle Vue Terrace, Guiseley, Leeds LS20 9BU
Marching Altogether: free from Leeds Trades Club, Savile Mount, Leeds 7
The Hanging Sheep: 40p from 41 Woodhall Terrace, Thornbury, Bradford BD3 7BZ
The Peacock: 50p from P O Box 442, Sheffield, S1 3UN

Leicester City:
The Fox: 50p from 36 Main Street, Huncote, Leicestershire, LE9 6AU

Leyton Orient:
Leyton Orientear: 30p from 1 York Road, Leyton, London E10 5QG

Lincoln City
The Banker Magazine: 40p from PO Box 1211, London N3 1RF
Deranged Ferret: 50p from 3 Doman Road, Norwich NR1 3AW

Linfield:
Blue For You: 50p from P O Box 51, Lisburn, BT27 5DN
One Team In Ulster: 50p from 9 Belvoir Park, Lisburn Co Antrim, BT28 1TZ

Liverpool:
Through The Wind And Rain : 60p from PO Box 23, Bootle, Merseyside L30 2SA
When Sunday Comes: 50p from 2 Maybury Court, Shaftesbury Road, Woking, Surrey GU22 7DT

Macclesfield:
Silk Yarns: 50p from 96 Branksome Road, Brixton, London SW2

Maidstone Utd:
Yellow Fever: 50p from 402 London Road, Aylesford, Maidstone, Kent ME 20 DA

Manchester City:
Blue Print: 50p from 9 Lathom Street, Chesham, Bury, Lancs BL9 6LX
King Of The Kippax: 50p from 25 Holdenbrook Close, Leigh, Greater Manchester WN7 2HL
Electric Blue: 50p from 8 Pentwyn Grove, Wythenshawe, Manchester 23

Manchester Utd:
Red News: 50p from P O Box 384, London WC1N 3RJ

Mansfield:
Size 10 1/2 Boots: 40p from 10 Dollis Avenue, Finchley, London N3 1TX

Meadowbank:
AWOL: £1.00 from 11a Forth Street, Edinburgh GH1 3LE

Merthyr Tydfil:
Dial M For Merthyr: 50p from 9 Linden Way, Trefechan, Merthyr Tydfil, Mid Glam CF48 2EL

Middlesbrough:
Fly Me To The Moon: 50p from 14 Selkirk Close, Saltersgill, Middlesbrough

Millwall:
The Lion Roars: 50p from 24 Woodham Road, Catford, London SE6

Montrose:
Mo Mo Super Mo: 50p from P O Box 3, Broughty Ferry, Dundee DD5 2YG

Morton:
The Cappielow Bugle: 35p from AKA Books & Comics, 33 Virginia Street, Glasgow G1 1TU

Motherwell:
Waiting For The Great Leap Forward: 40p from PO Box 2, Wishaw, Lanarkshire ML2 8DZ
Wherever You May Be: 50p from PO Box 2, Lanark

Newcastle United:
The Mag: 50p from 404 Warwick Court, Gateshead NE8 1EY
Jim's Bald Heed: 30p from 44 Shafto Street, Rosehill, Wallsend, Tyne and Wear, NE28 7AH

Northampton:
What A Load Of Cobblers: 30p from 3 Stag Court, Shire Lane, Chorleywood, Herts

Northwich Victoria:
Resign Roberts, Re-sign: 50p from 488 London Road, Davenham, Northwich, Cheshire CW9 8HW

Norwich City:
The Citizen: 40p from 53 Newton Park, Newton St. Faiths, Norwich NR10 3LR
Never Mind The Danger: 50p from 77 Belulah Road, Walthamstow, London E17 9LD

Notts County:
The Pie: 40p (plus 26p SAE) from 61 Stratford Road, West Bridgeford, Nottingham NG2 6AZ

Nottm Forest:
The Almighty Brian: 50p from 6 Grays Inn Buildings, Roseberry Avenue, London EC1R 4PH

Oldham Athletic:
Beyond A Boundary: 60p from 31 St John's Walk, Werneth, Oldham

Oxford United:
Raging Bull: 50p from 8 Nixon Road, Oxford, OX4 4BU

Peterborough:
The Peterborough Effect: 40p from P O Box 16, Huntingdon, Cambs PE18 6NH

Plymouth Argyle:
Central Heating: 40p from 9 How Street, Bretonside, Plymouth, Devon

Portsmouth:
The Greatest City: 25p from 12 Swallow Close, Havant, Hampshire PO9 2RA
Frattonise: 50p from PO Box 122, Southsea PO4 9UL

Port Vale:
The Memoirs Of Seth Bottomley: 35p from P O Box 418, Longton, Stoke-on Trent, Staffs ST3 6SB

Preston:
The PNE View: 45p from 58 Coombe Rd, Farncombe, Godalming Surrey GU7 3SL
53 Miles West Of Venus: 60p from PO Box 172, Preston PR1 4BU

Queen's Park:
The Web: 40p from 89 Busby Road, Clarkston, Glasgow G76 8BD

Q.P.R.:
In The Loft: 40p from 24 Woodham Road, Catford, London SE6 2SD
A Kick Up the Rs: 50p from 6 Mill Cottages, Chester Road, Grindley Brook, Nr Whitchurch, Shropshire SY13 4QH

Raith Rovers:
The Wild Rover: 40p from 113 Greenloanings, Kirkcaldy, Fife KY2 6NL

Rangers:
Aye' Ready 50p from P O Box 356, Glasgow G44 4DW
Follow,Follow : 50p from P O Box 539, Glasgow G11 7LT

Reading:
Elm Park Disease: 30p from P O Box 51, Reading, RG1 7JB
Taking The Biscuit: 50p from 5 Fetlock Close, Clapham, Bedfordshire MK41 6BG

St Johnstone:
Wendy Who?: 40p from P O Box 36, Perth, PH1 1YB

St Mirren:
There's A Store Where The Creatures Meet: 40p from 14 Eildon Drive, Barrhead, Glasgow, G78 2EA
Love Street Syndrome: 30p from P O Box 27, Helensburgh, G84 7EF

Shamrock Rovers:
Glenmalure Gazette: 30p from P O Box 2443, Dublin 17, Rep Of Ireland

Sheffield United:
Flashing Blade: 30p from 4 Cross Myrtle Road, Sheffield, S2 3EL.

Sheffield Wednesday:
Just Another Wednesday: 50p from 52 Ullswater Road, Handforth, Wilmslow, Cheshire SK9 3NQ

Southampton:
The Ugly Inside: 50p from 6 Dimond Close, Midanbury, Southampton

Stirling Albion:
The Beanos: 50p from Tamane, Brace, Dunblane, Perthshire FK15 9LP

Stoke City:
The Jolly Potter: 20p from Box 257, 52 Call Lane, Leeds LS1 6DT
The Oatcake: 20p from P O Box 276, Stoke On Trent, Staffs ST1 5RU

Sunderland:
Wise Men Say: 40p from P.O. Box 2, Sunderland SR1 1NG

Swansea City:
Jackmail : 50p from P O Box 24, Port Talbot, West Glam SA123 1QN

Swindon Town:
Bring The Noise: 30p from 10 Devon Road Swindon, Wilts, SN2 1PQ

Torquay Utd:
Mission Impossible: 20p from 14 Conway Road, Paignton, Devon TQ4 5LF

Tottenham:
The Spur: £1.00 from 153 Upton Road, Bexleyheath, Kent DA6 8LY

Tranmere Rovers:
Friday Night Fever: 30p from 38 Stanton Drive, Upton, Chester, Cheshire CH2 2JF

Waterlooville:
Foul: 75p from 172 Francis Avenue, Southsea, Hants, PO4

Watford:
Mud, Sweat And Beers: 50p from PO Box 436, Hemel Hempstead, Herts HP3 8UF

Wealdstone:
The Elmslie Ender: 50p from 37 Grange Road, Kenton, Harrow, Middlesex HA1 2PR
Long Ball Down The Middle: £1 from 50 Hartington Close, Sudbury Hill, Harrow, Middlesex HA1 3RL

W.B.A.:
Fingerpost: 50p from 19 Ashville Drive, Halesowen, West Midlands B63 3SD

West Ham:
The Boleyn Scorcher: 30p from 311 Samuel Lewis Buildings, Liverpool Road, London N1 1LL
Fortune's Always Hiding: 50p from P O Box 664, London SW11 6AL
Never Mind The Boleyn: 50p from 19 Canada Road, Acton, London, W3 0NP
On The Terraces: 50p from P O Box 1511, London NW1 6RY

West Ham/Dundee Utd:
UTD United: 50p from 54 Chaucer Road, Herne Hill, London SE24 0NU

Wigan Athletic:
The Cockney Latic: 50p from 32 Walkden Avenue East, Wigan, Lancs

Wimbledon:
Roger Connell's Beard: 88 Farm Road, Morden, Surrey SM4 6RB
Yidaho!: 50p from 73 Smeaton Road, Wandsworth, London SW18 5JJ
Grapevine: £1.00 from 49 Durnsford Road, Wimbledon London SW19

Witton Albion:
Bishop 3-1: 20p from 122 Cromwell Road, Winnington, Northwich, Cheshire CW8 4BX

Wycombe Wanderers:
Chairboys Gas: 40p from Cedar Cottage, Green End Road, Radnage, High Wycombe, Bucks HP14 4BZ

York City:
Terrace Talk: 30p from 7 Copper Beech Close, Dunnington, York YO1 5PY

Getting a subscription means that you are certain of getting a copy of *WSC* every month before it hits the shops. So if you want to have some of the uncertainty and doubt of life removed, send us £8.50 and we'll do the rest.

Please make all cheques/POs payable to *When Saturday Comes*

When Saturday Comes 1-11 Ironmonger Row, London EC1V 3QM